D0828335

Dame Gillian Wagner has been Chair of Barnardo's and The Carnegie UK Trust. She is the author of *Thomas Coram, Gent*; *The Chocolate Conscience*; *Barnardo* and *Children of the Empire*.

'This book is a work of art: Ellen Palmer's diary, on which it is based, offers a fascinating glimpse into mid-Victorian high society – and into the mind of a beautiful, intelligent and self-aware young woman gifted with a trenchant turn of phrase.'

– Anne de Courcy, author of *The Viceroy's Daughters*

'Engrossing… a great piece of social history.'

– Katharine McMahon, author of *The Rose of Sebastopol*

'This is a compelling record of a woman stultified both by her family and even more by the rigid hierarchy of Victorian society. I know of no other record which so vividly charts the failed efforts at social climbing by a family that used their daughter, Ellen Palmer, as the wedge whereby to prise open the door upwards. They failed. The diarist herself emerges as a mass of contradictions, vivacious and musically accomplished, vain and strong-willed, snobbish and also lacking in judgement when it came to men. But other traits, like her journey to the Crimea, anticipate what womanhood was to become in the next century. In the end she found love but only after the diary closes … She died at thirty-three.'

– Sir Roy Strong

The Secret Journals of a Victorian Lady

GILLIAN WAGNER

Published in 2017 by
I.B.Tauris & Co. Ltd
London • New York
www.ibtauris.com

ISBN: 978 1 78831 006 2
eISBN: 978 1 78672 249 2
ePDF: 978 1 78673 249 1

A full CIP record for this book is available from the British Library
A full CIP record is available from the Library of Congress

Library of Congress Catalog Card Number: available

Typeset by Free Range Book Design & Production Limited
Printed and bound in Sweden by ScandBook AB

CONTENTS

LIST OF ILLUSTRATIONS

Family Pedigrees

List of Plates

ACKNOWLEDGEMENTS

I have to thank very many family members, friends and colleagues for all the help and encouragement I have received over the years that it took to unravel the secrets of Ellen's Diaries. But first and foremost I am indebted to the Graham Palmers, owners of Cefn Park where the diaries were found. Roger Graham Palmer has been key to finding the diaries and allowing me to make use of them, as has his son, Archie Graham Palmer, who inherited Cefn while the book was in progress. The late Betty Askwith's interest in Ellen Palmer's life inspired me to continue her work. The complicated Palmer family background was sorted out by Thomas Woodcock, Garter King of Arms, who kindly provided me with the family pedigrees and added to my knowledge of the family and to whom I am very grateful.

Staff at the Denbighshire Record Office and at the Shropshire Archives were very helpful in producing family records of the Palmers and I thank them as well as staff at the Principal Registry Family Division and Wendy Hawke at the Guildhall Library, London. I also thank the Department of Prints and Drawings at the British Museum. Special thanks go to Dr Alastair Massie, Director of the National Army Museum, for his help over matters relating to the Crimean War.

The manuscript was read by Lucy Mccarraher, Elizabeth Bonython, Vanessa Graham Palmer and Jo Godfrey of I.B.Tauris, and has been much improved thanks to their suggestions. I am also indebted to the late Frank Loeffler for reading and advising on the reasons for the death of Lady Palmer, to Dr Douglas Austin for guiding me through the complexities of the Nolan affair and to the late Jo Robbins for information on the cholera epidemic. I also thank Dr Spolidor for his help with the history of the Duc de Gramont's family.

The mysteries of preparing the illustrations for publication and putting them on a memory stick were solved for me by Dr Dick Foster, to whom I am very grateful, as well as for his help with added research at the National Newspaper Archive. I am particularly indebted to Sheri Bankes, who photographed the portraits at Cefn Park, and to Dorothy Hylands for her photographs of Kenure Church and the ruins of Kenure Park. Thanks also go to Aislinne Dunne, archivist at the Irish Architecural Archive, and to Irene Stevenson at *The Irish Times* for help with the story of Kenure Park. I am grateful to Elisabeth Balcombe, Roger Bragger, Katherine Cator, Jill Croft Murray, Glenn Fisher, Julie Kavanagh, Christine Kennealy, Mark Lance, Norman Lucy, William H.C. Smith and Philip Wilson.

To all who assisted me with my IT problems I owe thanks, but in particular to Zoe Wagner and Ro Williams, to whom I am very much indebted for their help. I thank Alison Heath for her meticulous work on the index, and my publishers for their encouragement and support during the production of the book. Without the help of Google and Wikipedia (with reservations) the writing of this book would have taken even longer.

PALMER PEDIGREE

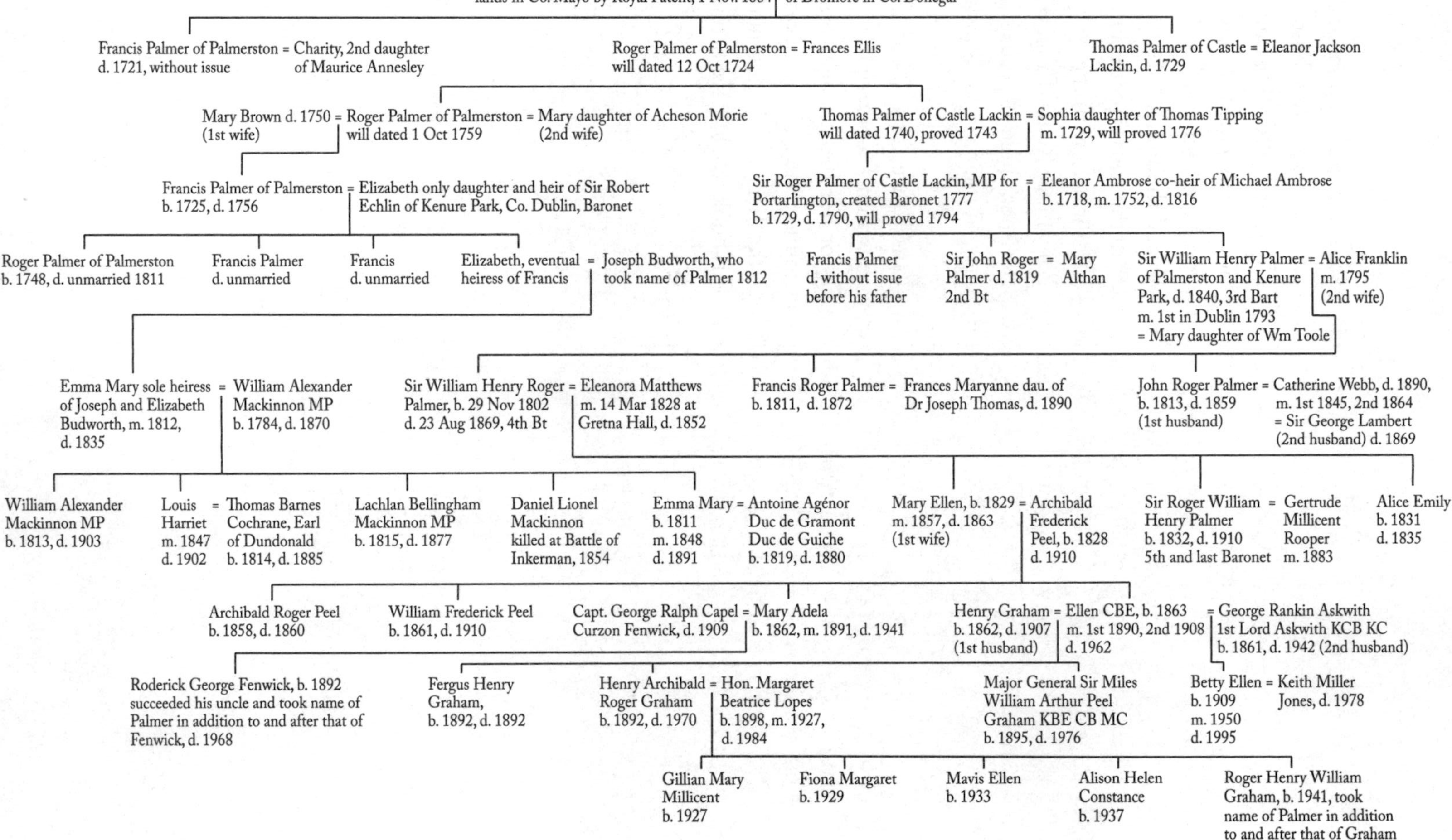

MATTHEWS PEDIGREE

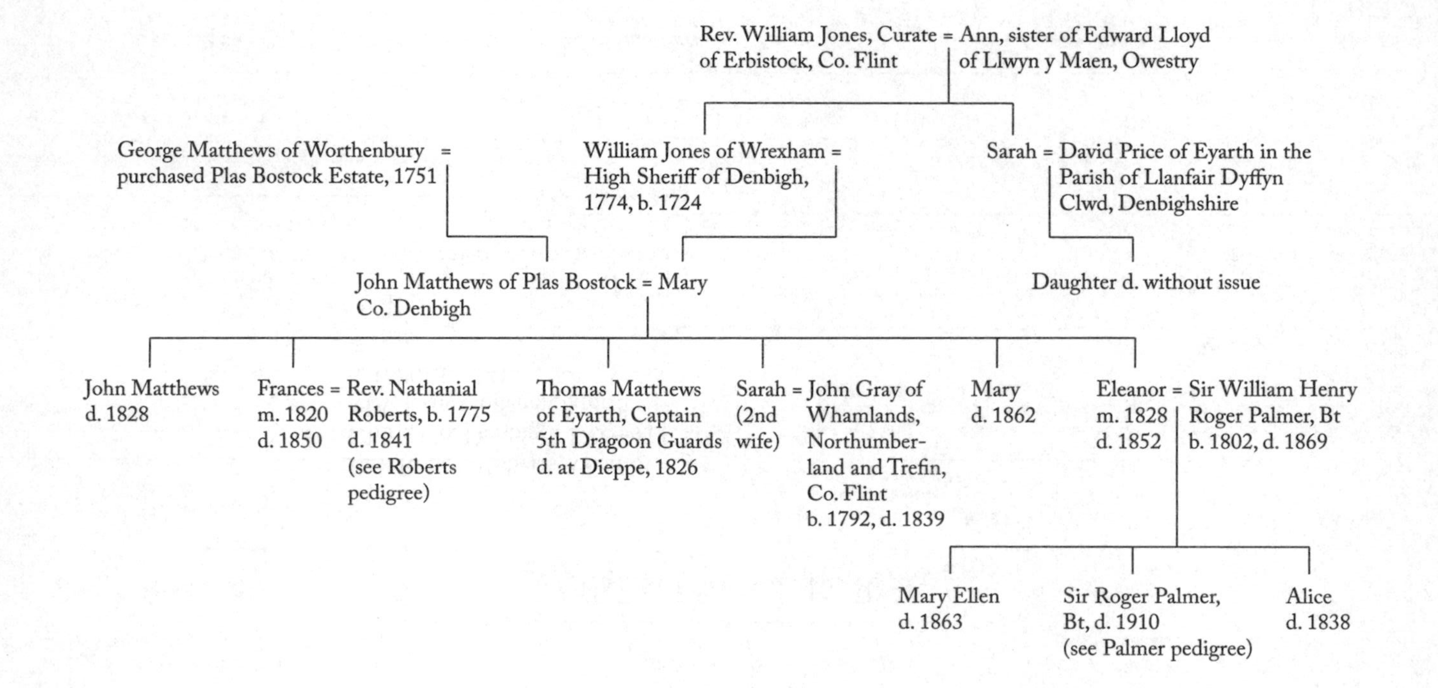

ROBERTS PEDIGREE

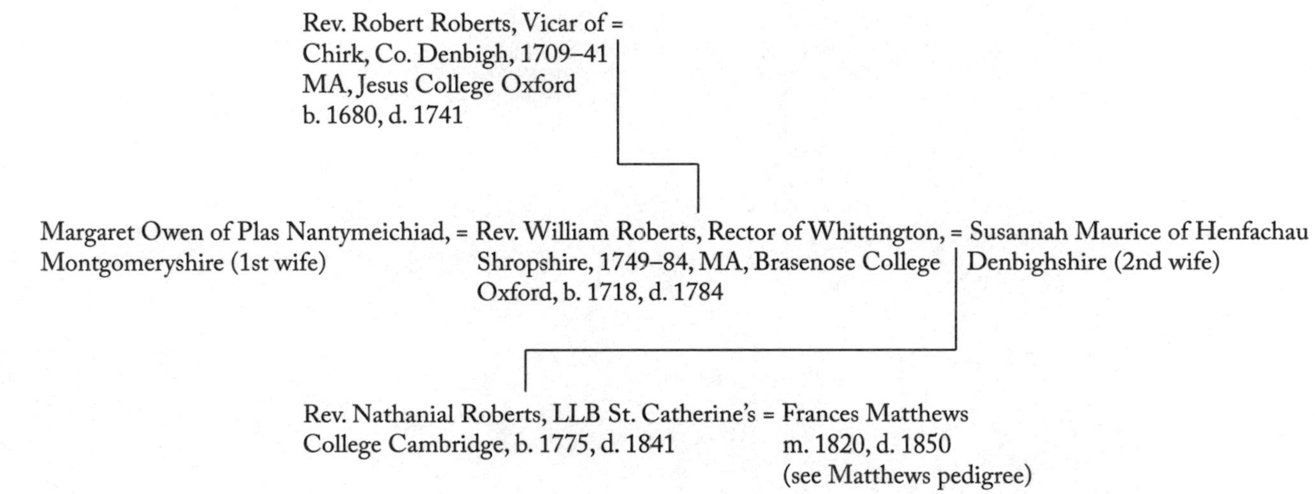

INTRODUCTION

Standing on the Galata Bridge in Constantinople, Ellen Palmer joyfully described the view: '*It stands in the midst of a forest of little caiques darting about on the sparkling waves, Constantinople arising on the either side, terrace upon terrace, in all its loveliness places of snowy whiteness overhanging the dark blue waters of the Bospherus, earth, air and sky all radiant with sunshine. It is a picture which words cannot describe.*'[1] She had only arrived in Constantinople thanks to a steely determination to escape another dreary winter in the country and the stale pleasure of a seventh London season in pursuit of a husband. Using the pretext of wishing to be near her brother, Roger, who had recently joined the 11th Hussars and been sent to the Crimea, and despite the dire warnings of all her friends and relations that it was madness to attempt such an expedition, Ellen had cajoled and bullied her father and her aunt into agreeing to make the journey east. She had yet to overcome the last obstacle, to reach Balaclava itself, but this remarkable woman had planned and overseen the whole expedition down the Danube and overland, facing real dangers en route, to arrive in Constantinople, where she revelled in the beauty and strangeness of the scene around her. She had written, aged 18, that '*I know that someday I am going to astonish the world*' and had she not died so tragically young at 33, she surely would have done so, for she was a woman ahead of her time.

Ellen Palmer was intelligent, talented, beautiful, wealthy and strong-willed. She was born in 1829 and her short life had much in common with some famous fictional heroines of her time, including Thackeray's Becky Sharpe and Austen's Emma Woodhouse, and was equally dramatic. Ellen's diaries, written between 1847, when she was 17, and 1855, provide an unusual account of a young woman struggling to satisfy the wishes of her rich and ambitious family, against her own inclinations, to make a marriage which would enhance their status in society: a classic story of love versus what she deemed to be her duty to her family.

Ellen's diaries also throw light on a newly wealthy family struggling to enter the first ranks of London society, yet never quite able to make it – all reported with unflinching honesty. The intricacies of the class system that operated at the highest levels in nineteenth-century society, as described and commented on through the eyes of a young woman, make fascinating reading. The diaries show that only after the death of her mother and one of her tyrannical aunts was she able to wrest control of her life from her frail and handicapped father, choose her own destiny and free herself from the gilded cage in which she had felt herself imprisoned.

For six years, she never missed a day of 'diarising', as she called it, until 1853 when her life changed. After she had journeyed to the Crimea to see her brother, who was with the 11th Hussars and took part in the Charge of the Light Brigade, she unexpectedly found the man who could offer her the unconditional love she craved. She then no longer needed her diaries as an emotional prop and record of her unhappy home life, so her writing tailed off and finally petered out.

Nothing would have been known of this unusual, wilful, beautiful and musically talented girl, apart from the fact that she married and had four children and died young, had it not been for the accidental discovery in 1983 of a small blue diary, tucked in the back of a bureau at her country home. The notes, a travel diary, describe her experiences in Constantinople and the Crimea. But inside this little diary were tucked four small sheets of paper covered with beautiful, miniscule copperplate writing which recorded the progress of her somewhat stormy courtship with her future husband. This discovery was enough to excite the curiosity of Betty Askwith, her granddaughter, who wrote a charming account of her grandmother's travels to the Crimea and her relationship with Archie Peel, entitled *A Crimean Courtship* (Michael Russell Publishing, 1985).

But this account was written without the benefit of the information contained in another three locked diaries, which lay unknown and unopened for over 150 years, and were only found in 1989 by Ellen's great-grandson, Roger Graham Palmer, at Cefn Park where she spent a large part of her life.

With the discovery of the three volumes of Ellen's diaries, we are able to construct a detailed and fascinating account as seen by a strong-willed girl trapped by the conventions of the day, of social life in London, Paris and Baden, as well as North Wales and Ireland where the family owned large estates. After her mother's death, she overrode all opposition and demonstrated her capacity to organise and assert her new-found independence by insisting on visiting Constantinople and Balaclava with her father and her Aunt Mary.

A further, small, earlier travel diary was discovered still later in 2008. It was written in 1844 while Ellen was on a tour of Europe with her parents at age 14. The tour lasted four months, but only the record of the first two months has been found.

Ellen's daily diary entries were first drafted as notes and then carefully copied, so that there were no amendments on the hundreds of pages of beautiful copperplate script. Each of the three main volumes is divided into three-year sections; the first two volumes, dating from 1847 to 1859 and 1850 to 1853 respectively, are complete, with every day accounted for. Ellen managed to fill each of the first two leather-bound volumes, their gilt-edged pages secured by a strong lock, so as to finish exactly at the end of the three-year period, on 31 December in 1850 and 1853. It must have meant meticulous planning, as the entries vary greatly in length.

A puzzling gap and blank pages appear in the third volume, covering the years 1853–4. Notes in the small blue diary cover some of the gaps in her formal diary, but she never wrote them up, as was her habit: the blank pages stare back, with nothing to say as to what happened during the missing months. The third diary, which she took to the Crimea, was carefully covered in blue cloth so as not to damage the binding. Her entries during her journey to Constantinople were particularly long as, she said, she had nothing else to do but diarise. The actual diary ends on 25 December as they steam into Balaclava on the *Caradoc*, but further notes exist in the small blue diary.

Ellen died giving birth to her fourth child, another Ellen and my grandmother, in 1863 at the age of just 33. My grandmother frequently remarked how much she regretted never having known her mother. If only those locked diaries, lying unnoticed among the game books and miscellaneous household accounts so carefully stored at Cefn, had been found earlier she would have known what a remarkable person her mother had been.

This is Ellen's story. I have let her tell it as much as possible in her own words.

CHAPTER 1

A Strange Family

Ellen Palmer was brought up in the expectation that she would make a socially advantageous marriage. She danced with Napoleon III while he was in exile in London,[1] charmed Lord Cardigan and was entertained by Lord Raglan in the Crimea. She was intelligent, beautiful, musically gifted and an heiress, but she was also demanding, spoilt and self-centred. Her family owned country estates in North Wales (Cefn) and in Ireland near Dublin (Kenure); they also owned extensive lands in County Mayo as well as a large London house in Portland Place, so she had all the attributes needed to attract a suitable husband. Ellen was also strong-willed and although she entered into the role her family expected of her, she nevertheless believed from an early age that she could only marry for love, an unfashionable concept among match-making parents who valued status and financial security above all else for their daughters. However, Ellen's family also hid a secret: her father was not only epileptic, but was mentally frail and unable to fulfil the traditional role of a head of family. The role was taken on by his wife, who managed the estates, and by Ellen after the death of her mother. This handicap, mentioned only once by Ellen, could be the reason for the family's failure to attain the place in society they felt they deserved.

Ellen, born in 1829, had a strangely solitary childhood, with only her brother Roger, four years her junior, for company during his school holidays. She felt misunderstood by her dull and dysfunctional family, as well as intellectually alienated by their limited interests and conversation.

This left her with the ability to disguise her feelings and conceal her thoughts from her immediate family. It also fortunately led to her using her diaries, not only to give an account of her inner life, but also to record with unflinching honesty the setbacks and snubs as well as the triumphs meted out to her family as they sought to move into the higher reaches of Victorian London society. Never intended for publication, they provide a rare view of that society seen from the point of view of a young girl, only 17 when she started writing and ending seven years later with her journey to the Crimea.

How and why Ellen Palmer's parents, Eleanora Matthews and Roger Palmer, ever met and then hastily married at Gretna Green, remains a mystery as their families came from very different social backgrounds. Roger Palmer, the son of Sir William Palmer, an Irish baronet, was living in Bruges in early 1828, probably because he was in debt.[2] Eleanora must have met him in Bruges, but there is no hint as to what she was doing there. She was the youngest of the four Matthews sisters, two of whom were married. Her family of modest means had lived in North Wales for several generations. As she was 32, well past what might be considered marriageable age, she could have gone to Bruges to act as companion to a lady or to work as a governess to a family living there, but it is impossible to know. Roger Palmer, who was 10 years her junior, was almost certainly living there to avoid his creditors. As has become clear from his daughter's diaries, besides his mental health problems and epilepsy, he had a reputation for running after women[3] and, as he was firmly excluded from any financial control of the marriage settlement,[4] he was probably also a gambler. Eleanora may have seen Roger, with all his disadvantages but nevertheless the son of an Irish baronet, as a means of escaping the dreary life of a Victorian spinster.

Nothing is known about their early relationship or how long they had known each other before their sudden arrival in early March 1828 at Cefn Park in North Wales, the home of Eleanora's eldest sister Frances and her husband Nathanial Roberts. Given Roger Palmer's reputation, the likeliest reason seems to be that he had seduced Eleanora. What is certain is that they were immediately packed off to Scotland to regularise their relationship by her shocked relations, who arranged for them to be married at Gretna Green on 14 March 1828.[5] Their descendants still own the small gold anvil they were given to mark the occasion.

A month later, on 12 April, the couple were married again by special licence at the parish church at Oswestry, with Eleanora's other brother-in-law, John Gray, and her unmarried sister, Mary Matthews, acting as witnesses. The only unusual fact concerning this second ceremony is that Eleanora is named as 'Matthews (alias Palmer)' on the marriage certificate, with the explanation that 'the parties had recently been married abroad which explains the lady signing in both her names'. It is unclear as to whether 'abroad' refers to the Gretna Green marriage or to some ceremony they may have gone through in Bruges before returning to Wales.

The most likely explanation for their sudden return and dash to Scotland would be that Eleanora was pregnant. However, their eldest daughter, Mary Ellen but always known as Ellen, was born 12 months after the marriage. It is possible that Eleanora was pregnant at the time and had a miscarriage. There is another intriguing possibility: could it have been that she had already given birth to another child in Bruges? Among the letters written by the family agent, Edwin Wyett, to Eleanora's wealthy elder sister Frances Roberts at Cefn Park, is one which is difficult to interpret, but which hints at such a possibility. The agent had already written to Mrs Roberts expressing some surprise at Eleanora's sudden marriage. In another letter to Frances he wrote that the family solicitor, Mr Jenks,

> has effected arrangements so as completely to arrange certain affairs and I believe the mother will come forward on the occasion that has been so prevailed upon. I therefore beg the favour of your not saying anything about the matter to your sisters who will be much annoyed at anything being said on the subject. I have no doubt that everything will go on quite straight. I am confident that I can rely on your honour of keeping the subject of our conversation entirely within your own breast […][6]

Whatever arrangements had been made, it is clear that money was involved, and it seems likely that Frances, the wealthiest of the sisters, needed to be told about the arrangements. Whether the mother referred to in the letter was paid to adopt the child, or whether the child had been fathered by Roger and the mother was being paid to keep quiet will never be known, but it is certain that there was something that needed hushing up. Edwin Wyett was more than just an agent to the family; he was a more of a friend and confidant to the elderly Nathanial Roberts who was nearly blind. His enigmatic letter to Frances Roberts provides only limited information but gives the sole clue as to the reason for the hurried marriage at Gretna Green.

But for the marriage of Roger and Eleanora, the Palmers and Matthews would almost certainly never have met, the social gulf between the two being almost unbridgeable.

The Palmers had lived in Norfolk before moving to Ireland. They had been strong supporters of Charles II, Roger Palmer having signed the loyal address to the king in 1662, and as a reward been given a grant of Castle Lackin (now a ruin) and large tracts of land in Co. Mayo by patent dated 1 November 1682.[7] The Palmers continued to live uneventful lives in Co. Mayo and settled around Palmerstown. The eldest grandson of Roger Palmer was known as Roger Palmer of Palmerstown; and the second grandson as Thomas Palmer of Castle Lackin. It was when Roger Palmer's son Francis married Elizabeth Echlin that the fortunes of the Palmers changed for the better: she was the sole heir to Kenure and the surrounding estates near Rush, Co. Dublin.

Elizabeth was clearly a strong personality: she had married Francis Palmer despite her father, Sir Robert Echlin, having disinherited her for making what he considered to be an unsuitable marriage. As a consequence, the estate and title had gone to a nephew, Sir Henry Echlin, but Henry turned out to be a profligate rogue who lost the estate to a gambling debt. Elizabeth, who was left only a shilling in her father's will due to marrying against his wishes, managed to buy back the estate. The house at Kenure, known as Rush House before the Palmers changed the name to Kenure Park, was an imposing, quadrangular building in the early-Georgian style, built in 1703. A portico consisting of a pediment supported by four Tuscan pillars flanked by a pair of fierce-looking lions guarded the entrance. Inside, a sweeping, dividing mahogany staircase rose from the hall; the ornate plaster ceilings were by Robert West; and the house was magnificently furnished with Sheraton, Chippendale and Regency furniture. Sadly for Elizabeth and Francis, their only child to marry and have descendants was a daughter, also named Elizabeth. She married Joseph Budworth, who took the name of Palmer *jure uxoris* in 1812. They in turn only had a daughter, Emma, who married William Alexander Mackinnon. Because there was no male Palmer heir to inherit, it seems Elizabeth gave up her claim to Kenure in favour of the male branch of the family in return for some financial compensation. Kenure passed to a cousin, another Roger Palmer, the son of Thomas Palmer of Castle Lackin. The Palmers now had a title and a country residence of some importance to go with their estates in Co. Mayo.

It was this Roger Palmer who in 1751 had married Eleanor Ambrose,[8] a renowned beauty. He was MP for Portarlington and she, besides being celebrated for her beauty, was also admired on account of her wit and intelligence. She was a Catholic, an heiress to her father's successful brewery and was known for her fervent patriotism – which made it all the more remarkable that she became the darling of the strongly Protestant viceregal court in Dublin. Lord Chesterfield,[9] the Viceroy, was so attracted to her that she was soon to be seen accompanying him to all official ceremonies, despite her religion. She took care to keep the relationship platonic and appeared at a Castle Ball to celebrate the anniversary of the Battle of the Boyne with an orange lily on her breast, causing Chesterfield to improvise the often-quoted lines:

Say, lovely traitor, where's the jest
Of wearing orange on thy breast,
When that same breast uncovered shows
The whiteness of the rebel rose.[10]

The white rose was the symbol of the Jacobites and the Catholic faction. By his marriage to this famous beauty, Roger Palmer brought a certain cachet to his rather ordinary family. It was said to be due to Eleanor's influence that he was created a baronet in 1777.

The title and estates passed in 1794 to John, their eldest living son, and on his death in 1819 to his son, William Henry Palmer. Sir William Palmer and his wife were living at Kenure in 1847 when the house was damaged by fire. Sir William employed the architect George Papworth not only to repair the damage but also to enlarge the house, and must have been busy overseeing the restoration when the news of his difficult son's unexpected marriage to Eleanora Matthews arrived.

The history of the Matthews family was much less colourful than that of the Palmers. A family of modest means, the Matthews had, for a considerable time, lived quietly in North Wales. Eleanora Matthews was the youngest of John and Mary Matthews' six children. John Matthews had acquired through a previous marriage an estate in Plas Bostock, and through his marriage to Mary Jones the Wrexham Fecan estate.[11] He had died in 1703 leaving £60 p.a. to his dear wife and the estates to his eldest son John, specifying that there was to be enough money to provide for an apprenticeship for the younger son Tom.[12] Tom died in 1826 and John died two years later, so there were no male Matthews left to deal with the difficult situation in which the family found themselves when Eleanora returned from Bruges with Roger Palmer. After John Matthews' death, the family estates were sold for £2,400 and the proceeds divided between the remaining four sisters.

Frances, the eldest and the most dominant of the four sisters, had married a very rich widower, the Reverend Nathanial Roberts, 34 years older than she was. Nathanial Roberts had inherited his wealth from his father who had married two heiresses in succession, Margaret Owen and Susannah Maurice. It seems that the younger Frances wanted more from life than Nathanial and left him, date unknown, to go and live in Dublin, as revealed in a letter from the agent, Edwin Wyett.[13] Wyett wrote to her in Dublin on 1 April 1825, at Blackhall Place, where she appears to have been staying with an unnamed colonel. He told her that he had been asked by her husband, who was now almost blind, to plead with her to return after a long absence. 'He says life is but short and at his age and situation renders the prospect of his own but very limited [...] his helpless situation and the distress he is in, he needs assistance of every description, so begs you to return in the name of propriety as well as to meet his wishes.' He added that her husband, who was in the process of making his will, wanted to provide for her and to make her comfortable but for him to do that she must return. With so much at stake Frances had returned to the marital home and whatever her relationship with Nathanial, and despite his anxieties, they lived together for another 16 years. But when he died in 1841 Frances duly had her reward. She inherited Cefn Park, which Nathanial had bought from the Kenyon family, together with his other properties, the house in Portland Place in London and the bulk of his fortune.

Frances' escapade occurred three years before Eleanora's unexpected return unleashed the possibility of a second scandal. Frances and Nathanial were living at Cefn in 1828 and it seems likely that the third sister, Mary Matthews, who never married, was living with them when Eleanora and Roger Palmer arrived. The second sister, Sarah, had married a widower, John Gray, and was living nearby at Mold. The family closed ranks: their first priority was to regularise the situation of their youngest sibling. Thrown together by the sudden and unexpected marriage of Roger and Eleanora, two very different families had quickly between them to agree some financial arrangement to provide for the newly married, improvident young couple.

Owing to the recent death of her brother, Eleanora had a small income of her own. Several draft post-nuptial agreements[14] show that Sir William was willing to forgive his son and pay his debts and that he also arranged for a new settlement of the Palmer estates in Co. Mayo and Sligo, as well as Kenure, providing for Roger to inherit on his death. The financially unreliable Roger was to have no part of the estate until then, but an allowance was agreed. The Matthews family for their part were determined that on no account was Roger to be allowed to touch any part of the income payable to Eleanora.[15]

Very little is known about the Palmers' early married life apart from the fact that they had three children: Mary Ellen was born in 1829; another daughter, Alice, was born in 1831; and a year later a son, Roger, was born. Alice was four when she died and was quietly buried in the catacombs at Kensal Green. Ellen mentions her only once in her diaries and that was to say that she was sorry never to have known her. It seems probable that Alice was very disabled, as she never came to live with the other two children and seems to have lived and been cared for in London, away from the family. The brutal truth was that, at this time, an abnormal child did not elicit sympathy and was thought to bring shame on the family, hence the need for secrecy. Prince George, the son of King George and Queen Mary, born more than 60 years later in 1905, was brought up in isolation from his family because he was epileptic. He died in 1919, a footnote to history. The behaviour of the Palmers towards their little daughter was in keeping with the mores of the time.

Everything changed for the Palmers in 1840 when old Sir William Palmer died, and they inherited Kenure and the fortune that went with it. Now the erstwhile plain Miss Eleanora Matthews became the wealthy Lady Palmer. Very little is known about those early years in Ireland apart from Ellen's description of her home life in her diaries. From this it would appear that it was Lady Palmer who was very much in charge of all business matters. It was she rather than Sir Roger who always dealt with the agents who managed the Irish estates. To cope with her husband's frailties Lady Palmer always employed a medical man, as much as to keep him occupied and out of mischief as to deal with the medical emergencies. The two men are frequently mentioned as going out fishing. A governess, Miss Ward, was also part of the household and stayed with the family for many years, becoming Ellen's close friend and confidante.

Before the family inherited Kenure they had spent their time between Frances' house at Cefn and the house in Portland Place, Her childhood does not seem to have been a particularly happy one. She wrote that she and her younger brother had no playmates and were entirely reliant on each other for company. Ellen gives no reason for the social isolation in which they passed their early childhood, but it could have been because their father's mental and physical frailties made the family averse to normal social intercourse. As a result, Ellen depended almost entirely on her brother for companionship. When he went away to prep school, and later to Eton where he made friends of his own age, Ellen was thrown back on the company of her mother, Aunt Mary who lived with them and Frances (always known as Aunt Abbey), a frequent visitor.

She had grown into an intelligent, gifted and beautiful girl, but looking back at her childhood she later wrote in unsparing terms about her family life:

> *I have lived ever since I was born amongst people who have not the slightest sympathy with emotions of any kind, indeed it is a curiosity to remark how utterly incapable they are of comprehending any deeper or more delicate feeling than those called forth by the common usage of everyday life. Now, likewise, I am so exceedingly sensitive that I feel acutely things which other people would hardly remark and consequently the certainty of not being understood and the dread of ridicule have induced me ever since I can remember to conceal every thought and feeling with the most jealous care […] no sister or friend to confide in, so have grown into a being apparently indifferent to everything beyond idle pursuits.*

The words 'no sister' were particularly poignant as Ellen was aware that she had had a sister, but had been told nothing about her and could only wish she had known her.

Ellen may have thought that she had concealed her feelings, but the very fact of her being so intelligent and strong-willed seems to have aroused powerful feelings of resentment on the part of her relatives. In every family there are rows and disagreements, but the extreme language used by her maternal aunts seems to hint at something more fundamental: '*The aunts flew at me like tiger cats, calling me every horrid name in the vocabulary of Billingsgate and said such slanderous and wicked things of me that had I been a kitchen maid I would have brought an action against them.*'[16] And she noted, '*this is not a once in a way but an everyday occurrence*', adding sadly that her mother nearly always sided with the aunts. There are other examples of the aunts not just scolding, but swearing at Ellen. She wrote that she did not record them all as they happened so frequently. It is understandable that if Ellen was constantly subjected to such abuse from her relations she learned to conceal her true feelings and emotion because any display of independent thought seemed to provoke an outburst. Ellen made no attempt to analyse the reasons for the hostile treatment she received but she may well not have concealed her true feelings as well as she thought she had done, and her relatives may have resented what they came to see as her superior attitude towards them. Her mother, feeling equally challenged, sided with her elder sisters during family arguments.

Ellen's role in the family was not simply that of an only daughter to be married to some suitable young man: she, rather than her more ordinary brother, was *the asset* that would propel them to the higher reaches of society. Beautiful, rich, clever and musical, she was expected to make a spectacularly successful marriage to a wealthy aristocrat. By the time Ellen was 16 she was well aware of what was expected of her; to some extent she accepted that was to be her destiny while still feeling distressed to hear her mother talking so openly about her ambitions.

When it came to the point, Ellen would allow her heart to rule her head and, although not wanting to disappoint her family, would not marry for the sake of a title and status without love. All girls were chaperoned at this period, but her family, perhaps sensing that their independent and strong-willed daughter was not entirely to be trusted to fulfil their wishes, subjected her to the strictest form of chaperonage, scarcely allowing her out of their sight and listening when they could to her conversation. Already emotionally isolated, she wrote of, '*the constant surveillance which never relaxes. Every word is watched therefore I feel the necessity of caution, a sense of oppression even when freed from danger I never feel perfectly at liberty, always a sense of weight upon my mind a sense of moral bondage*.'[17]

Ellen was 20 when she wrote of her unhappiness at home, but by her own admission this was a long-standing situation. Outwardly the spoilt darling of the family, she was more tightly controlled by her socially ambitious family than most of her contemporaries.

Ellen Palmer lived at a time when class distinctions were understood by all and particularly observed by the middle and upper classes. The hereditary aristocracy and noble families with large incomes and landed properties stood at the apex, confident and in no doubt as to their rights and position in society as part of the ruling elite. They were self-selected and could be numbered in a few hundreds. They were not, however, immune to change; events outside their control were beginning to affect them, but it would be some time before their dominant position in society would be challenged. The landed gentry, those who owned and lived in country estates and held sway locally, were the most threatened by a new wave of entrepreneurs and factory owners, which emerged in the early nineteenth century. The Industrial Revolution had brought financial success to a whole new breed of men: men who had seen new opportunities for trade and had taken advantage of the possibilities now opening up of capital investment in manufacturing, such as factories and mills. These new captains of industry were now able to purchase large properties, stand for parliament and entertain on a grand scale, and were looking for the same acceptance as the landed gentry, who by birth and inheritance formed a group as equally exclusive as the aristocracy. It was to preserve the difference between those who had inherited wealth and those who had made their own money that a new barrier to social advancement was erected. Being 'in trade' was seen as incompatible with the values of upper-class society.

Quite why the Palmers should also have found it so difficult to cross this invisible barrier is interesting. They had inherited wealth and property, but it could have been on account of their unusual marriage, or Roger Palmer's mental health together with his wife's relatively modest background, that they were prevented from being accorded the respect and status that they felt was their due. But Ellen made it very clear that this was the situation when she recorded a discussion with a friend who,

> *candidly told us our acquaintance and position was not what it ought to be considering our rights in every respect. We confessed this was true and so it is, for we have hitherto been like flying fish, would not enter the society offered to us and trying vainly to enter that to which we are really entitled.*[18]

Ellen's experience of navigating the intricacies of the social world into which she was plunged bear a remarkable similarity to those of a number of heroines imagined by novelists of the eighteenth and nineteenth centuries. Evelina in Fanny Burney's novel, *Evelina, or the History of a Young Lady's Entrance into the World*, describes Evelina as making '*at the age of seventeen her first appearance upon the great and busy stage of life; with virtuous mind, a cultivated understanding and a feeling heart.*' Ellen, who at the same age had the same attributes, writes in her diary, '*I naturally look forward to the coming season as one fraught with peculiar interest considering that I am to have a glimpse of the society I have only had so far a peep at in books.*'[19] Both had difficult family backgrounds and ambitious relatives. Evelina had to avoid the danger of being seduced, Ellen the danger of being married for her money, but both learned to navigate the complex layers of society, albeit in different centuries, eventually to find true love.

Society as portrayed by Fanny Burney was not greatly different from that depicted by Jane Austen, writing at a later date. As Ellen's story unfolds, there are many similarities with the fictitious Emma, heroine of Austen's novel of that name. *Vanity Fair*, the satirical novel by William Thackeray, was published in 1847, the same year that Ellen started writing her account of society from the perspective of a young girl expected by her family to enhance their social standing through marriage. In Thackeray's novel, the main character and anti-heroine, Becky Sharp, is strong-willed, intelligent and also determined one way or another to make her way in society. She speaks French fluently, has a beautiful singing voice and does not cultivate the society of women, all traits she shares to some degree with Ellen. In truth, Ellen was far removed from the cunning and amoral Becky Sharp, and it was her relatives rather than she who were so intent on her making an advantageous marriage. Ellen did, however, go along with her family's ambition, always excusing herself by saying that she saw it as her duty to do as her family wished. So it was not totally unfair when an unkind neighbour suggested that dining with the Palmers reminded him of Thackeray's novel with Ellen as the heroine.

The fact that Ellen embodied so many of the situations and characteristics of eighteenth- and nineteenth-century fictional heroines not only adds to their authenticity, but also shows that the problems Ellen faced and the choices she had to make were more mainstream than she might have realised. Plunged into society directly from the schoolroom, like Evelina, she quickly understood its dangers. Summing up her impressions after her first year as a fully fledged member of society, appearing in public alongside her parents, she writes:

> *This time last year I was anxiously expecting my debut in the world perfectly ignorant of what that world would bring forth [...] now I have been initiated into many of its faults and follies, but owing to my prudence in not expecting too much I have not been at all disappointed in the pleasures that I have experienced.*

She goes on to comment, '*I have heard and witnessed more manoeuvres and backbiting than I could ever have previously formed the least expectation of and on the other hand I (like others) have been flattered and praised more in a week than I had previously been during my whole existence.*'[20]

CHAPTER 2

The Grand Tour

Although so little is known about Ellen's childhood, the much later discovery in 2012 of her travel diary, written when she was 14, gives a fascinating insight into the diarist she would become. When the Palmers decided in 1844 to take their daughter on a tour of Europe, they were following a custom that had grown up in the 1660s. Known as The Grand Tour, it was seen as an educational rite of passage for the sons of the nobility and wealthy landed gentry, enabling them to see the historic and cultural places of Europe. The trips often lasted two or three years and it was hoped that these privileged young men would return with a new maturity, improved taste and an understanding of foreign cultures. The usual stops were Paris, Turin, Venice, Naples and Rome. By the nineteenth century, with the advent of the railways, travel had become easier, cheaper and safer, which led to a surge in numbers doing the tour. It became still more popular with the publication in 1836 of John Murray's guide, *A Handbook for Travellers on the Continent*.[1]

The Grand Tour had never played the same central part in the education of women, but in the eighteenth century Mary Wollstonecraft, Maria Edgeworth and Lady Mary Wortley Montague, among others, had all travelled on the Continent and published accounts of their experiences. It later became fashionable for young women with a companion to make short trips, but Ellen, travelling with her parents and her aunts in 1844, must have been one of the youngest to describe the experience. Her eye for the unimportant detail and the ridiculous enlivens her account of the tour. The Palmers were also travelling at a time when the railway system in France was incomplete, France having been slower to embrace the new means of travel, so coaches were still needed on parts of the route.

The tour, scheduled to last four months, was clearly educational in character and Ellen, travelling with her governess Miss Ward, was made to keep a daily record of her experiences. The small notebook she used to record her impressions of the tour was only found after the discovery of the main diaries. Unfortunately it covers just the first two months of the journey. Ellen certainly had Murray's guide, known as the Red Book, with her and the itinerary followed by the Palmers was very similar to that recommended by Murray. The guide was praised for being '*thoroughly English and reliable; for its history, hotels, exchanges, and scenery [...]*'. Besides Murray's Red Book, Ellen also had in her possession a copy of Byron's *Childe Harald's Pilgrimage,* a lengthy narrative poem, published by Murray in 1818. The poem, a loosely autobiographical account of Byron's continental tour combined with the world-weary reflections of a young man, had been an instant success. Byron had needed to leave England to escape the opprobrium his sexual exploits had incurred and Ellen was delighted to discover that they were following much the same route taken by Byron some 25 years earlier. An enthusiastic admirer, she never failed to mention any association with her hero when visiting places associated with his travels.

Besides her parents, the party consisted of her aunt Mrs Frances Roberts, now a rich widow and always referred to by Ellen as Aunt Abbey; her spinster aunt, Mary; Sir Roger's medical man; Miss Ward, the governess; a valet, a lady's maid, the coachman Kersley and a groom. They travelled partly by coach, complete with coat of arms, as well as taking a briska (a new type of landau which had seats that rose six inches when the top was lowered[2]) to accommodate the servants and the luggage, and partly by train and steamer. Apart from the coachman, the servants are never mentioned, but they must have played an essential, if unacknowledged, role. Kersley is probably only named because he was responsible for the hire of horses and for organising the loading of the coach and briska on the steamer as they travelled down the Rhine; from time to time he also arranged for them to go by train.

The party embarked for Antwerp from Tilbury on 1 September and sailed on the steamboat named *Antwerpen*. The day they spent in Antwerp set a pattern for their visits to other cities on their route. With Murray's Red Book and a hired local guide they set off after breakfast on a whirlwind tour of the city. They visit the cathedral and admire Rubens' 'Descent from the Cross'. Ellen dutifully mentions the other paintings they looked at and writes down details as to the length and height of the cathedral. Then on to St Paul's, '*which is a handsome church likewise adorned with fine paintings, specially the "Flagellation" and the nativity done by Rubens and pupils.*'[3] Ellen's attention is caught by two English ladies in dispute with the concierge because they will not give him a gratuity and he will not let them out unless they pay. She has mislaid her pencil case and when she returns to retrieve it, to her amusement sees that the argument is still going on.

She is less than impressed by a mound outside, intended as a representation of Mount Calvary with the Saviour on the cross. Describing the grotto, she writes, '*the walls are painted with the agonizing countenances of the sinners in purgatory interspersed with flames. Looking through the window you see our Saviour on a bed covered with silver offerings supposed to be sleeping tranquilly amidst the torments which surround him.*' She scornfully adds, '*altogether it is a most singular exhibition but one not calculated to impress the beholder with veneration for a religion which is interpreted with such gross superstition.*'

They then visit a small private collection of paintings belonging to a Mlle Herry, before setting off to drive round the town. Ellen notes that

> *the streets are mostly handsome, some of them are built in the Spanish style, several houses of 7 feet high which has a solemn and gloomy effect, but most of the bridges we passed were very bad, mere planks placed across the river. Having now satisfied our curiosity by examining as far as time would allow all the principal objects of notice in this venerable city we left our hotel [...] and took our places in the train for BRUSSELS [...] We were nearly two hours going to Brussels and on our arrival we proceeded to the Hotel de l'Europe and after a hot supper at 10 o'clock consigned ourselves to repose.*

The party abandoned sightseeing in Brussels, instead opting to go to Waterloo, but only Aunt Abbey, Miss Ward, Sir Roger's medical man and Ellen made the trip, as, Ellen wrote, the other three had seen it several times. The journey to Waterloo from Brussels took two hours and their first port of call was the house where the Marquess of Anglesea had had his leg amputated, which had already become something of a tourist attraction. Riding beside Wellington as the battle was in its final stages, he was hit by a stray bullet and said to Wellington, 'By God Sir, I have lost my leg.' Wellington replied, 'By God Sir, so you have.'[4] Anglesea was said to have smiled and joked during the operation to remove his leg and, when Ellen visited, there were both the table on which the operation had been performed and Anglesea's boot. A tomb had been raised over the remains of the leg and Ellen wrote derisively about the '*pathetic and pompous inscription*[5] *as if it were composed to deplore the loss of the Marquess himself. We then saw the table upon which the operation was performed and the boot cut from his leg which in duty bound we contemplated with more reverence than is usually vouchsafed to old tables and rusty boots.*' Someone else shared Ellen's sense of the ridiculous and in 1862 wrote on the tombstone:

> Here lies the Marquess of Anglesea's Limb
> The Devil will have the remainder of him[6]

The party then engaged the services of a guide, one Edward Cotton, who had actually fought at Waterloo. He took them to Hougoument and then to the monument erected to commemorate the battle, and pointed out the various points of interest. Standing overlooking the field of battle Ellen allowed herself '*a spark of national pride in the prowess of our country. Men who almost singly dared to resist the hitherto all powerful army of the oppressor who would fain have reduced their island home to a province of his empire and lowered the pride of free born Britons to wear the badge of servitude and dependence.*' Her reaction to Waterloo was very different from that of Byron who had made the same journey from Brussels to the battlefield, where he borrowed a Cossack horse and galloped over the field of battle. Visiting Hougoument, despite detesting the cause of the victors, he could not resist buying a few battle souvenirs; but he refused to associate himself with Britain's triumph: 'How that red rain hath made the harvest grow,' he wrote, and pointed up with passion the horrors of war.[7]

After a night at the theatre they left Brussels at 7am, having been woken at 5.30am, and took the postchaise to Louvain, where they breakfasted. Kersley had already put the coach and briska on the train, but unfortunately for the Palmers there were no seats left, so they were forced to sit in their own coach and briska on the train (no doubt a comic sight) for the journey to Cologne. Passing through Liège and Aix-en-Chapelle, they arrived at a quarter to nine at their destination. Such were the inconveniences of travel, they had to wait an hour before their coach was unloaded. There was a further delay because no horses were available and they did not reach their hotel until midnight.

During the half day they spent in Cologne, Ellen most enjoyed the military band playing a *fantaisie* from *Lucia di Lammermoor*, and was delighted by their harmonious performance, '*so different to our English bands*,' before being dragged off to visit the cathedral and the church of the 11,000 virgins. Then they travelled on again to Bonn by train, arriving at 2pm at the Grand Hotel, '*and like indefatigable sightseers set out immediately to view the university which is a handsome building [...] there being nothing else for ladies to see we engaged two carriages and went up to the Threnzberg, a mountain a little way out of town*.'

The coach and briska had to be loaded on to the steamer for their journey down the Rhine. Ellen was enchanted by the scenery. They disembarked at Coblenz but finding there was '*nothing very particular to admire*' they hired a coach to take them up the mountain to enjoy the view. Sunday was spent sailing down the Rhine to Mayence, where they planned to stay for two days, using it as a base for expeditions to Wiesbaden, and the Frankfurter Fair.

The trip to Wiesbaden was a disaster. They were unprepared for the violent thunderstorm accompanied by torrents of rain that broke out when they got there and were drenched to the skin. When they sought shelter in the Kursaal, Ellen doesn't hesitate to admit they caused great amusement and '*certainly we made a rather poor appearance among the gay company assembled there [...] this was at 2 o'clock and the table d'hôte*[8] *was not until 5 [...] and to add to our misfortunes there was not a train going back so we were compelled to hire two carriages into which we all crept after promenading through the gayest walk in Wiesbaden we returned to Mayence.*' How they managed to dry their clothes is left to the imagination. But, nothing daunted, and most probably urged on by Ellen, after resting and changing they returned to Wiesbaden, having been told that the gardens would be illuminated and that there would be all sorts of amusing goings-on. Unfortunately for them there was nothing to be seen but two large gambling tables at which rouge et noir and roulette were being played. Having watched one young man '*who seemed to have lost as much or more than he could afford walking up and down the room in great distress and an elderly gentleman by his side trying in vain to console him*', they decided to order their carriages and return to the hotel in Mayence, having sacrificed their dinner for the supposed attractions of Wiesbaden.

The excursion to see the famed Frankfurter Fair[9] was not much more successful as the weather was bad and they got caught in another shower of rain; they were, however, able to shelter until it was over. But when they went into the fair, perhaps their spirits had been dampened by the weather as Ellen has hardly a good word to say for it:

> *The articles for sale were of a common description and very dear. Altogether Aunt Abbey declared it was no better than the Wrexham Fair used to be [...] I certainly saw nothing in Frankfurt Fair worth coming over from England to see as some persons do. There were a great many people walking about among the shops but they all seemed to be of the lower orders.*

With that put-down they returned earlier than planned to Mayence, which they then inspected as was their custom.

Leaving Mayence for Heidleberg, they stopped off at Mannheim to visit the castle belonging to the Duke of Baden, but then lost their way to the rail station and missed the train. '*We were actually obliged to sit down 8 of us on the steps of a house a little way out of town and close to the station where we were happy to eat a crust of bread and a bunch of grapes which by good luck we were able to get [...] we waited until 6 o'clock when the next train left for Mannheim.*'

At Heidelberg, visiting the castle, Ellen was intrigued to notice that '*the students of the fine university of the Heidelberg fight duels with sabres and we observed several young men whose faces were covered in scars, not at all an extraordinary occurrence as there are several combats taking place sometimes in one day.*' The practice of duelling started around 1825 and was an indication that the students had courage; the scars were also a status symbol.

Their next port of call was Baden Baden, where they arrived at their hotel in time for the *table d'hôte* which, as Ellen explains, was a very pleasant custom: '*almost all the guests at the hotel meet together for the principal meal which must at least for sociable dispositions be much pleasanter than each one having a small, bad, private dinner sent up into their bedrooms.*'

Travelling could be very trying. Their arrival in Basel, Switzerland, after a long and disagreeable journey was made even worse as they had to walk into town and then could not find a hotel that would take them in. '*Let a person only picture themselves in our situation wandering about in the streets of a foreign town at half past ten o'clock half dead with fatigue already turned back from 3 hotels and only one remaining in the whole place*' – which luckily had rooms to let.

From there they went to nearby Neuhausen to look at the celebrated waterfall, the highest in Europe, which Murray called 'a hell of water', whilst Ellen writes of the stupendous grandeur of this splendid cascade. Very unusually Ellen describes the meal they were given, although, as she admits, it is not done to talk about food. However, on this occasion they were given '*two dishes of fumy bread, excellent honeycomb, a dish of diced pastry, preserves, fruit tart, pudding together with all the other etceteras upon these materials we contrived to make a very good feast*'.

As they travelled on through the Alps, it is clear that Ellen, although dutifully sightseeing, really revelled in the rugged mountain scenery of Switzerland. Trapped by bad weather in Lucerne, she was determined to climb to the top of Mount Rigi,[10] known as the Queen of the Mountains. Now, of course, the Rigi is accessible by cable car, but in

Ellen's day the only way up was on horseback or on foot. After waiting until the weather had cleared, they made the ascent from Reggio. Ellen records in triumph that she walked the whole distance which is excessively steep, keeping up with the horses and getting to the summit in two hours and a quarter, which was faster than Murray's allowance of three hours and a quarter to reach the top. Fog meant that there was no view to be seen from their hotel that evening, but when they were awakened by a Swiss horn at four the following morning to admire the view as the sun rose, Ellen was enchanted: '*altogether the view is certainly one of the most magnificent that can be imagined and we remained gazing on this splendid spectacle until 7 o'clock.*'

On the way to Berne they stopped at Interlaken and hired two carriages to take them to the Staubach Falls, passing '*through scenes the most savage and grand which we have seen. Here Byron planned his immortal tragedy of Manfred […] the scenery here is perfectly awful and its gloomy aspect has beheld a deed "suited to such a place" a fratricide committed in one of the wildest spots in the valley.*' Ellen must have had a copy of Byron's three-act tragedy *Manfred* with her as well as *Childe Harald*, because when they reach the falls she feels Byron's description is much more appropriate than her feeble attempts to describe the cascade[11] and quotes from the poem: '*It is not noon – the sunbow's rays still arch […]*' Byron was much influenced by the scenic splendour of the Bernese Oberland while he was writing his dramatic poem. The tragedy is focused on a reclusive magician figure, 'half dust, half deity', living alone in his mountain eyrie, tormented by guilt for his mysterious sin.[12]

From Interlaken they made their way to Grindelwald and rode on mountain horses specially trained to navigate the ragged and steep mountain path to the foot of the Upper Glacier, where they dismounted. They then had to creep almost on hands and knees through a low, winding passage and walked on the glacier for about five yards, the distance most people go. Ellen, naturally, was not satisfied, and holding on to the guide went on climbing up. '*The precipice (of solid ice be it remembered) being very steep every now and then we were obliged to cut steps with a hatchet to rest our feet upon and despite this precaution even the guide himself often slipped.*' Aunt Abbey, thoroughly alarmed but unable to stop Ellen, had sent Massone, their groom, up to join Ellen and the guide.

> *The danger was that if we should all three lose our footing we should have rolled to the bottom without possibility of stopping ourselves [...] in this manner we clambered up to the highest peak of the lowest range of ice and elevation of about 200 feet and would have gone further, but were obliged to return to Interlaken in time for the packet.*

Ellen consoled herself with the thought that she had been higher than any lady had as yet ever been, but of course had to pay for her adventure by a scolding from Aunt Abbey, who was doubtless also very relieved that she had got down safely. This was just one among many examples of Ellen's courage and fearlessness, and it must be remembered she was climbing in long skirts.

The making of literary associations was one of the educational benefits of the Grand Tour. While staying in Lausanne on Lac Leman at the Hotel Gibbon the party naturally wanted to see the place where the famous historian had written *The Rise and Fall of the Roman Empire.* When Byron had visited in 1816 he had found only a decayed summerhouse, and had plucked a sprig of acacia from the terrace which he sent to his publisher Murray.[13] When Ellen visited 28 years later even the summerhouse had disappeared and she regretted that there was now nothing to see except a portrait of Edward Gibbon in the hotel dining room, at which they gazed rather forlornly.

The following day they made the obligatory visit to the Château de Chillon, a massive, turreted stone castle built out into the lake, made famous by Byron's poem, *The Prisoner of Chillon.* Bonivard, a libertarian prior, was shackled and imprisoned in the deepest dungeon of the castle in 1530 by the Duke of Savoy for trying to free the Genovese from his rule. Ellen writes that the stone floor at the base of the pillar to which Bonivar was attached is worn into a hollow by his walking up and down. The pillars are covered in inscriptions, and Ellen believed Byron's to be among them, but she could not find it, or even what may have been a nineteenth-century addition.

Continuing her interest in literary associations, while visiting Geneva she writes dismissively, '*There are very few sights for the passing stranger to visit at Geneva, it is however interesting as having been the birth place of Rousseau and Calvin [...] Fernay, only five miles distant from Geneva was the residence of Voltaire, Rousseau's great rival.*' Even if she had never read any of their works it pleased her to know that they shared with her hero, Byron, a love of Lac Leman and quotes Voltaire's description, 'mon lac est le premier'. They did visit Rousseau's little island just off the bridge, but she thought the statue of Jean-Jacques very inferior.

The party had been travelling for just over a month when they set out to cross the Simplon.[14] They left Brig at 6 o'clock in the morning and Ellen and her father walked the whole way to the summit, a distance of 15 or 16 miles, uphill all the way. Ellen claimed to be not in the least fatigued and could have done it again. Nearing the summit, she writes,

> *the sight is a perfect picture of desolation, not the smallest flower dares to pop above the earth in the savage solitude of lofty mountains covered in snow, the transparent glaciers, the roaring cascades combine to form a scene of grandeur and sublimity which is almost terrifying. On the summit of the pass is situated the hospice, a large white building inhabited by a few brothers of the Augustinian order who freely give hospitality to anyone who asks it.*

Another famous author, Mary Shelley,[15] had passed through the Simplon the year before and in her travel narrative, *Rambles in Germany and Italy*, published in 1844, describes the Simplon in a short and telling sentence: 'There was a naked simplicity that inspired awe; the naked bones of a gigantic world were there.' The book was published too late, however, for Ellen to have known of it before the start of their tour. The Palmer party arrived on the Italian side of the pass at Domodossola at 8 o'clock in the evening.

The next morning brought them to Lake Maggiore and Ellen simply wrote that '*absolutely no words can do justice to its beauty*'. Taking time out to row across to the Isla Bella, a small island on the lake, to visit the palace belonging to the Count Borromeo, they were particularly struck by the curious mosaic-like grottos in the gardens. They were also shown an immense laurel on which Napoleon had cut the word 'Battaglia' in 1800, just before the battle of Marengo, and they could still see traces of the letters.

While they were staying in Como, doubtless at Ellen's request, they took a rowing boat and rowed down the lake to see the Villa Pasta, home of the famous singer Giuditta Pasta,[16] who was the reigning Italian soprano and had enchanted London in 1824 in a series of Rossini roles. Although Ellen would never have heard her sing, such was her love of opera that she wanted to see where Pasta lived. She was all the more thrilled to see the '*celebrated singer herself who was walking along her pleasure grounds close to the lake. She is about 50 years old and certainly must have been a very fine woman, but is now plain and fat.*'

Unlike in Geneva, in Milan they were assured of a wealth of artistic delights. After visiting a couple of churches they went to see Leonardo da Vinci's celebrated depiction of the Last Supper. It had already been the subject of three botched attempts at restoration when Ellen saw it, but she wrote prophetically of her fears for its future.

> *This splendid picture has been so much injured by repainting, patching, and altering that scarcely a trace of the original remains. We can yet, however see enough to justify the reputation it enjoys but it is scaling off so rapidly and incessantly that in a few more years this transcendentally beautiful work of art which should have been immortal will probably exist no more.*[17]

She was not the only writer to comment on the sad condition of 'The Last Supper'. Mary Shelley had also written of its parlous state, but Ellen at 14 must surely have been the youngest visitor to record her impressions.

Journeying on to Brescia, they saw what they could of the town in the short time before breakfast but then had to wait three-and-a-half hours at the next staging post for horses, which meant they could go only as far as Verona instead of to Vicenza as planned. Despite all its Shakespearean associations, they preferred their beds to looking for Romeo and Juliet's supposed tomb or walking where the two gentlemen had walked. They finally arrived in Vicenza the following day. While the horses were being changed they just had time to visit the Teatro Olimpico and to see Palladio's private palace before continuing on to Padua. Arriving there at about 7 o'clock they had to wait an hour and a half before they could eat.

The Palmer party was not only following in the footsteps of Byron and Mary Shelley, but also of Samuel Rogers, the celebrated romantic poet, now almost forgotten, eclipsed as he is by Wordsworth and Coleridge. He had done the continental tour in 1814. Ellen uses a quotation from his poem entitled 'Venice', to describe the city she is about to visit:

> *Now is the glorious city in the sea,*
> *The sea is in the broad and narrow streets,*
> *Ebbing and flowing and the salt sea weed,*
> *Clings to the marble of her palaces.*

Embarking on a gondola at Mestre, she notices with dismay that a bridge is being constructed to link Venice to the mainland and writes, '*how effectually will that do away with all the romance and charm attached to the entrance of this singular city*'. (The bridge was completed in 1846.) She is truly shocked by this manifestation of the advance of civilisation which she thinks '*certainly destroys the last dying gleams of romance and the world is getting as matter of fact as it possibly can*'. To add to her disappointment they go in a closed gondola to their hotel, the Hotel Royal, which no longer exists but was just behind the Piazza San Marco. However, she is soon captivated by the view from the hotel windows: '*The prospect was lovely, before us lay a wide street of water with several islands on which houses were grouped and the blue Adriatic covered with vessels of all sizes, washing the long amphitheatre which formed altogether a scene never to be forgotten.*'

As their first day in Venice was a Sunday and there was no English service, they felt they could allow themselves the pleasure of visiting St Mark's, afterwards climbing to the top of the campanile. Here Ellen comes to the gloomy conclusion that

> *despite the aristocratic luxury and majestic appearance of this beautiful city it is evident that this splendour is but a shadow of days gone by. The numerous palaces are falling into decay, the neglect of all its ancient customs and privileges, its present servitude* [Venice was at this time part of the Austrian empire] *contrasts with the times when its proud Doges ruled the state inspire a melancholy which is not diminished by the sight of gondolas with their black canopies gliding along the street in melancholy silence, so different from the crowds and bustle of other cities.*

She could have been writing about the state of Venice today, apart from the gondolas, which are no longer enclosed and are full of noisy, happy tourists.

Sightseeing on that first day had been taken at a slightly more leisurely pace and limited to churches because it was Sunday, but there was to be no let-up on Monday. Ellen wrote, '*Having resolved to work from morning to night to see the sights of Venice as quickly as possible, we engaged a gondola and set off at half past eight to the church of San Giorgio Maggiore beautifully situated on an island.*' After visiting the Treasury of St Mark's they went to see a private collection of paintings, where Sir Roger bought a fine picture by Bassano, and then continued their sightseeeing. After such a hectic day they took a turn in the public gardens, '*which are not very pretty being composed of nothing but short straight walks and ugly little trees*'. They arrived home at 6 o'clock '*after which I think everyone will consider it a pretty good day's work*'.

Their itinerary the following day was more varied. Another gondola was hired and they visited the Arsenale and then the island of Murano to watch glass being manufactured. Back in Venice they visited the splendid Frari church at a time when Canova's great monument to Titian was still under construction. It had been commissioned by Venice's Austrian rulers, and Ellen thought the design was cold and tame. Titian died in 1576 and it is said that no one knew where he was buried as there was no memorial to mark his grave. Ellen recorded that the spot where his body is said to lie at present was marked by the inscription:

In grazie Titziano de Vicelli
Digni emulo de Zeus e degli Agnelli

The visit in the evening to the Isola di San Lazzaro must have thrilled her. While in Venice her hero, Byron, had rowed back and forth to visit the monks who lived there to learn the Armenian language. He delighted in the monastery's collection of old manuscripts, becoming at the same time an admirer of the monastic way of life and a champion of the Armenian territory against Russian encroachment. But his interest did not last, and four months later Byron had deserted Lazzaro for the joys of the Venice carnival.[18] The monks showed the Palmer party round the convent, which then contained an Egyptian mummy said to be 3,000 years old '*and in perfect preservation but quite bruised by time and exposure with a piece of money in the mouth supposed to be intended to pay for the passage over the Styx*'. The money has since disappeared. They inspected the printing press the monks used to publish books in Armenian, and also the library containing some 200,000 books and 4,000 manuscripts, as well as Byron's work.

The Fenice opera house had just been rebuilt and for the first time Ellen finds herself out of sympathy with Byron who wrote that '*it is the finest he ever saw and that of Milan and Brescia bow before it*'. Ellen disagreed with his lordship: '*La Scala has more rows of boxes and is more handsomely decorated. The stage is of great extent and no doubt when well lighted looks very well.*' After one further visit to a private house their commissionaire told them that there was nothing more for them to see, excepting the churches. Perhaps he was tired, but even Ellen, having visited 15 churches out of the total of 85, felt that enough was enough, so they enjoyed themselves that evening listening to the band and walking round St Mark's Square. They made a quick visit to the Cannaregio the following morning to look at the paintings in the Palazzo Manfrini. Leaving Venice that afternoon, Ellen in romantic vein wrote, '*I was very sorry to bid adieu to the enchanted scene and as we saw this dreamlike city of the hundred isles gradually recede from our sight I think we all felt as though we were leaving a happy realm we should never behold again.*'

They had only two hours to see Padua before breakfast, but Ellen, her governess and the doctor must have walked extremely fast over the cobbles to see as much as they did. They went first to the church of Santa Giustina, they then entered the immense hall of the Palazzo della Ragione where the meridian line crosses the hall, and watched numbers of people busily employed in testing the accuracy of their watches. On to the university, which houses among other treasures a first folio of Shakespeare's plays, but Ellen did not know that. What did interest her was the statue of Elena Piscopia, the first woman to receive a university degree. '*She knew Hebrew, Greek and Latin and Spanish, French and Arabic perfectly and who was at once a musician and a poetess, a mathematician and an astronomer. The students however have almost demolished all the fingers and toes because they do not like a woman among them. I shrewdly suspect jealousy has a little to do with that.*'

The Palazzo Pappafava, which was their next port of call, and which contained paintings and sculpture, no longer exists as such and is privately owned. Passing the famous Café Perdochi, which remained open night and day for the benefit of those arriving late by diligence, they reached the Roman amphitheatre and the little church of Santa Maria della Arena, known as Giotto's Chapel. The three of them were able to go straight in to enjoy some of the finest frescos by Giotto which cover the walls. Ellen noted that '*the tints of these paintings are somewhat dimmed by time, having never been cleaned or restored but they are still very impressive*'. The paintings have since been restored. Fifteen minutes is all the time allowed to today's visitors, after having to wait in a decontamination chamber before entering so as not to damage the paintings. Ellen and her party probably did not spend as much as 15 minutes inside the chapel before rushing off to see the tomb of Antenore, the founder of the city of Padua. After breakfasting at the hotel, they even managed one more visit to the church of St Anthony before leaving for Ferrara. Even with all the good will in the world it would be impossible to see so much today in such a short time.

Leaving Padua, the Palmer coach trundled south over the flat, uninteresting Piedmontese countryside to Ferrara where they spent the night. By setting out at seven in the morning the usual party had just three hours to complete their sightseeing in Ferrara before leaving for

Bologna, where they arrived in mid-afternoon. Nothing was going to stop Ellen making the most of her opportunities. '*We arrived in Bologna at 3 o'clock and immediately set off sightseeing despite the weather which was really dreadful, but this was not so great an inconvenience here as it would be in England for in the city as well as in Padua and others there are covered portions along the sides of the principal streets.*'

Crossing the pass over the Apennines they finally arrived in Florence, where they were to spend a week. There was so much to see that they needed the extra days and, as Ellen puts it, each morning '*according to custom we set off sightseeing*', and lengthy descriptions follow of what they saw. So it is a surprise to read the brief entry for 24 October and a relief to know they could relax: '*Very wet morning but cleared up a little later in the course of the day. Aunt Abbey and I went out shopping.*' Normal visiting of sites of interest took place over the next two days, and on Sunday they found the English chapel, which was simply a middle-sized but very crowded room. They went to both of the church services. Sunday was very strictly observed by the Palmers so it seems a little strange that after the service they should have attempted to find the casino, but it was their last day in Florence. It was also sadly the last diary entry, for although there must be another volume recording the next two months spent mostly in Rome and Naples, it has not been found.

The views of the other members of the Palmer party are never mentioned in the diary, and Ellen often has recourse to the royal 'we' when giving an opinion, sweeping up any differences they may have had. Except for the fact that Aunt Abbey, Miss Ward and the doctor were nearly always the ones who went sightseeing with Ellen, we know nothing about their views or what they thought, nor do we know how her parents occupied themselves in the meantime. So it is all the more amusing to read about the one small personal disaster that Ellen allowed herself to record. Written upside down on the back cover are the words,

> *The reader will doubtless notice a very sensible alteration in the colour of the ink. As I have said before I was writing at home and sleeping in the same room as Aunt Abbey. I was staying up to write while she undressed herself. All at once she was startled from a cry from my table*

and looking round saw a dreadful disaster, there was my unfortunate inkstand spilt all over on the table which had two [words blotted out] *on it. Everyone else was in bed and we had a regular washing up operation to perform on the cloth which hopefully did not suffer much. I must add that next morning Aunt Abbey broke a large frame of glass in the window which deprives her of the right to laugh at me.*[19]

CHAPTER 3

Preparing for the London Season

It is clear from the very first entry in her diary, written on 1 January 1847, when she was 16 years old, that Ellen had reservations about the joys of a London season, and did not expect to find '*a fairy land of unalloyed pleasure*'. However, she much enjoyed her first taste of this new world despite the fact that it got off to a rather embarrassing start.

The Palmers were spending Christmas at Cefn. Nathanial Roberts had purchased Cefn from the Kenyons, a local Welsh family, after the house had been rebuilt following a fire in 1794, when all the records had been burnt. Frances had inherited the house – an unpretentious Georgian mansion standing in parkland on the outskirts of Wrexham – after her husband's death in 1841 and shared it with her sisters. The Palmers must have been pleased to be invited to dine at Wynnstay by their neighbour, Sir Watkin Williams-Wynn, to celebrate the New Year, and particularly so as Ellen was included in the invitation. It would be the first time that she had officially left the schoolroom and been treated as a member of society. Perhaps Sir Watkin, a young man, unmarried, in his late 20s, was curious to meet Miss Palmer. The Williams-Wynns were the largest landowners in North Wales, with over 100,000 acres in Denbighshire and Shropshire. Sir Watkin's grandfather, the 4th baronet, had done the Grand Tour and as a result of his interest in painters and paintings had played a significant part in developing the arts in North Wales, in addition to purchasing works of art for Wynnstay and commissioning

Capability Brown to lay out the grounds. He had also commissioned Robert Adam to build him a house in St James's Square, Nos 20/21, where his grandson was born in 1820. The 5th baronet, like his father, was an MP and held the seat for Denbighshire until his death. As the largest landowner in North Wales and controller of many parliamentary seats he was known as 'The King in Wales'. His son, the 6th baronet, who succeeded his father in 1840, inherited the estates, the parliamentary seat and the sobriquet.

Ellen was not yet 17 when the Palmer party set out to dine at Wynnstay, the occasion specially chosen to mark her entry into adult society. The two houses were only about 10 miles distant, but somehow the Palmers had mistaken the time and Ellen's first grown-up social engagement got off to an inauspicious start. Dressed appropriately in white muslin with a pink rose in her banded hair, she reported that

> *After we had waited about a quarter of an hour we heard a tremendous clatter on the stairs, the door opened and in bounded Sir Watkin who had just returned from hunting. I was expecting to see a perfect monster from the exaggerated reports of the country people & was really almost disappointed at seeing a very personable young man whose only remarkable point was a great breadth across the shoulders. He evidently was much astonished at seeing us there so early [...] after about ten minutes conversation he retired to dress and in an hour from the time of our arrival the guests were all assembled in the library.*

After dinner Ellen was called upon to play the piano, and Sir Watkin was very attentive, telling her all sorts of funny stories. Obviously the centre of attraction, she wrote '*that for my part I was delighted with the dinner party*', making no further comment about their early embarrassing arrival. It was the first of several *faux pas* the socially inexperienced, but ambitious Palmers were to make over the next years.

From this time onward Ellen began to keep a daily account of her life, not only to record her social life and everyday events, but also as a means of expressing her frustrations as well as her triumphs. The diaries reveal her unhappiness at home and the difficult relationship she had with her family, which was to blight her young life. She felt that the family tried to regulate not only her behaviour, but even what she thought. An expression of opinion with which the aunts did not agree led to both Ellen and her brother Roger being punished and forbidden card games, their regular evening entertainment. '*One dare not even think differently from the old folk. They must always be right & won't allow anyone to think at all,*' she writes. The next day she was in trouble again. Meeting her aunt Mary while cantering her pony with her brother, she was scolded for '*such a dreadful lack of decorum [...] was told I was a harridan, a bumpkin, a romp, a disgrace to the family etc*'. Her aunt was doubtless hoping to mould her into a prim and proper young lady now that she had come of age, but it left Ellen feeling deeply resentful. Her aunts did not just try to monitor her behaviour and opinions but tried to control her conversation. She soon discovered that it was very unwise to sit opposite her Aunt Abbey at any dinner party as she watched and listened to every word. This was not just a spirited, intelligent young girl being chastised by her elders for being rude and bumptious, it was treatment that persisted throughout her youth, leading her to say later that she felt like an '*imprisoned girl*'. Her family evidently feared that her independent-mindedness would damage the prospect of her making a suitable marriage. When later she was accused of appearing cold and unfeeling she thought it was because early on she had learnt to suppress her emotions so as not to provoke confrontations with her relatives.

Following the dinner party at Wynnstay, Sir Watkin arranged for the hunt to meet at Cefn. This must have been the first time such an event had taken place at Cefn because not only were the new carpets to be uncovered in honour of the occasion, but a great number of dishes were also made ready for the visitors. With undisguised glee, Ellen tells of the preparations for lunch that Aunt Abbey was to give for the foxhunters the following Monday:

> *Sir Watkin is coming with a large party from Wynnstay [...] the house has been turned quite topsy turvy in the expectation of this visit & we have been worried out of our lives with the preparations [...] after hearing the number of dishes till we know them off by heart, after taking*

the pains we did to wipe our shoes clean that we might not dirty the new carpets in all their undruggated splendour, after all this the affair turned out a dead failure.

A hard frost during the night meant that the hunt was cancelled and as a kindly gesture Sir Watkin and Mrs Williams rode over and showed the hounds at the back door. Ellen must have enjoyed writing her sarcastic description of the lunch and it also served as a personal revenge for the many scoldings she had received.

There was Dobbin [Aunt Abbey's nickname] *at the top of the table smirking so amiably as if she had 100 people looking at her, there were all the smoking chicken & fat moulds of blancmange really pathetically imploring to be eaten […] There were ourselves doing our little endeavours to consume as many provisions as 20 expected guests […] but nothing could prevent us reflecting that our grand party was dwindled down into […] oh dear me […] one miserable Wat and a Williams.*[1]

Ellen's diary, which she kept firmly locked, as well as being a record of her daily life became a safety valve for the expression of her thoughts and feelings without fear of reprimand. The other weapon she used to ensure she retained some semblance of independence from the regimented life imposed by the aunts and her mother was music. She wanted to stand out, to excel, and music was her chosen option. To underline her dedication she imposed a rigid discipline on herself.

I declare I have almost forgotten to chronicle one heroic effort I daily make, that is getting up at 7 o'clock by candle light every morning (be it ever so cold) to practise. No one else in the house thinks of stirring till broad daylight & although it certainly is an effort to leave one's comfortable warm bed & brave the bitter cold of a day wintery morning, to dress by candlelight, still if one hopes to attain eminence in anything one must make some sacrifices & this is one.[2]

This was not just a one-off fancy; the diaries show that Ellen regularly devoted up to seven hours a day practising the piano and singing when she could, and only missed practice when there was no piano available or there was no time.

The Palmers visited Paris regularly in the winter to enjoy its delights, but their visit in 1847 had a different purpose. Ellen was no longer confined to the schoolroom and this year the visit was to be part-preparation and part-rehearsal for the coming London season. The Palmers spent a few days in London before crossing to the Continent. Life might be dull in Cefn in the winter, but life in London could be worse. Ellen laments, '*Oh, the horrors of London in January. Fogs so thick you can scarcely see your right hand from your left, streets in a deplorable condition between snow and rain, a few miserable individuals hurrying hither & thither with blue cheeks & red noses formed a tout ensemble which looked perfectly dismal after the country.*'[3]

The family had meant to spend only a few days at their house in Portland Place before journeying on to Paris, but their departure was delayed by Miss Ward being ill, and the fog getting worse. '*It is only 11 o'clock, all I know is that I can scarcely see at all owing the fog,*' wrote Ellen in despair. Miss Ward recovered, the family arrived in Paris, but not without much grumbling. They had to take a hired carriage for the journey from Boulogne to Amiens and to add to their discomfort it started to rain and the carriage turned out not to be waterproof.

> *Let anybody fancy our miseries, three good sized people squeezed up on one seat & getting wet and dirty as fast as possible, Papa scolding, Mama wishing she had never come, and all three jointly abusing me for having brought them to this outlandish place […] we were obliged to put up an umbrella […] we did not get into Amiens until half past nine after thirteen hours.*[4]

Finally they arrived in '*dear delightful Paris*' and installed themselves in the Hôtel du Rhin on the Place Vendôme.

Their first concern was the all-important matter of leaving their cards at the British Embassy, so as to signal their availability to receive possible invitations. They had to find a friend to do this for them. The following days were occupied by more mundane matters: they ordered a piano and a pair of stays for Ellen, visited two dressmakers, Mme Soigny and Mme Camille, to order two 'robes de bal'. The fashion-conscious Ellen was much mortified at being laughed at for wearing an unfashionable straw bonnet and greatly relieved to be able to buy a black velvet bonnet, '*not before I wanted it for our straws are the laughing stock of Paris and during our promenade in the Boulevards we were made fun of unmercifully.*'[5] Ellen does not mention her mother also buying a bonnet, but one hopes she did to avoid the ridicule occasioned by their straw bonnets. They called on friends and Lady Palmer took tickets for a 'grand bal' in aid of the distressed Irish from a friend, Mrs Tudor, for the following week.

It was ironic that the tickets acquired by the Palmers for Ellen's first ball should be for the benefit of those affected by the disastrous potato famine in Ireland. By 1847, the famine, which had begun in 1845, had reached epic proportions. Irish peasants mainly subsisted on a diet of potatoes, as farmers could grow triple the amount of potatoes as of grain on the same small plot of land, so when the crop was attacked by a blight which turned the life-giving potato into a slimy, decaying mass of rottenness, famine inevitably followed. Although Irish Catholics made up 80 per cent of the population, English and Anglo-Irish families owned most of the land, and the Palmers, who owned vast tracts of land in County Mayo and in Sligo, were among their number. Although they owned Kenure, an Irish property which they visited two or three times a year, they were as much absentee landlords as the English aristocrats who never visited Ireland. The Palmers employed agents to manage their estates and extract rent revenues from their tenants as did so many of the ascendancy class, who saw their Irish possessions as income-generating, giving little or no thought to the plight of their tenants, who mostly lived in conditions of the utmost poverty and who were now dying from starvation in their hundreds.

By 1847, when *The Times*[6] was reporting details of the famine in Ireland, public concern was growing, and charitable events, including fundraising balls, became fashionable as a way of raising awareness of the unfolding tragedy. It is perhaps no surprise that Ellen, protected and cosseted as she was, made no comment and appeared unaware of the link between the charitable objects of her first ball and the fact that her lavish lifestyle was partly underpinned by rent money from the very same impoverished Irish for whose benefit the ball was held.

Sundays were strictly observed by the Palmers, and if unable to attend a church service they read the service at home, sometimes twice. A wet Sunday in Paris was no better than in London. Not allowed to read books or newspapers – '*it is about the greatest trial of mental patience that ever was*,' wrote Ellen – their only entertainment was to read the service. To compensate for the dreary Sunday, they were invited the following day to a small soirée by Lady Sanderson. This would be Ellen's first introduction to Parisian society and she did not expect to enjoy the occasion; a dreary evening with 40 guests sitting in a formal circle listening to music did not sound like much fun. But fortunately for her there were other young people at the party, so after tea and music, dancing began in another room and this Ellen enjoyed immensely. She met several young men, one a Mr Ledru, who was evidently much taken with her, as he subsequently put himself out to help the Palmers. He appears to have arranged introductions for them and got them invitations to balls and other functions during their stay in Paris.

After attending one or two musical soirées, going to the opera, shopping and walking, at last it was time for the big event – Ellen's first ball: the charity ball for the distressed Irish at the Hotel Lambert,[7] a 'hôtel particulier', or grand town mansion, belonging to a Polish nobleman, Prince Adam Czartoryski. As usual, Ellen, to avoid disappointment, and thinking they would know no one and that it would be excessively crowded, had discounted the possibility of actually enjoying it. She was amazed at how the courtyard had been boarded over and transformed into a ballroom, most elegantly hung with blue and white drapery and splendidly illuminated by chandeliers. She had been provided with a partner, a Captain Ogilvy, who danced a polka with her, and afterwards escorted her and her mother through the splendid suite of rooms including the *Salle de Jardin*, which she compared to a fairy bower. But, duty done, Captain Ogilvy abandoned the Palmers and went away to dance, leaving them sitting with nothing to do but watch the dancers. Following the English custom of not allowing anyone to ask a lady to dance without being formally introduced, Mama refused to let Ellen accept the request of a tall, moustachioed Frenchman, only to be told afterwards that he was a Vicomte and one of the stewards of the ball, and it was a great honour to have been invited to dance a quadrille with him. Despite this setback, Ellen did have one more dance – not with the Vicomte, but with a friend of his. They then had to wait two hours in the anteroom for the carriage and arrived home at half past two, heartily tired. It was not a very encouraging start.

Her first ball may have been grand but dull, but two days later Ellen attended another ball, this time in her new ball dress: three skirts of net over white silk looped up with green flowers, a wreath of the same in her hair which had been dressed by Hippolyte:

> *the whole toilette in perfect taste [...] altogether everyone agreed that I looked exceedingly well. Mrs Dansey was quite in extasies about it. We saw several people we knew but the Sandersons and Jenkins who had daughters on hand kept at quite a laughable distance & would not even speak to us. It is really surprising how afraid people are of other young ladies nipping in and stealing their beaux, however the gentlemen I met at their house would dance with me & so I got plenty of partners but no thanks to anybody.*[8]

This is the true voice of Ellen, confident in her own appearance, perhaps aware for the first time that she is attractive to the opposite sex, and not afraid to use her looks and personality to make an impact in the ballroom given half a chance.

Lady Palmer was very particular as to which invitations she accepted and only chose those occasions that were very grand or given by grand foreigners. Invitations to several English balls were refused, including one given by Lady Sanderson, as Ellen explained disingenuously – '*not wishing me to go to any but very grand affairs for fear of tiring me for the London season.*' The idea of tiring Ellen was laughable; her mother's real reason was doubtless to impress other mothers by her daughter being seen only at the most exclusive events. However, Mama had no problem in allowing Mr Ledru, who had called to ask if they were going to

Princess Czartoryski's[9] 'little evening', a less formal occasion where there would be dancing, to procure tickets for them. They had been preparing to go to the opera, but appreciating the chance to accept such an enviable invitation, stayed only for the first part of *Don Giovanni* before going on to the Hôtel Lambert, now no longer decorated as for the Charity Ball.

For the first time Ellen really began to enjoy herself, and found the French custom of being able to accept invitations to dance without a formal introduction very liberating. '*We found it very common practice to invite people you had taken a fancy to whether you knew them or not at least among the French.*' The evening ended with her taking part for the first time in a mazurka. In the 1830s and 1840s the mazurka enjoyed the greatest popularity, as it served as a sign of solidarity with the oppressed Polish nation[10] and was championed by Polish exiles and their aristocratic patrons. As there were no set figures and more than 50 steps, the dance could last for several hours. Uncertain of the moves at first, Ellen boasted she had soon mastered the intricacies of the dance. Only after she was exhausted from dancing energetically for two hours did Ellen take pity on her tired mother, and they returned home at 4 o'clock in the morning.

Ellen's accounts of subsequent balls underline her successes. She revels in the fact that so many young men beg to dance with her that she gets into trouble for double-booking her partners. She is still amazed that she can dance with a stranger and enjoys the lack of formality. At the Thurlows' ball she had engagements three or four deep and by the time they returned home at 5 o'clock in morning, '*I really had had enough dancing by the time I got home having sat down for one polka the whole evening and steadily refused all invitations being tremendously warm and rather tired.*'

As well as a little gentle sightseeing, walking in the Tuileries Gardens and going on shopping expeditions, Ellen was enrolled at Cellerini's dancing establishment where she enjoyed practising the polka, the waltz, the mazurka and the cotillion. Having discovered that there was to be a ball at the Hôtel de Ville, Ellen persuaded her parents to write to the ambassador, Lord Normanby, with a request to be introduced. The ambassador did not respond and Mr Ledru, who had tried to help, was unable to get tickets for them. There is a curious entry in the diary to say that the Palmers had refused an invitation to dine at the embassy with the excuse that they had flu. Perhaps this obvious lie was the reason for the lack of response to their request; Ellen says they had to stay in pretending to have flu. Were they fearful, perhaps, that Sir Roger might have one of his epilectic fits?

Ellen persuaded her parents to defer their departure for a week on the pretext of the ball at the Hôtel de Ville, but it was unfortunately cancelled. Her diary entry of 12 March shows how much she was enjoying continental life:

> *Awoke in a shocking disconsolate humour about leaving Paris tomorrow. Yesterday evening was our last pleasure in this gay metropolis and the thought of our approaching departure prevented me enjoying a single thing all this day. Really, truly I never felt so unhappy about anything since leaving Naples and yet I should be puzzled to say what grieves me so much in the circumstances. I suppose I must have an innate love for the continent, indeed which I am sure I have for whenever I am comparing it with England I catch myself constantly dwelling on the greater vivacity, gaity & sociability etc., prevailing in foreign countries. I am always sighing to return to dear Italy with such a love for travelling as I have it really is peculiarly unfortunate my parents should always have such a taste for remaining in stupid old England or stupider Ireland. In fact they only came abroad this year because they had nowhere else to go and I am sadly afraid it will be impossible to move them again for a very long time.*[11]

Mama went ahead to get the house in Portland Place ready and the rest of the family were left kicking their heels in Boulogne for a week. On their final day, which had been designated as a day for fasting and humiliation as a consequence of the Irish famine, they received a message to return to London. Instead of fasting, they embarked on the steamer and so were unable to mark the occasion. It is the second and only other time that the Irish famine is mentioned in the diaries; although Ellen occasionally talks about the possibility of unrest or even of riots, she never makes any comment as to the cause of the unrest.

CHAPTER 4

The London Season

The return to London had been timed to fit in with Ellen's presentation to Queen Victoria at Court, an essential event for any girl about to be launched in society. Two days after her arrival back at Portland Place, Ellen found herself in a coach bedecked with crimson liveries and gold lace, driving to St James's Palace with her mother who had returned to London early to ensure that everything was in order for this most important occasion. They found themselves in a crowd of other mothers and daughters, all heading in the same direction, and eventually reached the first anteroom. '*Oh what a scene it presented, lords and ladies dressed in their best, court trains, plumes, uniforms, epaulettes, counsellors wigs, all pushing and jostling one another quite as vulgarly as any low mob and intent only on getting near the railed off space so as to be in a good situation for progressing forward when the door was opened.*'[1]

Ellen, determined not to be overawed by the occasion, had been quite calm until the moment she discovered she had forgotten to take off her glove and was so flurried she almost tore it off. Mama told her to look for Prince Albert on the right and to curtsey to him.

> *Following these instructions I cast my eye around a group of gentlemen standing near the throne and after great indecision as to who I should fix upon I started a low reverence to the Lord Chamberlain taking him in my anxiety for the Prince. He however called out 'Kiss the Queen's hand Miss Palmer' upon which I bent very low to salute the hand that was held out, and then curtseying very low to a tall figure glittering*

> *with stars and orders on the Queen's left hand, saluted a row of ladies whose plumed heads nodded in response then escaped from the semi circle with the whole scene dancing before my eyes and a confused idea of having been close to the Queen and Prince and the Royal Duchesses.*

Although being presented at Court was an important rite of passage for a young girl, and meant that she was now considered an adult and a full member of society, able to attend Court functions, balls and parties as well as being officially in the marriage market and able to look for a suitable husband, Ellen seems to have taken the whole affair remarkably casually, apart from being a little flustered by being in the presence of royalty for the first time.

Unlike some girls, Ellen could not wait to get to her room when they arrived home and take off her finery: a dress composed of three layers of tulle over silk looped up with bouquets of cactus and heather, a train of white *gros de Naples* silk trimmed with *bouillons* (gathered or shirred bands of material) put on in waves and fastened in bouquets, the same as on the dress. Madame Flexon had come to do her hair, a little flatter than she wore it normally, but with bandeaux to accommodate the obligatory three feathers, lappets and flowers. But she made no mention in her diary of practising her curtsey, learning to walk elegantly, or fussing over her dress beforehand.

Attendance at Almack's was another important milestone on the route to social recognition, and acceptance as a member was a sign of approval. Almack's, on King Street, St James, was the first social club to admit both men and women. It was governed by a select committee of high-society ladies, called the Patronesses, who met every Monday and decided, on grounds of breeding and behaviour, who might be admitted or who should be made to leave. Obtaining a voucher for admission meant you were seen to be among the social elite, and was most keenly sought after. Lady Palmer appears to have asked a Mrs Drake to obtain vouchers, having decided that Ellen should make her debut in London society at a ball at Almack's. Indeed, to Ellen's annoyance, her Mama had gone without her to several soirées and once to a ball alone to make sure she understood the form. Finally, Ellen went to Almack's:

> *At 11 o'clock Mama and I went to Almacks where I made my first debut [...] we took the bench near to the Lady Patronesses and were much amused by Lady Jersey,*[2] *Lady Villiers & party who were the only grandees there and appeared to look upon the rest of the company as being from another sphere [...] the ball was very poorly attended and exceedingly stupid. Positively the only danceable person of our acquaintance we saw was Mr. Milman and I had a quadrille with him [...] oh how different these stiff and formal reunions are from the brilliant and delightful fetes of Paris. Even the dancing is as distinct as possible. There they dance for the pleasure of dancing, here they stalk about as if they were going to be hanged & looking deplorable in the extreme.*[3]

Captain Gronow,[4] the contemporary social observer, wrote, 'one can hardly conceive the importance which was attached to getting admission to Almacks, the seventh heaven of the fashionable world'. Not to be seen at Almack's branded one as outside the '*haut ton*'; it was the smartest marriage market, as only young men of decent background and respectable expectations were admitted, giving them the chance to seek out a suitable bride. Ellen was not impressed. '*It soon became very late & unbearably stupid so we took our departure, I being not at all charmed by this specimen of English society.*' A second visit did nothing to change her mind.

It was only an invitation to take part in a Polish mazurka at Almack's that caused her to relent. It seemed that Lord Dudley had been present when Ellen had danced the mazurka for the first time at the ball at the Palais Lambert in Paris. He was an enthusiastic supporter of Polish independence and had noticed how enthusiastically Ellen had thrown herself into the dance, quickly understanding some of the different moves involved. He wanted to introduce the mazurka to Almack's and persuaded Lady Agnes Duff[5] to hold some practice parties at her home. When he called on the Palmers, without the customary introduction, to ask if Ellen would join the group, this social solecism was overlooked because he also offered an invitation to Lady Palmer to be one of the patronesses of that ball. This was seen for what it was: a great honour.

Lady Agnes, the beautiful daughter of the Earl Erroll, was the same age as Ellen. She had been married young to a much older man, the Earl Duff, and was already pregnant with her second child. At the numerous rehearsals Ellen, self-importantly, instructed the group how to dance three of the chosen moves and was looking forward to performing the dance at Almack's. She had gone to enormous trouble to have a Polish costume specially made, consisting of a red cashmere tunic trimmed with swansdown, showing a silver embroidered bodice, little red boots and a red velvet cap with a feather and diamond clasp on her head. Her hair was arranged in ringlets with four long plaits with blue rosettes hanging down her back, something none of the other girls had thought of. With the patronesses in place, those dancing the mazurka were summoned upstairs. To her disgust, however, Ellen found herself in the worst place in the whole set, opposite the two worst dancers, including one girl who was so fat that when she did the kneeling position opposite Ellen she looked so ridiculous that the audience tittered. This was only one of the many occasions when Ellen's wish to excel proved to be a double-edged sword. Hiding her disappointment at having been so unfairly treated, Ellen wrote that the mazurka had been a success.

A box at the opera, either at Her Majesty's Theatre or at Covent Garden, was mandatory for anyone aspiring to acceptance in fashionable society. The King's Theatre on Haymarket, founded in 1821, had changed its name to Her Majesty's Theatre with the accession of Queen Victoria in 1837 and was run by a manager and a committee of noblemen who had transformed the meaning of opera-going, making it a social imperative. The supremacy of Her Majesty's Theatre was challenged in 1846 by the Theatre Royal in Covent Garden, when, after remodelling, it opened in 1847 as the Royal Italian Opera and some of the most famous opera singers came here to perform. A fierce rivalry developed between the two. A box at either was an expensive undertaking for any other than the very rich: at Her Majesty's Theatre it could cost up to 300 guineas a season. Opera was popular, not simply for the music, but because it mattered with whom one sat, where one sat, what one wore, whom one saw – all contributed to defining one's status in society. In the world of high society the importance of image made attendance at the opera a necessary part of the social round. The hierarchy of boxes was based on their visibility from the pit. First tier boxes and those with a view of royalty fetched premium prices.[6] The more visitors one had to the box the better, and one society lady described having no visitors to her box as a near-death experience.[7] Many ladies kept lists of the people they met and entertained, as did Ellen, but there are few known comments about the music they listened to. Ellen was no stranger to opera – during her European tour she had heard performances at the Scala, at the Fenice in Venice, in Rome and in Naples. For her, attendance at the opera was more than a social obligation; it was also a real pleasure. Her musical ability and knowledge enabled her to comment on the merits or otherwise of the singers, and for her the quality of the singing really mattered. The Palmers took a box at the opera in April and their first visit was to see *L'elisir d'amore* by Donizetti. Ellen was more interested in one of the new London productions of Verdi's *I due Foscari*,[8] an opera that appealed to her as it was based on a play by her hero, Byron. Her verdict:

> *I like the opera very much and the performance did it justice. Montenegro, the new prima donna, I did not so much admire. She sings with great energy and is a good actress but is not the sort of person to create a furore. Traschini, our old Neapolitan favourite, pleased me as much as ever, but Colettin certainly deserves the honours of the opera. His impersonation of the poor broken hearted old Doge was splendid and was tumultuously applauded.*

A month later, in May, they went to hear Jenny Lind in *La sonnambula* for a second time and Ellen writes: '*She was truly superb in it and was enthusiastically applauded. It appeared to me however that her voice was not quite so clear as on the first night, and I heard afterwards that she had a cold. However we were all highly delighted, especially with the two sleep walking scenes which were perfect.*' It takes a good ear to notice such a slight variation in performance. On another occasion, when Jenny Lind was singing the title role in *Norma*, Ellen writes, '*Jenny Lind delighted me exceedingly in her part of the Druid Princess. Her interpretation of it is not energetic and violent like Grisi*'.[9] Jenny Lind[10] had made her London debut on 4 May singing the part of Alice in an Italian version of *Robert le diable* in the presence of Queen Victoria, as she was to do two years later when she gave her final operatic performance, also with the Queen present.

The aristocratic ladies, like Lady Holland, Lady Jersey and Lady Palmerston, had the power to choose whom they would admit to the upper ranks of society, a role they clung to in this period of industrial change as the relationship between the upper and middle classes was constantly renegotiated. Their authority was rooted in polished manners, deportment and personal knowledge of the most important people in society. Status was not given lightly to families like the Palmers; it had to be acquired by hosting private gatherings, attending musical and literary parties, giving grand dinners, going to concerts and balls, taking a box at the opera, being seen at Ascot races and the Derby, and driving or riding in Rotten Row.

Having a beautiful, wealthy daughter to marry must have been useful to Lady Palmer in her quest to make the grade in society, but the family would have been much helped by their relationship with their distant cousins, the Mackinnons. William Mackinnon, a solid establishment figure and an MP, was a Fellow of the Royal Society and of the Society of Antiquaries as well as being head of Clan Mackinnon. One of his daughters would marry the heir to the earldom of Dundonald; another would become the Duchesse de Guiche. What Ellen did not know until much later was that William Mackinnon believed his family were the rightful heirs of Kenure and he held a strong but unspoken sense of resentment towards the Palmers.

William Mackinnon's wife, Emma, was the granddaughter and the sole direct descendant of Elisabeth Echlin who had bought Kenure from her bankrupt father, Sir Robert Echlin, after he apparently lost the Kenure estate on account of a gambling debt. Elisabeth had married Francis Palmer and this was how Kenure came into the Palmer family. Emma Mary Mackinnon, née Palmer, their daughter, was said to be the sole heiress, but probably because she was female the estate had passed to Sir William Henry Palmer, from another branch of the family.[11] Although William Mackinnon was outwardly helpful and friendly towards the Palmers, his relationship with them was always to be ambivalent.

There was much visiting and inter-dining between the two families. On one occasion, at an all-male party at the Mackinnons, Ellen was upstairs with two of the as yet unmarried daughters waiting for the men to come up. She describes how '*Mr Mackinnon walked in bearing two wax candles and announcing à haute voix "Sa Majesté". A stream of gentlemen walked in and at their head the Comte de Montemolin.*[12] *This unfortunate Prince appears an amiable and prepossessing young man and spoke to us all most affably and chatted upon everyday subjects just as if he were any private person.*'[13] The Count was the Carlist pretender to the Spanish throne and one of London society's most intriguing, high-ranking émigrés. Despite his seeming ordinariness, Ellen was dazzled by this encounter with royalty, as doubtless William Mackinnon had intended.

The Palmers were in the process of giving a number of large dinner parties, as was customary for parents with daughters doing the London season. The Conde, a name by which the Count of Montemolin was also known, together with his aide de camp Colonel Merry, was promptly invited as guest of honour at the next big dinner party given by the Palmers. He was also invited to the opera, with Colonel Merry, Ellen and her mother driving to Mortimer Street to pick them up. Ellen may not have paid much attention to the opera on this occasion as she recounts, '*The Conde handed Mama upstairs and Col Merry took me in and on entering the box HRH had one front seat and I the other. We were all very merry and talked and laughed almost all the time [...] in fact there was no more ceremony than among ordinary people and we enjoyed ourselves very much.*' The opera they watched was *I puritani* by Bellini, but Ellen was obviously so thrilled at being able to show off her royal acquaintance that there are no comments about the singers or the performance in her account of the evening. Unfortunately for her, émigrés princes did not rate very highly in the social hierarchy in nineteenth-century London, and as for the Conde, he was never to realise his hope of ascending to the Spanish throne, being taken prisoner on his way to lead a Carlist uprising.

The Palmers had brought Ellen's horse, Nonesuch, to London from Cefn and, as riding alone with the groom was not ideal, Lady Palmer was always on the lookout for a suitable riding companion. At first, Mrs Mackinnon occasionally accompanied Ellen, but at one of the many parties they attended they met a smart young married couple, the Hon. Charles and Mrs Rowley, who were promptly invited to another of the large dinner parties at Portland House. Very soon after that Ellen writes that she went to Berkeley Square to take her first ride with Mrs Rowley in Rotten Row on the edge of Hyde Park.[14] It is not clear if there was some financial understanding with the Rowleys but from then on Ellen often rode with Mrs Rowley, took part in expeditions arranged by her and was introduced by her to another group of young people.

Ellen was delighted to be invited to join an expedition to Greenwich planned by the lively Mrs Rowley. She already knew Sir Watkin Williams-Wynn and drove down in his drag – a lighter, more elegant version of a road coach – sitting on the box with Mrs Rowley. After a quick visit to take in the sights, they ran races up and down the hill; Ellen beat Lord Ranelagh[15] even running backwards, to his great astonishment. Although Ellen didn't know it, Ranelagh had a reputation as a womaniser and would later have relationships with Annie Miller, the pre-Raphaelite model, and Lillie Langtry, the society beauty. They dined well with '*oceans of champagne*' and when they set out on their homeward journey '*were excessively jolly on the road. I sat on the box with Sir Watkin and prevailed on him to sing Old King Cole, all the gentlemen joining in the chorus and making a very considerable row to the excessive astonishment of the other nearby passengers on the road*.'[16] They stopped off at Vauxhall Gardens and Ellen returned home in Mrs Rowley's brougham, having thoroughly enjoyed herself, free for once from the suffocating supervision of her mother and aunts.

Other expeditions followed, and Ellen became part of a set that included Lord Ranelagh, the two Miss Gleggs, Miss Cotton and Captain Percy Williams, as well as Sir Watkin and several other young men. One day they went to Epping Forest and six days later to Windsor, about which Ellen wrote, '*I never was so delighted in my life, the beauty of the views, the interesting old ruins, the splendid trees and above all the exhilarating sense of freedom experienced in galloping over the unbounded arena of green turf, uphill and down dale formed a "tout ensemble" quite novel and enchanting*'. After seven hours on horseback, part of the time galloping as hard as they could, they returned to the hotel to dine. The party visiting Edmonton days later was a large one, and included several carriages, but after dinner at 4 o'clock, the elders set off back home while the young, including, on this occasion, the Conde, went boating on the lake and danced to an impromptu band on the lawn. On the way home, Lord Ranelagh purposely led them astray, an action much approved by the party '*who were all ready for any larks so our escapade was universally approved, excepting for the good folks at home*', where they arrived at two in the morning.

The decision for all the party to visit Bedlam, or to give it its correct name, Bethlem Royal Hospital,[17] was arrived at by mutual consent; public displays of 'madness' were still, at this time, considered a popular attraction and a form of entertainment. After a not very agreeable ride to the site at St George's Fields in Southwark, they were conducted through the building by one of the keepers. Ellen found it interesting and thought the accommodation quite perfect. They spoke to some of the inmates and '*found them all labouring under different delusions [...] we saw Edward Oxford, who attempted the Queen's life but he appears not mad at all and is employing himself in learning different languages*'.[18] In June 1840, Oxford, a disgruntled barman aged 18, had fired twice at the Queen riding in her carriage in Hyde Park. He was tried for high treason, found guilty but acquitted on the grounds of insanity.

After spending an hour and a half at the hospital, they galloped home quickly. The same party, for the same reason, also visited the new model prison at Pentonville, but Ellen found this '*an onerous thing*' and did not enjoy seeing all the poor prisoners having their supper.

Mrs Rowley made Richmond the destination for their final expedition on 8 July. Ellen writes joyously that the Count de Montemoulin and Col. Merry came to fetch her and she found the usual party assembled: '*the 2 Miss Gleggs, Sir Watkin, Lord Ranelagh, Mr Conway, Mr Percy Williams and his brother, Col Williams. This is our usual party and a merrier one it would be impossible to find anywhere, not one individual but what is up to fun and jolly as jolly can be, in short we understand each other perfectly and consider ourselves "société charmante"*.' They rode in the park, dined at the Star and Garter, changing from their riding habits into their ordinary clothes, the girls helping each other, and after dinner had fun rowing on the river. Ellen particularly records that she had a very nice talk with Mouse Glegg; as she had no sister and had never had a female friend in whom she could confide, this was important for her. All except Lord Ranelagh drove to Portland Place where they sat down to another jolly meal, and then played Blind Man's Buff until 5 o'clock in the morning, although Ellen records that there was a certain gloom hanging over the whole party as the ebullient Mrs Rowley was leaving the next day. The weeks that Ellen enjoyed the company of the fun-loving Mrs Rowley and the expeditions she organised were possibly the happiest and most carefree of her life, away from the watching eyes of her censorious female relations.

On 24 June, Ellen recorded that Portland House was made unliveable as it was prepared for their ball. Two large rooms were set aside for dancing, the carpets taken up and the floor covered with brown holland tightly nailed down to make a '*parquet*', and the hall stairway and landing were ornamented with flowers. Guests started to arrive at 10 pm but dancing didn't begin until 11. '*I opened the ball with the Count de Montemoulin and Prince Louis Napoleon*[19] *and Lady Georgina Packenham were our vis à vis. After the first quadrille the dancing began in earnest and of course I was overwhelmed with engagements.*' She was too excited to eat supper and forgot many of her partners' names, but for the benefit of posterity she mentions that she danced with Prince Louis Napoleon as well as Lord Ranelagh. To her great annoyance the ball ended at 3 o'clock, but she rated it a great success. Doubtless the Palmers thought they had done well to have their daughter open the ball with the Bourbon pretender to the Spanish Throne and the nephew of Napoleon Bonaparte and future President of France (as Napoleon III), but it did little for them so far as English high society was concerned.

One day soon after, while walking with her mother in Kensington Gardens to listen to the band, Ellen noticed two gentlemen, '*apparently foreigners coming out of the gardens at the same time as we did [who] kept very near us all the time staring as much as was consistent with politeness and rather more*'.[20] Little did Ellen know then of the far-reaching consequences that would follow from this chance encounter. A week later she hurried home to change for what she called a '*little soirée dansante, to take advantage of the fact that the druggets have not yet been taken up, meaning the floor was still covered in a rough sort of over carpet to facilitate dancing*'. They had about 150 guests and this time Ellen did note her dancing partners. Among the usual names of the Conde and Lord Ranelagh was a new one: the Count de Bark.[21] He had to get Miss Disbrowe to introduce him (he must have turned up at the party uninvited) and Ellen immediately recognised him as one of the two foreigners they had seen out walking. The party ended earlier than expected and they had to persuade the guests to stay on to dance the cotillion. Ellen records that it was a very pleasant occasion, '*though there had been numberless disappointments*', but gives no details as to what constituted the disappointments. From then on in her accounts of the remaining London social occasions, the Count de Bark is frequently mentioned, as is Lord Ranelagh, who on one occasion asked her if she loved him. This is written in Italian in the diary, as are extracts detailing other romantic encounters. Lord Ranelagh continued to make himself useful, obtaining tickets for them to go a musical party with dancing at Richmond, where she danced twice with the Count. When they went to the opera, Lord Ranelagh and the Count de Bark were the most frequent visitors to their box.

It was also through Lord Ranelagh's good offices that they obtained tickets to see Queen Victoria prorogue Parliament in the newly built House of Lords. The construction of the present Houses of Parliament had begun in 1840, with Charles Barry the chosen architect. By 1847 only the House of Lords had been completed, and this was the Queen's first state visit to the new building. It was also the last time that a monarch was to prorogue Parliament in person. The Queen was accompanied by Prince Albert, and while her throne occupied the whole space under the canopy, his chair was positioned lower down to her left. Today, the Queen and Prince Philip sit on identical thrones beneath the canopy. The official account notes that the Queen spoke in her usual clear, distinct voice. She first of all dismissed her subject with the words, 'I have the satisfaction of being able to release you from the duties of a laborious and anxious session'. She then went on to talk about measures taken to deal with the Irish famine: 'I rejoice to find that you have in no instance proposed new restrictions or interfered with the liberty of foreign trade as a mode of relieving distress [...] I cordially approve the acts of large and liberal bounty by which you have assuaged the sufferings of my Irish subjects. I have also readily given my sanction to a law to make better provision for the permanent relief of the destitute in Ireland.'[22] If Ellen thought at all about the consequences of the Irish famine, and she could not have failed to know that her family lived off the rents of their Irish holdings as their Irish agents were frequent visitors to Kenure to discuss business, she might have been reassured by the Queen's speech. But the reality was that the measures promised did little to assuage the terrible plight of the Irish peasants.

Ellen's account of the occasion was relatively brief.

> *We had very good seats in the gallery and from thence had a very good view of the scene, the peers in their scarlet robes, ladies in gay attire and the throne itself surrounded by the courtiers. When the Queen arrived she took her seat most majestically and after a few interesting ceremonies she read her speech most emphatically and in a clear and distinct voice.*

Lord Ranelagh then showed them over the building, but when it came to leaving, the crush was as great as at a royal reception and they had a long wait for their carriage.

Ellen's brother Roger was now home from Eton and he was able to accompany her on early morning rides, when they would meet up with the Count and Lord Ranelagh. The group often went to listen to the band in Kensington Gardens or to spend an evening in Vauxhall Gardens. One way or another, Ellen was seeing a lot of the Count de Bark, who was very attentive. The London season was drawing to a close. Ellen and her mother went to the final ball at Almack's, a very select one, given by the Lady Patronesses. It was mentioned in the *Morning Post* with the comment that the Lady Patronesses remained until a very late hour, and the presence of Miss Palmer, Lady Palmer and the Count de Bark was also noted,[23] but for Ellen it proved a real disappointment. '*For some time after our entrance no one came near us, not even to ask me to dance. It seems as if there was a sentence of excommunication hanging over us and I was quite au désespoir for such a thing never happened to me before.*' Ellen was at last rescued and danced a waltz with Lord Henry Loftus. She had a few more dances, including one with the Count de Bark, but unsurprisingly she did not enjoy the ball very much. '*Indeed it was the least agreeable I have been at, the Jerseys and all the grandees were there.*' Ellen's surprising lack of success may well have been caused by her association with Lord Ranelagh. His reputation as a ladies' man would have been known to the Patronesses, who would not have approved of Ellen's behaviour towards him. They had ways of making their disapproval known, and others took note, which perhaps explains Ellen's lack of dancing partners.

When they left London for Kenure, with their departure noted in the *Morning Post*,[24] Ellen had to say farewell to her governess, Miss Ward. '*It is really a hard thing to separate after being constantly together for eight years and I could not restrain my tears, although I am not a crying subject in general.*' Miss Ward was to remain a friend of the family and frequently stayed with the Palmers, acting as companion to Ellen from time to time. Lord Ranelagh was also at the station and gave them two magnificent bouquets and a basket of peaches. Ellen had time on the train to reflect on the events of the season '*and finally settled that although I have of course experienced vexations and disappointments like other people, still on the whole not having made up my mind to enjoy perfect felicity I was not disappointed. Indeed I was agreeably surprised for I have enjoyed my season very much and had a great deal of pleasure*'.[25] From her family's point of view the season must have been counted a success. True, she had not found a husband, but she was still very young. She had been seen at all the right places, done all the right things and had been much admired for her looks. There was always another season to look forward to.

CHAPTER 5

Country Life in Ireland

After the excitement of the London season, continually rushing from one engagement to the next, life in Ireland could not have provided a greater contrast. The family journeyed to Kenure by way of Cefn and there, during the remainder of Roger's school holidays, brother and sister spent a lot of time together walking by the seashore in the early morning, guzzling gooseberries from the garden, practising running races and seeing how far they could jump. Roger devised what he called six training canters which meant he cantered for 100 yards on his pony while Ellen ran alongside as fast as she could. As well as running she trained herself to jump. She wrote that she had cleared 20 jumps nearly 10 foot wide and it was no wonder she felt tired out by the end. If what she claimed she was able to accomplish is true, her feats of athleticism were out of the ordinary for any girl, let alone one in her position.

After Roger went back to Eton, it was no wonder she found having to toddle round the grounds with her elderly relatives a sore trial. Not allowed to walk outside the park on her own, she was reduced to taking her maid with her when she went down to the seashore, commenting,

> *I dare say these constitutionals are very healthy, but they are anything but pleasant in the long run as only a ladies maid is very stupid company. I have no other. Indeed my situation is dreary in*

> *the extreme, one young person without a single companion within 30 or 40 years of my own age to whom I can talk or confide a single thought. Of course three old aunts who watch every word and look and continually read long lectures are worse than nobody and added to all this the perfect solitude we live in, never setting eyes on a human being except the Rush folk. I sit in my own room all day long glad to escape the business which is continually going on below and I often think what a lucky thing it is I am fond of music else I really don't know what I could do.*[1]

The day she wrote that entry she had sung for two hours and played for over five, '*being resolved to use double diligence in practising so that I may astonish Crivelli next year.*'[2] Crivelli taught most of the English opera singers of the period so Ellen was in good company.

Of the two special occasions that autumn, a dinner at the Vice Regal Court in Dublin and an excursion to Lambay Island, there was no doubt in Ellen's mind as to which was the most enjoyable. Her mother had long promised an excursion to Lambay Island, about three miles distant from the mainland. At that time it was owned by Lord Talbot of Malahide, from whom they must have asked permission to visit. There are steep cliffs on all but the western side and Ellen, true to form, chose, with the younger members of the invited party, to make a tour of the island. Even she said it was pretty fatiguing, scrambling up and down narrow precipices, knowing that one false step could send you rolling into the sea. But Ellen enjoyed physical exercise as much as she disliked formal occasions.

Attendance at the Vice Regal Court in Dublin was a social necessity, and the Palmers duly accepted an invitation to dine at the Castle. The Clarendens kept to the same rigid formality that obtained at the court of St James. Lord Clarenden had recently been appointed by Lord Russell, the Prime Minister, as the Lord Lieutenant of Ireland, an appointment he had reluctantly accepted, being more interested in European foreign policy than the rapidly developing famine crisis in Ireland, as well as having to deal with the Young Ireland Movement, Orange disturbances and economic disarray. Clarenden, liberal and learned, believed that no matter what the conditions of the times, traditional hospitality had to be maintained, although he had difficulty meeting expenses.[3]

The Palmers booked in at Gresham's Hotel, where they dressed for the occasion, and then drove to the Castle. Dismounting at the lodge,

> *we found ourselves in the dreaded presence of the representative of Majesty. And regal etiquette was indeed kept up for the aspect of the circle was in the last degree formal, solemn, so much so that I felt on entering the room as if I had been plunged into ice. Lord and Lady Clarenden received us with a condescending bow and we sat down to twiddle our thumbs till dinner time. All my pleasing notions of agreeable neighbours were doomed to be awfully deceived [...]*[4]

Ellen was taken into dinner by a hobbling, white-haired Sir Compton Domville who had lost his palate and all his teeth so that Ellen could not understand a word he said. Dinner lasted for two hours and had it not been for Lord Loughborough, who sat opposite and occasionally addressed a word to Ellen, she might have fallen asleep she was so bored.

> *To my great joy the moment of liberation arrived at last and Lady Clarenden having made a slight inclination to the ladies marched out of the room with a stately step. It was triste enough in the drawing room, but I whiled away the time talking to Mrs Butler who is an agreeable person [...] Not long after this Lord and Lady Clarenden, bowing and shaking hands with their friends retired from the circle just as the Queen does.*

The only moment of light relief came when the aide-de-camp (ADC) on duty, Mr Ponsonby, '*rather a good looking agreeable young man*', came over to talk to Ellen. Otherwise it was '*the dullest of all dull dinner parties I have ever been at*'.

An invitation to stay with her friends the Gleggs for the Knutsford races taking place at their home, Whithington Hall in Cheshire, a stone-built house set in a handsome park, was a welcome relief. Ellen, who had never had occasion to have an intimate relationship with girls her own age, was '*delighted to meet my friends again and the dear girls really gave me a most affectionate and cordial reception possible to be*'. Ellen was not interested in racing or races, but they provided the excuse for the visit. The party drove six miles to the racecourse, and the following day they attended the Knutsford race ball, where the only dances, apart from the final country dance, were the waltz and the polka. Nonetheless, they enjoyed themselves and did not leave until 2 o'clock in the morning for the long drive home. Apart from her enjoyment in being able to chatter with her friends, it was Mouse Glegg's generosity in lending Ellen her horse so that she could join the local hunt, which met at Withington Hall,[5] that gave her the most pleasure. '*The hounds assembled in front of the house and with the scarlet coated whippers in and huntsmen, the large party from Astell who were likewise congregated on horseback and the joyous character of the whole meeting formed a scene especially striking to me who had never witnessed anything of the same sort before.*'

As precedent demanded, Ellen was presented with the brush of the only fox killed, and rode about for the rest of the day with this trophy around her horse's head, enjoying the gallops across the fields. At one point during the visit the girls stole Ellen's diary; it was always kept firmly locked so they were none the wiser. The diary had become for Ellen more than just a record of events; it was a means for her to acknowledge her unhappiness and feelings of despair at her situation, emotions which outwardly she firmly repressed.

Once back home and missing the companionship of the Glegg sisters, she started writing a poem about Mouse Glegg and five days later completed 74 verses of which she was very proud. She had it made up in a smart little book and posted it to Mouse Glegg. Driving home after a boring dinner party with neighbours, she thought enviously of the ball given by Lord Derby at Knowsley Hall to which the Gleggs had been invited and which would then be at its height, but hoped to have a full account from Mouse in a day or two. When no immediate answer came in response to the poem, Ellen fretted that she might have offended them, but was delighted later by a letter saying Mouse thought the poem great fun, and asking her to write the prologue to a play about Charles II that the officers at Manchester were getting up. She decided to write an epilogue as well. She was not so pleased to be asked to write a duo in verse to reclaim a parasol from Mr Western, and still less when Mouse wrote that she would be taking credit for the prologue and the epilogue as well as the verses. '*I thought it a very unhandsome proceeding and would not allow myself to be done in such a way. Actually she told me she intended to make me her "poet laureate" for the future so I might find plenty of occupation in building her a reputation at my expense.*' The correspondence continued after this interchange, but it was both a recognition of Ellen's superior intelligence and an indication of her outsider status. The families remained friendly, and after Mouse Glegg got married, Emily Glegg became Ellen's special friend.

The Vernons[6] were one of Ireland's oldest families, having lived in Clontarf, situated on the north side of Dublin, continuously for over 300 years. The manor house, on the same site as Clontarf Castle, had been rebuilt several times and the Castle itself, in its present form, was only completed in 1837. The weather at Kenure had been wet and cold for days and Ellen was so bored that an invitation to stay with the Vernons at Clontarf Castle just before Christmas was welcome. A dinner party was given in the Palmers' honour, and Ellen saw to her horror that Sir Compton Domville, her erstwhile neighbour, was a guest, but fortunately for her she did not sit near him this time. Ellen never liked dinner parties, and her diary report of this one is filled with disobliging accounts of the other guests. She excels herself in describing the unfortunate Lady Domville:

> *Let anyone imagine the fattest woman they ever saw multiplied by three, and let them further imagine on this woman's head a hat to which all other hats in existence are a joke. It was I should say about two foot square surmounted by flowers innumerable and crowned by a plume of feathers very much like those adorn a hearse. Altogether she looked like a moving monster and I should not have been more astonished if I had seen one of the pyramids moving into the room.*[7]

To make matters worse, they had music afterwards and as no one appreciated Ellen's contribution she grew nervous and cold and did not perform well.

Two more dinner parties followed, and matters did not improve, prompting Ellen to analyse the way she performed as a singer.

> *For me in particular, everything depends upon the reception I meet with from my audience. If once I begin to feel that I cannot inspire them with the sensations I feel myself then my enthusiasm cools at once and I sing like a machine, but if on the contrary I see them inspirited and warmed by the strains then I am stimulated to double my efforts, and confident of possessing complete power over their sensations, my own energy increases fourfold and I surprise myself. This is not the same with regard to playing for to begin with you can be more independent of your own feelings with your fingers than with your voice [...] in the meantime I will not be discouraged.*

Mrs Vernon enjoyed a good gossip, and Ellen heard, to her astonishment, that Mrs Vernon had been told by the Taylors, their neighbours who lived at Ardgillan[8] '*that I could not ride at all and that I went about on a pony like a four posted bedstead with a servant holding the bridle, myself being in terror the whole time. I really was astonished at this for Mrs T had seen me on horseback and must have known better.*' This must have rankled with Ellen because she was a good horsewoman and fearless rider as she was soon to prove. But she recognised the report for what it was: malicious gossip.

On her return home, she told her brother, whom she always referred to as Doddy, that the visit had been rather slow, in spite of the good intentions of their kind hosts. It remained wet and cold up to Christmas Day when,

> *We wished each other a Happy Christmas (a merry one being out of the question) first thing, and afterwards set out for Balbriggan Church [...] we walked about in the grounds in the afternoon but could hardly fancy it a real Christmas day as until now we have always spent the festive season either at Cefn or abroad. Certainly our first specimen of*

> *Christmas in Ireland was not very gay, but it was comfortable enough demolishing roast beef and plum pudding. Played spec* [a card game] *in the evening.*

Seeing in the New Year was hardly more cheerful, in spite of Roger and Ellen's efforts. Having spent the day walking by the seashore and in the grounds, they '*had a little feast upstairs of roasted apples, welsh rabbits and flips, but the affair was rather a failure as the cheese wouldn't toast well, the apples wouldn't roast well and the flip to my mind didn't taste well.*'

So ended 1847.

Outside events rarely impinged on the gentle rhythm of life at Kenure. Balls at Dublin Castle were a welcome diversion as were the first invitations to hunt. There are few references to the troubles and only one to the revolutionary fervour that was sweeping the Continent. The nearest Ellen and Roger came to the reality of the troubles was when they went wandering outside the deer park and got lost. Making their way outside the boundaries of the park, they observed a man also creeping cautiously along. Having been warned by several people not to be out at dusk even in their own grounds,

> *we crept quietly along close under the wall scarcely daring to breathe but luckily for us we did not see any more of the dreaded man, (who I think must have been a poacher) crossing several tremendous fences, in an agony of fear we at last got home [...] for if the man had found himself detected there is no knowing what he might have done in that solitary spot where no one could possibly either see or hear us. In Ireland it must be remembered they are not quite so scrupulous as in their sister Isle.*

Later on in March, Ellen commented that '*the newspapers this morning contained most alarming accounts of the revolutionary feeling about in this country and they say we were on the eve of a rebellion*'. In a throwaway remark, Ellen comments, '*Glorious fun this and it is consoling to think that after all we shall have some small ennuis in our own country for all the grand doings we were so shamefully cheated out of in Paris.*'[9] In this casual way Ellen was referring to the revolutionary uprisings that were taking place all over Europe, and particularly in France during 1848, which meant Paris was considered too dangerous for the pleasure-seeking visitor, as well as the possibility of trouble in Ireland. The political upheavals in Europe beyond France were taking place in Germany, Poland, Italy and the Austrian empire and ended by affecting over 50 countries, although they were swiftly put down and had few lasting effects.

In France, poor harvests, economic depression and the crushing of the peasants' revolt had stimulated the activists, largely middle-class, to agitate for change. Since demonstrations and public gatherings were outlawed, a series of banquets, known as the 'Campagne des Banquets', was held to raise money and demand changes. In response, Louis Philippe,[10] who had been elected King of the French in 1830, abdicated in favour of his nine-year-old grandson, but public opinion rejected this solution and the Second Republic was proclaimed. Louis Napoleon Bonaparte, the man who had been Ellen's dancing partner at her coming out ball one year earlier and who had been entertained to dinner at Portland Place, was elected President of France.

Although there would be no visit to her beloved Paris, Ellen found some compensation in being allowed to accept invitations to hunt. As this was the first occasion she had been permitted to hunt, apart from going cubbing with the Gleggs, she and Roger were accompanied by Kersley, their coachman, who made them wait and took them through the lanes instead of through the fields. Ellen wrote that

> *I was heartily sick of Kersley's sneaking ways of proceeding and despite his earnest entreaties that I would not risk my neck I decided that a 'tumble' was fifty times better than safety purchased by crawling along the roads and having elected Mr Moore for my guide I bade goodbye to the fat coachman and boldly plunged into the open country. Now came the glorious part of the chase. We took the head of the entire field and kept it for 3 miles as stiff a country (they all said) as is to be met with anywhere. I grew perfectly dauntless, dashed at everything, cleared them without moving in my saddle and completely astonished the whole field, myself into the bargain [...] we crossed a railway just behind a train and took two boundary fences which even Daniel (the groom) advised*

> *me not to attempt. Even Roger who was some distance behind (the we refers to Mr Moore and I) told me afterwards that when they saw us nearing the fence cried out "she'll be down, a certainty" were astonished when they saw me clear it like a shot without the least injury [...] we pursued our cross country course and subsequently left two colonels on the wrong side of a tremendous brook which they could not get over and earnestly tried to prevent me from crossing, however I was so plucky that I verily believe I should have gone over a six foot wall had it come my way.*[11]

The hunt ended at Ardgillan, where they assembled having lost the fox. Then came the compliments: '*They all said they had never seen a lady ride like me and I was told afterwards that Colonel Campbell, (who is one of the best horsemen in Ireland) declared that in all his life he never saw 3 ladies who could really ride and of these 3 I was the best horse woman.*' In a letter to her son Richard, Mrs Taylor from Ardgillan corroborates Ellen's account: 'There was a grand hunt at Kenure yesterday, Miss Palmer riding fairer than any of the other hunters, to the horror of her old mentor the coachman, Roger, the poor foreshortened brother, attending and a Mr. Moore, M.P for Mayo you never saw so happy a girl as the heiress, it was her first hunt and she is up to anything, but she will never be Mrs Colonel Taylor, not to say the truth I should wish her to be so notwithstanding her £100,000 and her musical talents.'[12] Mrs Taylor seems to have disliked the Palmers, never missing an opportunity to run them down, and certainly did not wish Ellen to marry her son.

With this triumph under her belt Ellen was impatient for the next opportunity to show off her riding skills. At last the day dawned and Ellen was invited to join the hunt starting from Howth Castle.[13] She set out with Merk, her maid, by train and was met by Mr Vernon and Lord Howth and his family, who were waiting on the bridge on horseback. She mounted her horse, Nonesuch, which had been brought over, and the party set off for the Castle where they met up with the hounds. There are still people in Rush who remember the story of what happened to Ellen on the hunting field that February day, such was the scandal. Ellen herself was brutally honest in writing her account of the disaster. After wondering whether she would add to her laurels, to be or not to be, she answered her own question:

> *Not to be, that is for certain for instead of adding to my laurels I have thoroughly disgraced myself and I can hardly find courage or words to relate the mournful tale. However it must be done [...] as it was intended that we were to chase an outlying deer before lunch, off we set at once to the Hill of Howth, I, for my part, little anticipating the ignominious plight in which I should shortly return to those friendly halls. When we reached the covers the hounds soon started the deer and as they broke into full cry and the hunters swept after them the spectacle was quite beautiful.*

After being thrown and quickly remounting without any trouble, she came to a small ditch between two and three feet wide. Then disaster struck:

> *How it happened I cannot even surmise, but the fact is lamentably certain that I was first thrown on my horses shoulder and careered half over the field with my arms clasped affectionately around his neck in a remarkably happy and delightful state of mind. The animal, I suppose, not relishing my change of position, plunged wildly, thereby throwing me quite to the ground and my habit being caught in the pommel he dragged me after him at full gallop until the cloth gave way and I was left sprawling on the grass. When I arose from the ground, oh dear! What a spectacle was presented to the delighted eyes of the crowd of strange gentlemen who thronged around to know if I was hurt [...] My habit was torn off about 3 inches below the waist and unluckily all my petticoats had given way also so that when I recovered myself sufficiently to cast a glance at my nether garments to my horror and astonishment I saw myself standing not 'en chemise' but actually 'en pantalons' in the middle of the field [...] Daniel* [the groom] *in agony cried out 'what shall I do Miss' and in answer to my frantic enquiries of 'where is my habit' the miserable man handed me a strip of cloth about 4 inches wide which I endeavoured to wrap round my legs. Poor Mr Vernon in his*

> *anxious regard to decency attempted to conceal me from eyes profane by standing before me, but unfortunately he was not attired in petticoats so the effort proved abortive. Lord Howth's plan was a better one for he rushed to a gentleman standing nearby, tore off his upper coat and wrapped it around me, but when I tried to walk in it I found I could only proceed in a succession of hops so in the end I was compelled to wait until a riding skirt was procured from Lady Emily's maid and when that was done I remounted and rode home to lunch.*[14]

Although Ellen says she felt more annoyed than she had ever done in her whole life, yet she felt obliged to laugh and joke about her misfortunes. After lunch, Lord Howth and several gentlemen accompanied her to the station, and she jumped several decent hedges on the way, thereby gaining much praise for her pluck in not minding the spill. Not unnaturally, she felt very downcast that evening and went to bed early.

Such a dramatic mishap on the hunting field was too good a story not to make the rounds with suitable embellishments. Mr Workman, one of the Irish agents, coming to talk business with her mother at Kenure, said he had heard of her tumble in Dublin and that it was reported at the Castle that '*I had split my drawers in the act*'. Col. Taylor from Ardgillan called to ask after her health, having heard of her unlucky spill. His mother had already written to her other son,

> there was never such an expose as poor Miss Palmer made on Friday. She was out with Lord Donoughmore's hounds and got two falls, tore all her clothes to ribbons and remained (a ce qu'on dit) [as one might say] in her habit body, a pair of grey worsted stockings, no drawers! Yet in this condition wanted to go on hunting but Lord Howth called off the hounds and she rode home to Kenure across the country. Such was the account given at dinner at Howth that day – allowing for exaggeration – it is sufficiently an untoward thing for a young lady. Women have no right to hunt.[15]

It is fortunate that we have Ellen's own brave account of what actually happened. Lady Palmer also received a letter from Mrs Vernon, dwelling on her 'most mortifying disaster' in such a spiteful way that the Palmers felt it was a definite attempt to annoy. Ellen was also informed by Mr Workman that her tumble had afforded fine fun to the Castle people and that the aides-de-camp were calling her 'Venus with a jacket on'. This was probably one of the least scabrous of the jokes that were being bandied around. However, nothing daunted, Ellen longed for an invitation to the Castle ball, which arrived at the very last minute, and she found that the incident did nothing to diminish the number of partners wishing to dance with her. In fact, two of them persuaded her mother to stay on in Dublin so that Ellen could attend the ball at Clondarf.

Apart from balls at the Castle, the Palmers now received invitations to a whole clutch of other balls. When an invitation to Mouse Glegg's wedding arrived, Ellen was more interested in the social life she was enjoying in Dublin, than having to make the somewhat tedious trip across the water to England to attend, and she tried to excuse their non-acceptance with the bother of having to make a double crossing of the Irish Sea. This reason was not accepted by Lady Glegg, so the Palmers resorted to the age-old excuse of indisposition and they did not go to Mouse's wedding. Compared to society weddings today, such weddings in the nineteenth century were relatively modest affairs and Ellen would not have missed much by her absence, although she did offend the Gleggs.

Quite why Ellen was so often described as an heiress seems a little odd when she had a brother, who, in the normal course of events, stood to inherit the estates as the only male in the family. But as the Palmers were known to be wealthy it was assumed that Ellen, the only daughter, would also share in the inheritance. All through her life she dreaded being married for her money and not for herself. This fear may have resulted from a letter that her mother received at the end of February.

> *Mama received an anonymous letter in the post warning her to beware of that notorious 'liar, profligate and fortune hunter now pursuing her daughter' and went on to say that he would not scruple to slander and traduce me in order to compel me to marry him and thus gain possession of my fortune. It was a most atrocious letter and this was not the worst of it and made me feel thoroughly uncomfortable.*[16]

There are no clues as to who was being referred to but it could have been Lord Ranelagh, because Ellen, having enjoyed flirting with him during her first season, would subsequently only acknowledge him with a cool bow. Lord Ranelagh or not, it seems that Ellen did indeed know to whom it referred and had been conducting a flirtation with the gentleman, so that when she writes, '*and this was not the worst of it*', it could be taken to mean that further embarrassing details were included. She went on to lament her fate in such dramatic language that perhaps this was not the first time she had heard this said.

> *Oh, the miseries of money! No sooner does a person look at me twice than some kind friend immediately tells us to beware of fortune hunters and this besides the very humiliating idea that one owes every common attention entirely to one's reputed wealth, there is super added the disagreeable necessity of suspecting everyone who approaches to be actuated by some sinister motive [...] Doubtless many are unjustly suspected of fortune hunting but how is one to distinguish between one class and another. The very fact of being constantly obliged to suspect and suspect is of itself painful to a naturally open and generous mind. Doubtless it sounds romantic and ridiculous but I declare I speak from my heart when I say that I would rather have been a portionless girl so that I might at any rate have had the consolation which alas I do not possess now of knowing I was sought for myself alone.*

Ellen attended a fancy dress ball for the first time:

> *I had never seen a fancy ball before and was quite delighted at the novelty and brilliance of the scene. Indians, Germans, Sultanas, gipsies, Quakers, Greeks, Albanians, Highlanders, Chinese, etc., were mixed up in a strange confusion and putting dancing out of the question, it was exceedingly amusing to sit quietly and look on as the motley groups passed in succession.*

When dancing did begin, Ellen had enough partners not to care that two of the ADCs, the Ponsonby brothers, cut her as far as dancing was concerned, and wrote, '*now I know so many people I don't care a fig for them as I always dance the entire evening*'. However, she did note that she was also cut by Lord Atho and Mr Standish. Her Polish costume was much admired but she also overheard a lady ask, '*"Which is Miss Palmer?" "Just before you" was the answer. "Goodness how she is got up," was the polite rejoinder.*' '*This is a la mode Dublin*', was Ellen's comment.[17]

Before leaving for London, the Palmers felt emboldened to invite a large party of their new friends, including Lord Howth and Lady Catherine St Lawrence, to spend the day at Kenure. After a tour of the house they visited the gardens and then the young people went down to the seashore where they ran and jumped over fences. After lunch Ellen was made to sing, but soon persuaded the fiddler to play on the terrace while they danced on the grass: a quadrille, a country dance and the Roger de Coverley. The party seems to have passed off very well despite Ellen writing of many disappointments, including the non-appearance of the Vernons and Lord Mount Charles, all having promised to attend. The fact that many of the party were going on to Lady Castlemaine's ball that evening and there was still no invitation to the Castle ball may have added to her feeling of despondency after the guests had gone.

Finally an invitation to the Castle ball did arrive, and the last week in Dublin was a busy one socially. Ellen's friends the L'Estranges called for her and took her riding in Phoenix Park, which she enjoyed as it combined the advantages of seeing friends, as in Rotten Row, and galloping over a splendid extent of turf, as in Windsor Park. '*We saw everybody there, Lord Atho and Lord Mount Charles, Capt. Bagot and Captain Lindsay came and rode a long time with me. I had some good gallops with them [...] We returned home in time for dinner which we had at half past six o'clock then set off for the private theatricals which took place at the Queen's Theatre.*'[18]

Besides the Castle ball, the Palmers attended one given by Lady Blakeny at the Royal Hospital. Although Ellen danced the whole time, she records that her '*former friend, Lord Dunkillin cut me completely, made the stiffest of all possible bows and never once spoke to me the evening through [...] the reason for such extraordinary conduct I am at a loss to imagine, but these young gentlemen do give themselves the most extraordinary airs and I believe they fancy themselves "monarchs of all they survey".*' This was particularly so with regard to two of the ADCs. '*Capt. Ponsonby and Mr Standish also cut me completely as far as dancing is concerned, but they generally do so that is nothing wonderful.*' Playing games, cutting and snubbing each other was all part of the life of the small Dublin social world. At Mrs L'Estrange's ball she records some successes: Lord Mount Charles not only danced with her twice, but took her down to the supper room and would have stayed with her had her next partner not arrived, wanting to dance. Mr Vernon told her that one of the officers had named his horse, down to run in the garrison stakes, 'Nelly Palmer' in her honour.

It was perhaps fortunate that the Palmers were planning to leave Kenure at the end of the week because at Mrs Boyd's ball a number of friends, including the two lords, were absent, and as a consequence Ellen did not dance as much as usual. '*Owing to some extraordinary unprecedented circumstances I actually sat down for three dances running, so finding it very flat we left early.*' Rumours abounded in the small world of Dublin society and Ellen found herself married off to several different gentlemen. Her mother received a letter from Aunt Abbey saying she had heard at Miss Williams-Wynn's that everybody in London believed she was to be married to either Mr Moore or Mr Scrope Bernard. The week before she had been congratulated on her approaching marriage to Lord Howth, and there had even been a rumour that she was to marry the French President, Louis Napoleon. Ellen wrote, '*Nobody must mind any stories they heard of my proceedings here as Dublin is full of stories of my sayings and doings which to say the least of it are as surprising to myself as to anyone else.*'[19] Interest in her sayings and doings was no doubt partly fuelled by the memory of her disastrous fall on the hunting field. She may have missed Paris, but Dublin had not been without its compensations and had helped to relieve the boredom of Irish country life.

CHAPTER 6

A Fatal Attraction

Back in London in April 1848, the same social round of parties, dinners, balls and visits to the opera started up again, with her mother and aunts still hoping that this season Ellen might find a suitable husband. Almost immediately on their return they met up with the Conde de Montemolin and his circle and the Count de Bark.

At first Ellen was dismayed at what she saw as Count de Bark's detached and cold manner towards her, but when she discovered what she thought was the reason – that he had sent her music at the end of the previous summer season and her mother, without telling her, had returned it together with his unopened letter – her main concern was to let him know what had happened. She was anxious to find ways of being with him without causing too much attention as she knew her growing attraction to him was being noticed by the family.

Rehearsing for another mazurka to be danced at the Polish Ball at Almack's provided a good opportunity for them to meet. The Count de Bark came to a rehearsal, as they had previously managed to arrange, and took his place as Ellen's cavalier as they led off the dancing together. At the following rehearsal, with the Count de Bark as her partner, they managed to get enough time together for Ellen to explain to their mutual satisfaction about the music being returned by her mother. When Ellen arrived at Almack's on the day of the Polish Ball she was presented by the Count with '*the most beautiful bouquet I ever saw of scented geraniums and gardenias to match the colours of my dress. Some of the other young ladies had some of the same sort, but not nearly so handsome*'. The mazurka dancers had competition, for the first dance was the Duchess of Bedford's Oak Leaf quadrille and the Duchess of Leeds' White Eagle quadrille followed. In spite of suggestions that they would never get through the mazurka,

> *we danced it better than we had ever done before, there was not the faintest shadow of a mistake and the whole thing went in a way which commanded universal applause and astonished as well as delighted the bystanders. Indeed the remarks we heard on every side were complimentary in the extreme and we had the satisfaction of completely cutting out the quadrille.*[1]

Ellen had hoped that riding in Rotten Row might provide her with opportunities of meeting the Count in a more casual setting, but to her extreme annoyance her Aunt Abbey had taken to riding in the park and too often saw it as her duty to accompany Ellen home. Derby Day saw both the Palmers and the Count at the races, enabling the Count to make frequent visits to the Palmer coach. At the opera he came to the Palmers' box and as often as possible made himself available to hand them to their coach afterwards.

Aunt Abbey, who played a leading role in Ellen's life, also gave dinner parties for her, mostly described as stupid or boring by Ellen, but not the one given on 31 May. She took Emily Glegg with her and was able to sit next to the Count at dinner. However, in the carriage after dinner on the way to a subsequent ball she heard from Mama, '*that Mr Rowley and Mr Watkin told her people began to give me to the Count de Bark. This is really too bad and is the very thing I have been fearing for the last week since the Mazurka as now doubtless I shall be almost forbidden to speak to him.*' The curious thing was that although the Palmers were completely opposed to Ellen ever marrying a foreigner, and despite the fact that Ellen's name continued to be linked to that of the Count by gossips, he went on being invited to dinners at Portland Place and was often admitted when he visited at other times. Were they dazzled by his title and his good looks, as they undoubtedly were by their association with foreign royalty afforded them by the Conde de Montemolin, who again opened the dancing at Ellen's ball?

Although Ellen continued to enjoy her success in the ballroom, where she listed not only all her partners but also all those who asked but never got to dance with her owing to lack of time, she frequently notes that other occasions were not as enjoyable as they had been during her first year, when the irrepressible Mrs Rowley had organised so many happy riding expeditions.

The young lovers had tiffs, as young lovers do. The first of these occurred at the Fourth of June celebrations at Eton. The Count was standing by the river's edge and was invited by Lady Palmer to join them in their enclosed space. Having accepted with pleasure, he then disappeared and was seen walking arm-in-arm with a Miss Saunders, Mrs Dodd's sister. Ellen was furious, but her anger did not last. When she and the Count met up at Kew shortly afterwards, Ellen's horse was very obstreperous and the Count came up to take charge of her; he told her that he had foregone an invitation to Holland House to be with her and she was mollified. Going for country rides was another useful way to find time to be with the Count, although it was not always easy to arrange as Aunt Abbey often wanted to come too. On one occasion Ellen, accompanied by Captain Seymour, another devoted admirer, and the Count set off with Aunt Abbey in attendance.

> *We rode two and two and it was the greatest fun conceivable to see the young men relieving guard upon Dobby* [Ellen's pet name for Aunt Abbey]. *When one had been talking to her for ten minutes he thought it high time for the other to come to his aid, but when this was accomplished and he came to be my companion he was proportionably astonished that the other victim should get tired of duty after his turn was out. However we had a lovely ride and I had so many sweet things said to me that I cannot remember half of them. We only got home just in time to dress for the opera where Mama, Miss Ward and I went. We saw 'Nino' sung by Crivelli [...] Count Montemoulins and the Count de Bark visited us.*[2]

Mama put her foot down when Ellen proposed going to Twickenham with her cousin, Emma Mackinnon, and insisted that Dobby came too. A note was dispatched and Aunt Abbey came hurrying round, *full of bustle and importance and quite prepared to make a row. She vowed she had heard the Count propose to me* [at their last meeting he had offered her a gardenia saying it was a *fleur sacré*] *and told Mama his attentions were pointed in the extreme and finished with the intelligence that Dr Twiss,*[3] *who had been making enquiries about him had heard he was a Swedish adventurer of low family and poor to a degree. Of course I contradicted the story, but really it is a hard case that I cannot even speak or look at a person twice without some kind friend coming and trying to lessen the individual in my estimation.*

Here Ellen was being disingenuous. She listed a number of admirers, including Lord Ranelagh, who had proposed to her the previous year, in whom she was not in the least interested. Her flirtation with the Count was becoming altogether more serious. He was the only person who came to their box at the opera that evening and Ellen remarked that he had the sense not to stay too long.

A week before the Palmers were due to leave London at the end of the season, Roger, the Count and Ellen went riding together. Roger held back to ride with Kersley, giving the Count the chance to present Ellen with a beautiful ring which she felt unable to accept, telling him that she knew her '*parents would never consent to my union with anybody but who possessed the attributes likely to gratify their ambition*'. In her diary Ellen gave vent to her frustrations and what she saw as her fight between love and duty.

And oh, would that my hard fate did not forbid my following the dictates of my own heart and uniting myself to him forever. Gladly would I forgo all those so-called advantages which I might otherwise attain, for after all what real happiness do they ever bestow. I am tired already of the vain glitter of empty splendour and never did I feel obedience so hard a task as in the present instance. I rejected Lord Ranelagh and many others, it was an easy task, for my heart was not interested in them, but in this case, though I am no romantic girl I feel the case is fearfully different. However as I told the Count either my parents or

> *I must feel the pang and sooner that they should suffer I will sacrifice myself without saying a word to them about it.*[4]

Despite herself, Ellen shed some tears as she assured the Count that there was no hope of her family ever changing their opinions, at which the Count seized her hand and kissed it, seeing her tears as a sign of her love which she did not want to acknowledge.

They parted at the railroad, where the Count concealed himself behind a building to catch a last glimpse of Ellen. Although cheered by this demonstration of his regard for her, she was so distraught at the thought of not seeing him for a year that when her aunts fell out with her over some trifling matter and started abusing her she burst out crying. Noting that in other circumstances she would normally have answered them with spirit,

> *for the first time in my life I could do nothing but sobbed almost hysterically. The cup was quite full and one additional drop made it overflow. Really I do not think I ever felt so utterly miserable as I did during this morning's journey; at a time when I greatly needed affectionate sympathy and consolation, to be treated with cruel harshness and severity was almost more than I could bear. And then I have no creature to whom I can turn for advice and comfort excepting my brother, and he, kind and good as he is, cannot think or feel like a sister would. I am indeed lonely.*

Ellen knew only too well what was expected of her, as she continued,

> *It makes me sick at heart to hear them (my aunts and Mama etc.,) speculating on my forming a brilliant marriage and coolly talking over the various candidates as if wealth and consequence were really the only requisites in choosing a partner for life. I unfortunately know too well already how insufficient these are to constitute true happiness and yet is it not dreadful to think that if I resolve to obey their wishes I shall probably be obliged to sacrifice all my own hoped desires in order to grasp these brilliant nothings.*[5]

Torn between love and duty, Ellen was trapped by the system that in her heart she despised, but in her head she, too, wanted the social recognition her family thought they were entitled to. She did mind about the snubs and rebuffs and sometimes remarked on how she would like to get even with those who so ostentatiously put them down. Invited to the wedding of Louisa Pulestan, she wrote,

> *but to our great disappointment after being asked into the parlour where Sir Richard and one or two guests were, she never invited us upstairs or came to see us so the only glimpse we caught of her was in her passage from the door to the carriage. Such an insult after asking us to come I never heard of.*[6]

An invitation to another and far more important wedding brought Ellen and her mother back to London from Ireland where they were spending the winter as usual. Emma Mackinnon, a distant cousin of Ellen's, was to marry the Duc de Guiche and Ellen had been invited to be one of the two bridesmaids, the other being Miss Molesworth. This was a rather surprising marriage. Agénor, Duc de Guiche,[7] the eldest son of the Duc de Grammont, was a distinguished member of the French nobility. Seen as one of the most eligible bachelors on the French social scene, his name had been linked with that of the beautiful young Duchesse de Dino among others,[8] but he had chosen to remain single until he was 29, seeming to prefer the life of a playboy to the duties imposed by marriage. However, among the aristocracy marriage did not preclude mistresses, who were an accepted fact of life.

Agénor's scandalous association with Marie Duplessis, a young prostitute, was known to have taken place sometime in 1840 while she was working as a shop girl, having been abandoned by her rich elderly protector.[9] Marie, the daughter of a brutal father who had brought her to Paris from Normandy and abandoned her, had turned to prostitution to survive. Fascinated by her looks and her innate grace, Agénor fell for her charm and seductive beauty and, prefiguring Shaw's *Pygmalion*, became her mentor, teaching her to disguise her miserable past and take on the poise of a fashionable lady. Marie was a quick learner, with an instinct for dressing to maximum effect; with Agénor directing her reading and developing her sense of taste, she became one of the most distinguished members of her profession, a well-read woman with superior manners and cultivated conversation.[10]

Agénor's parents, alarmed at this liaison and Marie's extravagant tastes, dispatched their son to London where his uncle, the Comte d'Orsay,[11] was well established. Flouting convention, d'Orsay was living with Lady Blessington,[12] a close friend of the Duchesse de Gramont, at Gore House. The house had become the centre of a brilliant and fashionable circle where the young Agénor de Guiche would find plenty to distract him. Returning to Paris two years later, he knew that Marie had taken numerous wealthy lovers and was living a life of great luxury. Among her lovers, Liszt, at the height of his fame, had become completely fascinated by her and she in turn found him captivating. When they met, it is recorded that he 'totally abandoned himself to her, listening with uninterrupted attention to her beautiful language, so full of ideas, and, at the same time so eloquent and pensive'.[13] Lola Montez, of Irish descent but passing herself off as Spanish, was an inhabitant of the same *demi-monde* as Marie and had been among Liszt's many lovers and when she wanted to go to Paris it was he who provided her with letters of introduction.[14] She arrived in 1844, hoping to make a success as a dancer. Although very different in character, Lola flamboyant and fiery, Marie relying on a more discreet charm to entrance her lovers, the two women became friends.[15] They may have met both of the Alexandre Dumas, father and son, in the popular boulevards, cafés and restaurants that they frequented, but for Marie, without doubt her most significant lover was Alexandre Dumas, fils, who later used her as his inspiration for Marguerite in his novel, *La Dame aux Camélias*, published a year after her death in 1848. The book was an immediate success and prompted Verdi to use Marie's story as the model for his tragic heroine, Violetta, in the opera *La Traviata*. Had it not been for the book and the opera keeping alive interest in Marie's life, her name might be no more than a historical footnote.

All the de Guiche papers were destroyed in a fire at his château, so it cannot be known definitely, but it seems that Agénor continued to visit

Marie to the end of her life, although financially unable to compete with her rich lovers. He had been her first '*amant de coeur*', and despite taking other lovers himself, including Rachel,[16] the famous actress, he remained attached to her and is mentioned in one account of her funeral as being among the mourners.[17] It is believed by the family that Agénor did not marry while Marie was alive, and it was only after her death that he looked around for a possible bride. Alternatively it may be that in spite of his aristocratic background, his playboy reputation and his relative poverty made it difficult for him to find a suitable wife.

Whether Emma Mackinnon knew anything of Agénor's colourful past is not known, but her parents, who were frequent visitors to Paris, would have been aware of his reputation. The two families would have known each other from the time that the de Gramonts and their children spent in exile at Holyrood Castle. The French Revolution of 1830 and the overthrow of Charles X, the last French Bourbon king to reign by hereditary right, had resulted in his exile, and the staunchly monarchist de Gramont family went with the king to Scotland. There is a charming silhouette of Agénor and his brothers practising fencing and archery as young boys at Holyrood,[18] but the castle would have been a dismal place to bring up a family and to the boys it seemed more like a prison than a home. The marriage of Agénor and Emma had all the hallmarks of having been arranged by their families. The couple did have memories of their Scottish childhoods in common, but the strong-minded Emma liked riding and country life whilst Agénor liked neither. Pragmatically, Emma must have decided that life as a *duchesse* would be preferable to growing old at home, whilst Agénor, financially strapped and having known romantic love, must have been content to settle for a dull but rich wife who would provide him with heirs and financial stability.

The wedding took place at St Mary's Bryanston Square on 27 December 1848 and Ellen left a detailed description of the ceremony. Although she may not have realised it at the time, the connection with the de Gramonts and de Guiches would become increasingly helpful to the Palmers' social aspirations. Ellen was surprised to find the solitary groomsman was Lord Ossulston, who had cut them dead for a whole year, then introduced himself at the opera as though nothing had happened.

Lord Ossulston was heir to the Earl of Tankerville, whose wife had been born Corisande de Gramont, thus making the Duc de Guiche her nephew. Finding that she was now connected to Lord Ossulston by his cousin's marriage, Ellen wrote,

> *It is really very extraordinary but some things are strange in this world. The duc de Guiche whom I was so anxious to see rather disappointed my expectations. Certainly he is a handsome man and withal a very nice mannered one, but somehow he is not a person I should ever have fallen in love with. The ceremony was gone through very coolly by the parties concerned and after it we immediately adjourned to Hyde Park Place. Here we had to while away two hours before breakfast and Emma insisted on my singing, though I would rather have had a tooth drawn than comply, being unprepared and rather tired after the journey. However Lord Ossulton very kindly sang something first to give me time to pluck up my courage.*

Lord Ossulston was known to have a very fine singing voice,[19] and so they sang some duets together. Ellen was enchanted and looked forward to singing with him when next they met. They went into dinner together '*and sat immediately opposite the bride and bridegroom who looked comfortably blissful during the repast […] Lord O told me that the Duc is not a man of sentiment and I agree with him as a result of the morning's observations.*' It would seem from Lord Ossulston's remark he was aware of the nature of the marriage. The bride and bridegroom left for Paris and then drove to his château in the Pyrenees. There is no mention of what the bride wore, but Ellen was dressed in her embroidered muslin over pink, white lace scarf and chip bonnet, which she says was much admired. After this excitement the family returned to Kenure.

Ellen nearly always devoted the first page of her diary each year to both an assessment of the past and a guess at what the future might bring. In Ireland, in January 1849, separated from the Count de Bark, she wrote that she thought she had got over her infatuation. '*Now I am a young lady of two seasons standing, actually almost passée though yet in my teens. I don't think this has been altogether a happy year for most of it has been rendered uncomfortable by what I now begin to think was merely girlish fancy instead of a love on which the whole happiness of my life depended.'* Trying to convince herself that this was the case, she continued, '*Indeed I think I have got over it, and so shall be spared the misery I endured last season of having my whole thoughts and interest bound up in one object, which said object was perpetually kept away from me by interposing relatives.*' Considering her future, she assessed the chances of marrying happily as a thousand to one, as she thought the possibility of mutual affection springing up between her and the eligible candidates of her parents' choice did not exist. '*As for a marriage of convenience I hate the very word and I am equally averse to making a choice my parents would not approve. Look where I will the future looks gloomy and despite my apparent possession of all the good this world can bestow my real claims to happiness are small. However hope remains to cheer me up.*'

Passing through London on the way to Paris for their usual spring trip, Ellen was told that the Count de Bark had called at Portland Place to say he was leaving for Sweden. Far from forgetting him as she had thought, all her old feelings were aroused, and although she wondered where he had been and why he had not contacted Roger as arranged, she was full of hope that he would call again on Sunday. '*He* <u>*did*</u> *come after all [...] Merk* [her maid] *summoned me from my room telling me the Count de Bark was downstairs. I was in such a flurry that I could scarcely walk to the sitting room [...] when I did look at the Count I found he had grown very thin, but handsomer than ever.*' He told them he was going to Sweden to rejoin his regiment, but never explained why he had not got in touch with Roger, who was to have acted as a go-between during their absence from London.

Ellen's joy at seeing him again and the misery of the impending parting drove all other considerations out. '*If I could have said one farewell without the prying witnesses I could have parted with him with more resignation [...] the visit was miserably constrained and stiff as may be supposed but the count seemed as if he could not tear himself away and when he did take his farewell of me it was with tears in his eyes.*'[20] Ellen had a great capacity for interpreting events to fit in with her wishes.

After having to miss their usual time in Paris in 1848 on account of the revolution, the Palmers spent a very successful month there in April

1849 and enjoyed the social cachet that came from their new relationship to the de Guiches and the de Gramonts. The Duc had arranged for Ellen and her mother to receive an invitation to a concert given by the president, Louis Napoleon. Remembering the hospitality he had enjoyed at Portland House during his time in exile in London, Ellen writes, '*The President was extremely polite and came up to us several times. Once he told us that the Conde de Montemoulins had been taken prisoner and added that, I know he was an old admirer of yours – now don't blush.*'

Back in London at the beginning of the season, they attended the usual round of parties and balls. By way of distraction one morning they went to the sale of Lady Blessington's furniture at Gore House, being sold to pay her debts, the Duc d'Orléans having already left to avoid his creditors. A short while afterwards, on 15 May, Ellen read in the *Morning Post* that the Count de Bark had returned from Sweden, and couldn't help feeling delighted at the possibility of seeing him again. She thought the news that Lola Montez was to marry, imparted by her neighbour at a dinner party given by Sir John Hayes, was just an interesting piece of gossip.[21]

Lola, since her time in Paris in the mid-1840s, had become notorious, not just as a rather unsuccessful dancer with countless lovers, but because she had been the mistress of King Ludwig I of Bavaria. Her extravagance and the power she was seen to wield over the king led to unrest and to her house being attacked, forcing her to leave Bavaria for her own safety. Not satisfied with Lola's departure, the students who were at the forefront of the public unrest continued to riot and forced the king to abdicate. Lola, in the meantime, had come to London to try to mend her fortunes and to find someone to give her the security she now needed, despite the fact that Ludwig continued to pay for her extravagant lifestyle. Marriage was what she had in mind.

Ellen obviously knew who Lola was and asked in all innocence, 'Who to?' – little expecting to hear the answer,

> *to a Mons. de Bark whom you have probably met in society last year. At this I felt as if I had suddenly received a pistol shot so totally unprepared was I for the blow, but I controlled myself and heard, with outward*

> *calmness at least, the villainy of the man whom I have loved with all the warmth and purity of a first affection.*

Her companion then went on to give chapter and verse of the story of the Count's involvement with Lola.

> *They say he left Sweden originally because he was overburdened by debts; then he came here and tried his luck with three or four rich heiresses and fortunes (no doubt I was among the number). Finding he could not retrieve himself that way he made love to Lola Montes, promised to marry her and borrowed six hundred pounds in order to go to Sweden last March to arrange matters.*

He gave Lola the same reason as he had given Ellen, that he was going to rejoin his regiment on account of the war with Germany. Ellen continues her account,

> *Now Lola found out that he was not an officer at all and this awakening her suspicions she sent her lawyer after him to demand either restitution of £600 or else he should return immediately and marry the lady. This he refused to do and then he said it was quite out of his power and the lawyer only got £200 worth of jewels back out of the whole sum. Lola declares that if he does not pay she will publish some letters from ladies which he gave her (some from the Duchess of Somerset, Mrs Dodd and others, for it seems he has been a celebrated lady killer) […] bitter indeed was the awakening from my long dream, but if I ever see the count again I will tell him what I have heard and listen to his defence before I utterly condemn him […] it was a hard trial to hear all this from a stranger who repeated it all like some piece of amusing gossip, totally unconscious that every word he uttered went like a dagger to my heart.*[22]

Although this account of the Count's involvement with Lola does not appear in the latest biography of her, Lola's lovers were many and varied and the story does ring true. Installed in a house in Half Moon Street for a while, Lola found London more expensive than she had expected. No longer able to rely on Ludwig, except to pay her debts, even though he had made her the Countess of Lansfeld, she was desperate to find a husband to give her status and security. When she first met him, the Count de Bark must have seemed the answer to her prayers: a handsome man-about-town, a serving officer, a count with estates in Sweden, and if the price of a promise to marry was 600 pounds then that was easily found. Great must have been her fury when she discovered that she had been tricked. Soon afterwards she did marry the young, besotted 21-year-old George Trafford Heald, a cornet in the 2nd Life Guards with an income variously described as being between £3,000 and £14,000 per annum – a most unsuitable match as far as he was concerned and much against the wishes of his family.

Ellen's distress increased with a visit from Mr Mackinnon, who came to warn her mother about the Count, saying he was nothing but a notorious swindler. He then told the whole dreadful story of the Count and Lola Montez because he said he had heard about a flirtation between the Count and Ellen. Worse was to come when Mr Mackinnon said the Count had given Lola all the letters he had received from ladies and she was going to publish them. Ellen had never admitted even to her diary that she had written to the Count, but now with the threat of publication she wrote,

> *I grew so dreadfully terrified hearing that, that I was half inclined to throw myself on their mercy and confess everything, but I restrained the impulse by which I should have compromised everything and everybody and determined to brave the storm. Although I wrote in the most innocent spirit possible yet if the world got hold of the story I should be ruined forever and the bare thought makes me shudder, indeed the sad conviction that he never did love me and the distracting fear of being made the ridicule of the envious world form and accumulation of misery is almost greater than I can bear.*[23]

Her misery was made worse by being told that the Count had also proposed to Miss Sebastion Smith but refused to marry her when her father would not settle £1,000 on him. Then she took no more notice and dismissed the story as idle gossip.

At a ball given by Lady Johnston a Mr Pepys took the opportunity to talk to Ellen about the Count de Bark. He told her that the stories circulating about the Count were false from beginning to end. Obviously briefed by the Count to explain away his connection with Lola Montez, he gave a detailed account of what was said to have taken place between them. It was true, he told Ellen, that the Count had received a £600 loan, almost forced on him by Lola who threatened to burn the bank notes if he did not take them. She then demanded that he marry her, and when he refused she concocted this atrocious tale. Mr Pepys said that the story of the letters was equally untrue. Ellen was so relieved she never questioned the source of the story; she was grateful to be able to excuse the Count's conduct, and relieved to be able to refute the gossip about him, even going so far as to pretend to herself that she no longer loved him. Since Lola and the Count were both inveterate liars it is hard to know where the truth lay, but there can be no doubt that the Count had been attracted by Lola and seen her also as a possible source of income. To judge from their portraits Lola and Ellen were curiously alike in looks. Both had black hair framing pale oval faces, with large eyes and heavily marked eyebrows; both had big personalities, the one suppressed, the other given full rein.

Not only did Ellen miss the Count de Bark at her own ball, she also missed the Conde de Montemolin as she had opened the dancing with him for the last two seasons. She had enjoyed the kudos his admiration brought her and sometimes used his friendship to upstage others who wished to be noticed by him. She had heard only the day before that he was to marry Miss de Horsey.[24] She considered that she was the Conde's special friend so was vexed to learn that he had been not only seeing Miss de Horsey while paying court to her but had proposed marriage to her. '*I must say I was exceedingly astonished that a piece of my undisputed property like the Conde should take the liberty of breaking his chain and walking off in that independent manner. However it will not seriously affect my peace of mind,*'[25] she wrote on hearing the news of the engagement, but she no doubt did feel the loss of her connection with the royal house of

Bourbon. According to Miss de Horsey (the future Lady Cardigan), the Conde was a beautiful dancer and they discovered they had many tastes in common. The Conde being passionately fond of music they frequently sang together, and she fell in love with him. In her memoirs she admits that she had been 'dazzled by the romance of the affair and by the rank of my would be suitor, for I do not think that any girl in my position could have been quite unmoved if a Prince of the Blood had selected her for his wife instead of one of the royalties he could have chosen. The Count proposed to me in February 1849.'[26] Ellen had been equally dazzled, although not emotionally involved, her love for de Bark excluding any other romantic attachment.

Having endured the boredom of an appearance at St James's, the Palmers were rewarded with an invitation to the Queen's ball at Buckingham Palace. From Ellen's description of the event it might seem that her flirtation with the Count, since the Lola Montez stories had become public knowledge, was beginning to adversely affect her social life. She wrote,

> *The magnificence of the rooms was very striking indeed the whole scene looked truly regal. Almost the first persons we saw were Lord Howth and his daughter [...] then we moved into the room where the Queen was sitting and danced a quadrille with Mr. Clerk in the same set as Her Majesty. She seemed to enjoy herself extremely and certainly danced particularly well. After the quadrille was over a great many people walked past the throne making curtsies and Papa and Mama were among the number. Then we paraded about the rooms talking to our friends and occasionally obliged to form a passage for the Queen who was trotting about all night. It was a much better ball for dancing than it is usually, but I did not think it particularly pleasant for all my friends cut me in a most unusual and extraordinary manner.*[27]

It never seems to have entered her head that the reason she was cut by so many friends might have been because of her involvement with the Count and his association with the notorious Lola. The Count was careful to keep his distance, merely bowing to them at the opera, and when he did call at Portland House nobody told Ellen. It wasn't until a month later that they met in Rotten Row, where the Count said he had heard she was very gay in Paris and she just had time to tell him that she did not believe the stories that were circulating about him. But still the Count kept his distance, avoiding her at Lord Howth's ball and refusing to dance. For Ellen the agony of seeing him and not dancing was too great: '*If I did right I know I ought to behave frigidly and refuse to dance with him when he does come round [...] to part in anger would cost me too much to endure to try the experiment.*'[28]

The following evening at Lady Gage's ball the experiment was over. Ellen danced twice with the Count. He took the opportunity to turn the tables on her by telling her that he had heard from a gentleman that she was desperately in love with someone else, and furthermore, said she had told this gentleman that the Count de Bark liked her, at which she had laughed and shown the other his letters. This confirms the fact that Ellen and the Count had been writing to each other, although she never directly admitted to this in her dairies; but when in the country at Cefn or Kenure she arranged for his letters to be sent to Roger and passed on by him, doubtless feeling that their correspondence might be intercepted. Ellen was overjoyed to discover the reason for the Count's coldness and wrote, '*before the cotillion was over we were as good friends as ever. I think he likes me as well as ever for his eyes were scarcely off me the whole evening and he always continued to dance either next to me or opposite in the quadrille. Alas, I care more about him than the whole world put together.*' The following day she continued to analyse the Count's feelings and her own:

> *Altogether his manner was tender and affectionate in the extreme and quite free from that shade of coldness which has so often grieved and distressed me. I think he really loves me but gets impatient sometimes at the extreme fear I display of our love being discovered. Alas, I thought I was cured but I am worse than ever for that I could possibly love another even in years to come appears an absurd chimera.*[29]

These were no vain words; it was years before Ellen allowed herself to fall in love again.

The guest list for the second ball Ellen's parents gave for her that season included the Count de Bark's name so she must have persuaded her parents to forgive him. The ball gave the couple plenty of opportunities to talk. They made arrangements to ride together with Roger to provide cover, to walk to Primrose Hill, to meet at parties at Vauxhall and to go riding in the park. It was while riding in the park with Mrs Jones, who was often Ellen's chaperone during this activity, that she was introduced, at his request, to Francis Grant,[30] the well-known portrait painter, whom she had observed staring at her most intently whilst the band was playing. Mrs Jones told her that, not knowing who she was, he had said '*he had never seen such a pretty girl in such a pretty costume and that I only wanted a hawk on my arm to make me look like an ancient picture.*'[31] Ellen brushed aside the compliment, nevertheless taking care to record what Grant had said, with the comment, '*however I care nothing about beauty or any such vanities now*'. Francis Grant eventually got his wish to paint her; he would have liked to have painted her mounted on a horse, but had to settle for a more conventional pose. Her splendid portrait can be seen at Cefn.

Just before they left London, still using the good offices of her brother to disguise their meetings, Ellen managed to see the Count twice more. They met at Primrose Hill, where they strayed into the fields on the other side. The Count wanted to know if Ellen really meant to give up her parents' ideas of marrying nobody but some great *parti*, and if there was no hope for him, as he would wait any length of time. Trying to persuade her to marry him, he said that of course at first, for a year or two, her parents would be angry, but if they saw her happy they would relent. But Ellen could not put love before what she saw as her duty. After a long farewell, she and Roger went home. '*I spent a miserable evening, and what makes my grief almost intolerable is that there is no hope for me. I will not marry without my parents' consent and that is hopeless to expect. Indeed I could never summon up resolution enough even to ask it so sure am I of the result.*'[32]

Considering that on many occasions in her diaries Ellen writes of her miserable family life, and the dislike and contempt she feels for her aunts, the question remains, why does she feel so duty bound to obey their wishes? She is a strong character, yet she cannot bring herself to fail in what she conceives to be her duty. On one occasion she even calls it her '*sacred duty*'. It may be that having been brought up since childhood in the expectation of making a successful marriage, and so much seeming to depend on her fulfilling this role, she simply feels unable to disappoint her ambitious family. Although romantic to a degree, she herself is perhaps also ruled by her head rather than her heart, accepting and even partially agreeing with the role her family expects her to play in society.

CHAPTER 7

A Bleak and Cheerless Future

During most of 1849, while Ellen was preoccupied by her relationship with her Swedish count and torn by her duty to her family, she almost ignored the fact that she had other suitors with serious intent. Any letters proposing marriage were referred to her mother, who had no difficulty in refusing an offer of marriage from an 88-year-old peer of the realm; but there were other more interesting offers.

Early in the year a Shropshire neighbour, Jacky Leche, owner of Carden Hall, Cheshire,[1] had been captivated by Ellen's beauty and her exploits in the hunting field, and wanted to propose marriage. Ellen had carelessly given him a piece of gorse which he kept in his pocket for months, saying he would return it only if she promised to marry him. Having been invited for the first time to hunt at Carden, she and her aunt arrived early on the appointed day and so first rode round the park, which Ellen described as beautiful. '*Carden is a sweet old place, a black and white house as old as the hills and having that look of real antiquity which none of the modern mushrooms do. Mr Leche met us and conducted us to the dining room where a magnificent repast was laid out.*' In fact Carden was a magnificent white and black timber-framed house which had been in the Leche family since at least the sixteenth century. Ellen was, however, far more interested in recording her exploits on the hunting field. '*I rode over everything without looking at it, cleared them without making a single mistake and won immortal renown. I went over tremendous fences which numbers of gentlemen would not look at and rode at one where a red coat was sprawling horse and all [...] I think I have gained more credit here than in Ireland and as I had just cleared one immense leap half the field cried out, "Well Done".'*[2] She had the grace to admit that her brother kept up with her, but there is no doubt that she showed great skill and bravery.

When Sir Watkin came riding over to Cefn a few days later to fix a day for the Palmers to dine at Wynnstay, he was in a jovial mood.

> *Sir Watty began chaffing me about Jacky Leche and says the report is that we are to be married this month. Positively the 'King of Wales' was in quite a good humour today and consequently my respected relatives were quite in raptures when he was gone. I see very plainly what they are driving at but it is all of no use for I don't really think I could ever make up my mind to marry a being so perfectly 'antipatico', however luckily for the peace of the family I don't think I shall ever be asked.*[3]

Sir Watkin was often referred to as the 'King of Wales', a nickname which reflected his standing in the country. From the Palmers' point of view, marriage between Sir Watkin and Ellen would have provided an ideal solution; it would not only have enhanced their social standing, it would have meant Ellen living nearby. Sir Watkin certainly enjoyed her company and teasing her, but Ellen was right when she thought he would never propose. He married his cousin, Marie Emily Williams-Wynn, in 1852.

Dismissing Jacky Leche's increasingly desperate pleas to be taken seriously, Ellen told him it would be useless to write to her parents, knowing instinctively that despite his wealth and background he was not sufficiently grand to meet with her parents' approval. As he made no secret of his attachment, or of his determination to win her over, their names continued to be linked by county gossip. When, after a dinner party at Carden poor Jacky Leche was heard saying that he would cut his throat if Ellen did not relent, she did show some compassion. '*I really do think I never saw a young man so much in love as he is. However I fancy it is too instant to last long and I hope it is for I should be very sorry if I thought otherwise.*' Ellen was able to sympathise a little with his unhappiness, on account of her own feelings for the Count.

Jacky Leche next persuaded Roger to take a written proposal of marriage to Ellen, which her mother answered with a decided rejection. The day after his proposal had been turned down he asked Roger to come and see him. Roger returned from the visit thoroughly upset, according to Ellen, saying, '*he never saw a fellow so utterly floored in his life. He cried and sobbed as if his heart would break, and danced about the room like a madman – indeed Roger himself who is not usually very impressionable came back crying at the scene he had witnessed.*'[4] Jacky continued to send Ellen streams of letters which she returned unopened. However, she did open a parcel and found

> *a most magnificent bracelet of solid gold and diamonds in which was set a large medallion. On raising the lid which was also of solid gold ornamented with a profusion of beautiful diamonds one saw a miniature of Mr Leche himself exquisitely painted. Really the man's pertinacity and vanity are beyond anything I could have conceived but it is no use his obstinate perseverance for had he the wealth of the Indies I never could like him.*

Ellen was now feeling annoyed at his persistence in the face of her refusal. But she was nonetheless astonished to learn in May that he had become engaged to a Miss Corbett.

> *For my own part I am glad of it as I shall be spared an immensity of annoyance, but when I think it is only six weeks since he professed to be madly in love with me, and in spite of all my rebuffs passionately protested he could <u>never</u>, <u>never</u> care for anybody else I cannot help reflecting of the values of vows of constancy. It is actually no more than a fortnight since he wrote to Roger in the old strain, so how he can have managed to make up a match so quickly I cannot imagine.*[5]

Later that year she had news of 'poor Mr Leche' from Roger that told its own story.

> *His wife, he says, is rather pretty but he does not seem to care a pin about her, in fact he says poor Jacky does not seem to take an interest in anything, scarcely answers when he is spoke to and in short is a perfect wreck. Kersley told him that he had heard just the same account from the servants, they all think he married in desperation and I came home quite penetrated with pity for him.*[6]

Jacky Leche had not been the only one to make a bid for Ellen's hand and although she had many admirers there was another whom she viewed more favourably. Riding in Rotten Row with Roger and a Mrs Jones who sometimes accompanied her, Ellen wrote that

> *Mr Lane Fox joined us and remained all day as usual [...] He is the most persevering lover for he does not care how I am surrounded nor if I am talking to anyone else at the time, but waits quietly next to one if he cannot find a place by my side and coolly waits until my nearest neighbours decamp.*

This quietly persistent admirer might have had more success than other known suitors, the family having discovered that on Lord Conyer's death he was in line to become the Duke of Leeds.[7] Her mother had gone so far as to confide in Ellen '*that the thing was not to be sneezed at, to use her own expression*'. He showed his devotion by obtaining leave of absence from his regiment so as to be able to travel on the same day as the Palmers left for Wales, even altering his departure to suit theirs, and managing to catch the same train to Chester.

'*At this place we finally bade him adieu with the intention of going on to shoot at the Duke of Leeds in the Highlands, but his last words were not to be very surprised if we should meet him walking about the lanes of Wrexham some fine morning.*' He was as good as his word, for a few days later Roger and Ellen met him walking with his dog Rollo in the park, telling them he was staying for a few days at the Wynstay Arms in Wrexham, and there were several other 'accidental' but carefully planned meetings.[8] Unfortunately for him, the family read in the papers that Mr Lane Fox had got into a terrible scrape standing surety to bills amounting to £14,500 for his father and had been cheated by the money-lenders. He went from being 'a nice young man' to a 'nasty spendthrift' in the family's estimation, and was never invited to Cefn. When they said a final farewell,

> *he seemed grieved at the parting but after all his extraordinary proceedings he has not said a word to me beyond the most commonplace conversation which certainly is rather strange. Perhaps however he considers it indelicate to do so just after losing his trial which he actually did not know of until we told him. He wants to give us Rollo (his dog) which we cannot accept.*[9]

Ellen did, however, want the dog and was very pleased when Mr Lane Fox called on Roger at Eton and gave it to him. Mr Lane Fox may well have felt it better to say nothing; he must have been all too aware of Ellen's feelings for Count de Bark, as he often jostled with him for a place by her side when out riding. The two met socially from time to time after the Wrexham visit, but there was no further romantic involvement on either side. Rollo, very often mentioned in the diaries, continued to be a much-loved dog and a constant reminder of his previous owner.

There had been a cholera epidemic in Ireland in the early 1830s. In 1845, the disease came for a second time, travelling from Europe and arriving just as the famine was taking hold. But this time the epidemic was more severe; the starvation and poverty of a large part of the population reduced their ability to withstand disease so that the number of deaths was greatly increased. The epidemic was at its height in 1847, but swept through the whole of Ireland in the summer and autumn of 1849 and was rampant in Dublin, reaching Rush that autumn.[10] The park at Kenure extended to the edge of the town, and Aunt Abbey, who was already in residence, had written to the Palmers warning them not to come. Unfortunately the letter did not arrive in time and they set off for Ireland as was usual.

On arrival they were told by Dr Graves, the family doctor, that there had been 90 cases in Rush resulting in only five deaths, but that these numbers would probably increase – and increase they did. Fishing had been the mainstay of the town, but since the harbour had silted up there was much unemployment and poverty. Kersley, the head coachman, was one of those who had contracted cholera and the family were relieved to know that he had recovered. Three days later the impact of the disease was brought even closer to home.

> *This morning the first news we heard was that Martin, the carpenter who was working at Kenure, a healthy young man, died of the cholera after two hours' illness. It is a curious affair that he was the person sent for to make coffins this day week and now he himself and the man sent to fetch him are both dead. Echlin also made six coffins for immediate use before dinner today […] there were 15 cholera deaths today.*[11]

Roger and Ellen were allowed to ride their ponies on the seashore, but visiting was kept to a minimum while the cholera raged. On Wednesday, 5 September, Ellen records that

> *poor Father Andrews, the priest, died after a few hours' illness, also Jim, our old wood ranger. It is really awful beyond description every person that appears brings news of some awfully sudden death and gloom which is cast over everything is quite appalling. Dr Graves says has a great many cases today and has an assistant coming down tomorrow as it is impossible for him to do all the work alone. Many people have fled the town in fear and one family who fled on Monday were brought home corpses today. Everyone is perfectly panic struck and the general gloom is awful to witness. There were 23 cases of cholera and 12 deaths in the village today.*[12]

As so often with Ellen, music was her great refuge and she noted the number of hours she practised beside the daily number of deaths. '*Practised before breakfast as usual for I always get up at half past 6 […] Dr Graves called, 30 cases of cholera today […] played 3 and half, sang 2 and a half.*' The following day there were 20 deaths '*and in some cases entire families were swept away by this awful disease. Poor Green has lost his wife and four children in one week. Played 2 sang 2*'. They had few visitors. Dr Twiss came over to see them, probably on business, and even one visitor was better than nothing, '*This morning Dr Twiss left by train. A fussy old gentleman is certainly not a very amusing personage but really in these wild regions a visitor of any sort is acceptable and we were half tempted to regret the worthy doctor whose twaddle we can scarcely manage to listen to in London. However circumstances alter cases as the saying goes.*'

In an effort to provide some entertainment for Ellen and Roger, Lady Palmer had driven over to Ardgillan to try to arrange another expedition to Lambay Island, but the Taylors had vetoed the idea to Ellen's great regret.

Toward the end of September it was Roger's turn to succumb to a mild form of cholera, diagnosed as a bilious attack, but which prevented him from returning to Eton for a few days to Ellen's huge delight. By 25 September the disease was abating, and that week there were only eight deaths. Nonetheless, by the end of the month Ellen also succumbed.

> *After I was seized with diarrhoea which increased considerably accompanied with spasmodic pain in the stomach and shivering Dr Graves*[13] *was sent for. I was put in bed with hot water bottles at my stomach and feet. Dr Graves gave me a powder and ordered me to take a pill every quarter of an hour in case the symptoms did not abate. There was happily no occasion for this but I passed a miserable night [...] in short I had a slight attack of cholera.*[14]

The epidemic was finally declared over and a Service of Thanksgiving was appointed for 15 November, but the family had not been notified and were shocked when they discovered they had missed Divine Service that Sunday. Out of a population of 1,600 in Rush at the time, 824 people had contracted the disease and 176 had died.[15]

Ellen always missed her brother terribly when he went back to Eton and Miss Ward was invited to stay to provide some company. Ellen also worried that Count de Bark had not replied to letters she sent via Roger, and life at Kenure, besides being lonely when her brother was away, was continually punctuated by family rows. Only occasionally did Ellen record what was said, although she noted that rows were an almost daily occurrence. On 25 October, however, she obviously felt particularly strongly because a row took place at Kenure, where she felt that Aunt Mary was in a sense a guest as the house belonged to her father. She described the row:

> *This evening I had a row royal with Aunt Mary who, after interfering herself in everything and laying down the law all the day, chose to bid me to hold my tongue because I ventured to express a most harmless opinion of some point under discussion. Her excessive impertinence nettled me so I begged she would not interfere with my concerns. This was replied to in a flood of Billingsgate abuse in the midst of which I walked off to bed. It is really too bad that this old woman should be allowed not only to push me out of my place (which she does in everything) but also to silence me when I dare to speak in my own father's house.*

Family rows are part of the fabric of everyday life, but the frequency of the rows and the virulence of the language used by the aunts does seem strange, as though they were not only jealous of Ellen but resented her very presence, with her mother more often than not taking their part. It made for a very unhappy home life for poor Ellen.

For a long time music had been her solace and refuge, and the hours of practice that she put in had begun to show results.

> *I have some time ago attained a certain height in the vocal art, but the step beyond that is the most difficult to accomplish. It is in fact over leaping the barrier which divides good amateur singing from professional execution and this feat I have until lately almost despaired of achieving in spite of all the most unwearied endeavours. Now however to my great delight I begin to see my way clearly before me and the maxim of 'patience and perseverance' do wonders and seem in a fair way being verified.*
>
> *Certainly my exertions have been tremendous and I sacrifice all other amusements to the one great end and after all why should I not become eminent? As Crivelli* [her music teacher] *says, there is every reason why I should, and the fact of my studying for pleasure whilst others do it for bread seems to be in my favour rather than against me. My*

> *ambition is to not merely be a good amateur singer, but to attain artistic excellence and if time and labour can do this it shall be done. Even Jenny Lind and Sontag were mortals after all and however great their natural powers, sill their great facility and finished execution could only be attained by practice.*[16]

Her diary notes show that she was as good as her word. A few days later she wrote of her disciplined life: '*Even when it is a wet day instead of taking the surplus time for purposes of idle amusement I never indulge in such an idea instead of that sit down and practice steadfastly for so many extra hours.*'

Encouraged by her German maid Hermann, Ellen planned a Christmas tree[17] like they had in Germany and thought that making the little ornaments to hang on it would amuse her as life was so dull. She was very clever with her fingers and designed many pretty little objects for the tree, which occupied some of her time. She was still working on Christmas Eve:

> *This day I was awfully busy working for my tree that I could not find another moment to walk or ride [...] first I finished a scent bag then I wrapped up the bonbons. It was a very amusing occupation and an endless exercise for one's taste and ingenuity. The tree was decorated in the spare bedroom and brought down to the sitting room whilst we were at dinner. When the door opened and the tree appeared blazing with light everyone was delighted and it certainly looked very pretty.*

Roger and Ellen did manage to have some fun over the Christmas period and from the description of their feast on New Year's Eve it is obvious what an important role Kersley and other members of staff played in aiding and abetting their plans.

> *When they all retired to bed I went up to Eliza's room and Roger joined us and we sat down intending to make a regular night of it and see the New Year in in style. Between Kersley and Roger we managed to have everything arranged in a grand way for our gay doings and we sat down in the highest spirits to do justice to our feast. We had*

roast partridge and quails with capital bread sauce and splendid roast apples and cream for the second. In the drinking line they had brandy and whisky but I stuck to port wine as I particularly dislike spirits. We drank lots of toasts and enjoyed ourselves exceedingly until 4 o'clock in the morning at which time we broke up and quietly retreated to our couches.

After the excitement of the New Year's Eve party, life in Ireland continued even more drearily as Lady Palmer had a lingering cold and could not go to the obligatory Reception, known as a Drawing Room, and as a result there were no invitations to the Castle balls. Things got slightly better when the Sadleirs did invite Ellen to a Castle ball and Mama recovered sufficiently to go to the next Drawing Room. Ellen, according to her diary, had a terrific success at the next ball, a fancy dress ball, as Ondine,

in a sea green crape dress spangled with silver like drops of water, body girdle of pearls, sleeves looped up with shells and coral and pearl necklace and coral bracelets and wreath of water lilies on my head and my hair hanging at full length quite loose and waved. Altogether everyone said I had never looked so well before and declared my dress the prettiest in the room and my hair they raved about and would scarcely believe it could be my own.[18]

She enjoyed her success and covered several pages of her diary with accounts of the compliments she received from admiring young men. But such moments as these were the high points in a life that otherwise continued unhappy at home, apart from the pleasure she took in her music.

Back in London for Ellen's fourth season, the family were shocked and grieved to learn from Sir Benjamin Brodie,[19] one of the most eminent doctors of the day, that Aunt Abbey had cancer and that there was no hope for her, although she might recover in the short term. Ellen was upset to find the horrid story of the Count de Bark and Lola Montez had appeared in the *Post*, copied from the Paris correspondent of *The Globe*, however she was soon dancing with him again at Lady Gage's ball.

He for his part was anxious to know if her feelings for him had changed since last year and, when she repeated the mantra of never being able to marry him on account of her parents, he said he could not understand how she had so much self-control if she really loved him. They argued as to whether it would be better to break off their relationship and she was persuaded against this by his offering to wait any length of time for her. Seeking to justify his behaviour with Lola Montez yet again, she wrote, '*he cannot be a fortune hunter as they represent or else why not have yielded to Lola Montes solicitations and accepted the hand with £700 a year allowed her by the King of Bavaria besides her savings*', and concluded naively, '*Surely that would have been more advantageous from a worldly point of view than wasting his time in hopeless pursuit of me and offering to wait any time as he has done over and over again.*'[20]

She was reluctant to find anything wrong with his behaviour, although she saw him at the opera the next night with 'horrid' Mrs Dodd and her sister Miss Saunders, and noted that he did not come to their box. She excused this on the grounds of her having told him not to approach too much, '*but I still don't think he need have staid so long flirting with those two odious women*'. Whoever these ladies were – obviously carrying with them a certain reputation – Count de Bark was often in their company, to Ellen's great distress, although she never confronted him with the fact. However, his behaviour had not escaped notice, and after another visit to the opera when de Bark did come to their box, Mama '*complained of the latter visiting us and told Roger he must not encourage him. Now we scarcely ever see him at all and it is too bad to say this. I cannot bear to hear it and it makes me quite uncomfortable when I speak to him.*'[21]

On a visit to their friends the Lister Kayes, during a discussion of who should be invited to Ellen's ball, Lady Lister Kaye gave them her honest opinion of how they were judged by society. Ellen's record of what passed between them is both frank and revealing:

> *She candidly told us our acquaintance and position was not what it ought to be considering our right in every respect. We confessed this was true and so it is; for we have hitherto been like flying fish would not enter the society that was offered to us, and trying vainly to enter*

that to which we are really entitled. Consequently we have undergone a series of mortifications by not being admitted to the circles in which we wished to move, and being prevented by pride from entering society below our level. We have long brooded over these disagreeable things and our conviction of some desperate step being necessary induced us to listen to Lady Kaye's proposal of scratching out every objectionable person on it and replacing them by allowing her to invite some first rate acquaintances of her own.[22]

After some thought they agreed to follow Lady Lister Kaye's advice. It is tantalising not to have more information, but Ellen seldom comments on the mortifications they suffered or mentions any discussion about their lack of success in penetrating the higher reaches of society. It would make fascinating reading to compare the original and the edited lists of guests, but unfortunately neither has survived; there are only the few names of Ellen's dancing partners noted in her diary to record who was present at the ball.

But before the ball took place another social crisis confronted the Palmers. They had been seeing a lot of the Gleggs and Emily had become one of Ellen's few close friends. Ellen frequently rode with either Mr or Mrs Glegg, Emily's father and mother, now Aunt Abbey was too ill to ride and when Ellen's other chaperone, Mrs Jones, was not available. Emily Glegg, who was unmarried, had the misfortune to become pregnant. When the Palmers were told of Emily's pregnancy they were truly shocked. There was to be no casual acceptance of the odd illegitimate child as happened in aristocratic circles; strict Victorian moral values were invoked:

This morning Mrs Rowley came to lunch and shocking to say told us such an awful story of Emily Glegg's conduct with Mr Jervis that we can never notice her again. It has been whispered for some time but Mrs Rowley would not tell us until she was quite *sure of the fact and we never having had any suspicion of the rumour before, we were perfectly horror stricken at the idea. When Mrs Rowley was gone we went to the Lister Kayes and there heard the same story with additions. There appears indeed to be so little doubt about it that no one respectable can again be seen speaking to Emily.*[23] *Really it turned me quite sick to hear of it and I do think by degrees I shall be afraid to trust anyone for I should as soon have suspected myself as Emily Glegg. I am sorry for the infatuated girl herself, although her conduct has been little short of madness, but she was so pleasant and nice that she will be a terrible loss to me, and what a life of misery is before her, for her old friends will look the other way at her approach. I cannot help feeling for her and the poor parents I pity beyond measure.*[24]

The ostracising of the Glegg family was to be total as far as the Palmers were concerned; even though Mrs Jones was away, Ellen could not be seen associating with the Gleggs. '*I cannot ride as the Gleggs are of course out of the question.*'[25] Apart from the moral condemnation of Emily's conduct, Ellen felt betrayed, for they had been intimate friends for several years, and the loss of a confidante made her suppress her feelings to an even greater degree. Now there was no one except her brother whom she could trust.

On the day of her ball, Ellen describes the house as looking more beautiful than ever; every window was boarded in and filled with flowers, and the centre part of the balcony was fitted as a boudoir and lined with red and white draperies and mirrors. This time Ellen was introduced to a whole series of new young men, presumably those on Lady Lister Kaye's list, beginning with Count Ernest Schlimminpanssenck, followed by Mr Ashley Ponsonby, the Hon. Fitzgerald Foley and the Hon. Capt. Jocelyn, and danced with old friends, including the Count de Bark. He told her this was the first happy evening he had spent for a long time, fanning the flames of her infatuation.

So pleased were the Palmers with the success of their ball that they decided to have another one. With the new intimacy between the families, Laura Lister Kaye began to take the place of Emily Glegg as a confidante. She told Ellen that due to all the rumours circulating about de Bark, her family had decided to drop him and she was not allowed to dance with him. Now they knew the rumours to be false and they wanted to make it up. Ellen's pleasure at hearing this was somewhat marred shortly afterwards, when '*horrid Lord Ranelagh came up to me and began upbraiding me for not asking stupid vulgar Mr Lloyd Wynn to our ball, adding that he knew we were not allowed to ask our own friends at all. In fact he was so rude that I turned on my heel and gave him a very short answer.*'[26] No doubt Lord Ranelagh did not keep the knowledge that the Palmers had been seeking help with their guest list to himself, which would not have helped their social ambitions. But so anxious were they to build on their success that the Palmers went to Lady Macnaughton's party expressly to meet the Nepalese princes. '*We achieved our object which was to be introduced and get them to our ball, and then went home contented.*'[27] Alas, they had to cancel the ball as the date they chose clashed with the great agricultural meeting at the Albert Hall.

It was at a party at Ranelagh Gardens that Ellen came closest to believing that she might one day marry de Bark. She had never openly acknowledged her feelings to the Count, but that evening while they were waltzing together,

> *he asked me if I really loved him a little and actually drew from me the acknowledgement that I had never loved anybody else and this seemed to make him perfectly happy so that I had not the heart to check the enjoyment of the present by hopeless expectations of the future. And yet I begin sometimes to conceive a glimmering idea that all may not be so hopeless as I have until now invariably imagined. I just begin to conceive a possibility of time and patience overcoming the scruples of ambitious relatives and it occasionally crosses my mind that some day or other I might have the courage to mention my long hoarded secret.*[28]

After the dance, Miss Kaye accused her of 'spooning' and since half of London seems to have known that she and the Count were in love, it is very unlikely that her family did not know or at the very least suspect something was going on. Maybe that accounted for some of the abuse she received from her aunts.

Lord Glengall,[29] a friend of the Lister Kayes, called and persuaded Sir Roger and Lady Palmer to go to Mayo and 'to assist', as he put it, in the election. The election in West Mayo had been called for 20 July and the sitting MP, the conservative Joseph Myles McDonell, was opposed by George Henry Moore. With no time to spare, the Palmers set off that evening, but despite their support George Moore was returned as MP for West Mayo. Ellen was delighted at the thought that she would be going about under the care of Lady Lister Kaye, who had shown herself very sympathetic towards the young lovers. Sadly for Ellen, she woke the next day to find herself covered in a red rash: she had measles and was confined to bed,

> *instead of attending Mrs Stanhope's déjeuner and the Turkish Ambassador's ball. I don't remember ever in my life being so disappointed for besides being a very gay week there was the pleasure of going about with Lady Lister Kaye untrammelled and free from the excessive watching to which I am usually subject and as Mama is so very particular about my going out with anybody except herself, it is an opportunity which may never occur again.*[30]

Things were made worse by the behaviour of Aunt Mary,

> *My aunt blew me up and called me every vile name she could think of because I happened to be upstairs when a note came for me [...] in the afternoon Doddy and I took a stroll across the broad walk and back. It happened to rain a few drops just as we came through Park Crescent home whereupon the two aunts burst out again (although they had approved of our going) abused us so violently and then relapsed into a state of utter sulkiness as though they were the injured party.*[31]

The next day was a Sunday and Ellen said she had never spent such a horrid day in her life. But this was not the worst.

With Roger's help, Ellen managed to go riding with the Count de Bark several times and they were able to make arrangements to meet occasionally. But so much of their time together was taken up by the Count accusing Ellen of being cold and when on occasion he failed to turn up for a meeting, by Ellen suspecting that de Bark did not really care for her. Ellen knew that she appeared cold and this was confirmed in a conversation she had with Miss Lister Kaye who, '*suddenly exclaimed, well you are the most incomprehensible girl I know for with all the admiration you get you do not care a straw for anybody [...] and said she could not discover a single spark of love in my behaviour.*' In seeking to understand her own behaviour and the reasons that made her act the way she did, Ellen wrote,

> *I know that I do seem to be freezing at times, although heaven knows nothing is farther from my natural disposition but it is a curious instance of the force of habit on a character which is in reality warm and ardent to a fault. The fact is that I have lived ever since I was born amongst people who have not the slightest sympathy with emotions of any kind, indeed it is a curiosity to remark how utterly incapable they are of comprehending any deeper or more delicate feeling than those called forth by common occurrences of everyday life. Now unfortunately I am likewise so exceedingly sensitive that I feel acutely things which other people would scarcely remark and consequently the certainty of not being comprehended and dread of ridicule have induced me ever since I can remember to conceal every thought and feeling with the most jealous care [...] There is another thing that contributes to the same result and that is the constant surveillance to which I am exposed and which never relaxes. Every word and look is watched, consequently I feel a necessity of caution and a sense of oppression which filters every movement and restrains every impulse. Even when freed from the danger of something I can never feel perfectly at liberty there is always the sensation of a weight upon the mind, a sort of moral bondage which is the fruit of such a system.*[32]

Ellen recognised that the Count had cause for complaint, yet when he failed to turn up for a ride in Rotten Row she compared his behaviour to that of Jacky Leche '*whom I used to laugh at and who used to travel hundreds of miles for the wildest hope of catching a glimpse of me out walking.*'[33] She continued to be tormented by the thought that he did not care for her when he missed another rendezvous. Yet when they did meet, she wrote, '*and still with all this I love that man, yet though I would have died sooner than let him discover that I expected to see him when his own heart did not prompt him to come.*'[34] At the end of that final meeting before the Palmers left for the country, Ellen, despite all her doubts, was beguiled into accepting his ring, although of course she was never able to wear it. Did she secretly believe that she was engaged to him? She never admitted the fact.

They took the dying Aunt Abbey with them back to Cefn. Ellen, her emotions in turmoil, had accepted the Count's ring, yet believed that his cool conduct over the past few days meant that she must give up hope of his love.

> *But this conviction gave me inexplicable misery and the wretchedness of this morning's journey I shall never forget. I was obliged to make the most strenuous exertions to prevent the tears from overflowing, to laugh and talk while my heart was bursting. And after all it was but a sorry attempt for they all asked what was the matter with me and set it down to my not being well […] I cried half the night […] but the only thing I sought was his love. I care nothing for riches, rank and splendour, which are the idols of half the world. I might have grasped them over and over again, but they were nothing compared to him.*'[35]

A day later she confessed that '*I did my first Swedish exercise this evening. However there is no harm in learning the language though he may never know it, so why should I sacrifice the pleasure?*'

It seems probable that Aunt Abbey had lung cancer and as her condition grew worse the family could only wait and watch. There was a false alarm: after the family had gathered round her bed to say goodbye, '*she bade me read her the last prayer for the dying. I could scarcely obey her, but tried to command myself and when I had concluded there was an awful silence broken only by the sobs we could not restrain. Even the servants were assembled […] To the doctor's extreme astonishment however she rallied at 4 o'clock.*'[36]

Two days later she did die and again it had been Ellen who read the prayer for the dying and the Lord's Prayer as she breathed her last. Besides arrangements for the funeral, the dressmaker had to be sent for to measure them all for mourning dress. Aunt Abbey – Frances Roberts

– the eldest of the Matthews sisters, was buried at Oswestry. Only Roger and Mr Roberts (the medical man and no relation) attended the funeral. Her death changed the family dynamics because she was the one who owned Cefn and had inherited all her husband's very considerable wealth. Mentioning the legacy left to Aunt Mary of £300 per annum, Ellen revealed the animosity that Aunt Mary had always felt for her elder sister: '*Asked by Mama one morning when she was busy to take her place in the carriage and accompany Aunt Abbey on her daily drive, I heard her refuse and say in reply, "no indeed, Fanny says I shall never be any the better for her death so why should I trouble myself about her".*' However, when Mary believed her sister might leave her something, and it was only at the last moment that Aunt Roberts called a lawyer and did indeed leave her £300 per annum, her attitude changed. Ellen writes, '*Aunt Mary's subsequent devotion, the great care she took not to let Aunt Roberts out of her sight did not proceed entirely from sisterly devotion!!!*'

It was the first time that Ellen mentioned the relationships between the sisters in the diaries. Mary Matthews was unmarried, she had no home of her own and with a very small income had little choice but to be part of the Palmer household – not a happy situation to be in. Her three sisters were all financially independent, so it is perhaps understandable that from time to time she vented her frustrations on the two younger members of the household, Ellen and Roger, and especially Ellen. What is less understandable is that Ellen's mother nearly always joined in the abuse with her aunts.

The year ended badly.

> *At dinner today whilst I was talking quietly to Roger, Aunt Gray turned around and inquired in the most offensive tone and with one of her celebrated sneers, said 'pray what do you know about it?', alluding to the subject Roger and I were discussing. I was rather aggrieved at being set down in this way before the whole party, (Mr Roberts included) especially as it is part and parcel of a regular system of Mrs Gray's to sneer me down at every possible opportunity as if my opinion were below contempt so that I really scarcely dare open my mouth in my father's house. Accordingly I requested her very quietly not to address me in that*

> *impertinent manner and will it be believed although I have hitherto borne her insults without a word, yet because I dared at last to insinuate that I would not be sneered down any longer, Mama took me aside calling me an ill tempered girl and scolded me for my impertinence and joined my aunts in talking at me the whole evening. Is it to be wondered at that I should be tired of my home? Especially as this is not a thing which happens once in a way but is of everyday occurrence. I seldom note down the trials of temper which every 24 hours brings forth.*[37]

Things got even worse. The following day, 30 December, Ellen wrote,

> *Mama came and told me my two aunts had been recounting some odious slanderous story about Roger bringing Dr Kingsley to see me professionally when I was sick in bed during her visit to Ireland.* [While Ellen had measles.] *He certainly did so and with their full knowledge and concurrence, but to think of their raking up such a trifling circumstance 7 months afterwards and making it the foundation of a series of horrible accusations! Really the atrocity of these women (fiends would be a better name) is beyond belief.*

Caught between her impossible love for the Count de Bark, whom she could not give up, and her unhappy home life, it is hardly surprising that she could see her future only as bleak and cheerless.

CHAPTER 8

Heartbreak

Ellen was not under any illusions about her future, but she did enjoy herself on occasion; she loved dancing and music, rejoiced in her success as a musician and did not lack for partners at the balls she attended. But as was her custom, the entry in her diary for New Year's Day, besides summarising the main events of the past year, also tried to foresee what the future might hold. This year she was particularly gloomy as she remained obsessed by her love for her Swedish count, knowing that it was never likely to result in marriage,

> *Nor is it likely, as far as I can see, that anything will alter [...] I cannot shake off my long and deep attachment, nor can I summon up courage to make it known to my parents. Still less could I wed another; and therefore what can I have to look forward to but a blank and cheerless future. Hopeless of being able to forget, hopeless of consent to my long cherished wishes, doubtful even of my love being truly returned and with a home that would be misery to think of remaining forever. What ray of hope is there to light me on my solitary path. Without a friend who will truly sympathise with me (for owing to my terrible aunt's influence my mother is a stranger to my inward thoughts) there are moments when I feel deeply the loneliness of my condition. And yet indifferent observers think my fate a brilliant one and are disposed to envy me the advantages of my lot and my own great happiness.*

She could and did flirt and dance with a large number of young men who were attracted by her vivacity and lively sense of fun, the public face she used to conceal her inward unhappiness. Judging by her diary entries she had no very great opinion of her family and yet she could not bring herself to go against their absolute determination that she was not on any account to marry a foreigner nor any man who did not live up to their social ambitions. She was in thrall to the Count de Bark and, although this would be her fifth London season, clearly had no intention of looking for a husband, still less getting married to anyone other than the Count. All the hopes her family had invested in her making a successful marriage were therefore in vain; the dinners, the balls, the boxes at the opera, the dresses and visits to Paris – all centred round the belief that Ellen would make a suitably prestigious marriage. Ellen rarely mentioned the opinions of her aunts and mother, but perhaps their sense of frustration at Ellen's continued refusal to conform to their wishes lay behind her aunts' frequent outbursts. Their lives were dominated by their wish to marry off Ellen, and they had every reason – particularly Mary, with no future except as an unmarried maiden aunt – to feel jealous of their niece. She was clearly their intellectual superior, beautiful and talented, but never spoke to them of her thoughts and feelings. Worse still, she showed no sign of fulfilling their wishes and giving them the sort of prestige enjoyed by the Mackinnons, who now basked in the reflected glory of their relationship with the de Guiches and de Gramonts. They could well have felt a certain amount of resentment at her behaviour.

On their annual trip to Paris in 1851 the Palmers found the city very full, and it took them three days' hard searching and constantly being outbid before they finally found rooms in a house in the Place Vendôme. Very soon Ellen was writing about meeting the Count de Bark who had returned to Paris on learning that they were there. Fearful that the Count might be attracted by her fortune, Ellen tasked Roger with the mission to misinform the Count as to her prospects, and to say she had not been left money by her aunt nor would she inherit anything on the death of her father. When the Count went to Oxford to meet Roger, he probably saw through this clumsy attempt to underline Ellen's lack of financial expectations. De Bark had specifically asked Roger as to her fortune, but he must have been suspicious when Roger insisted that she would inherit nothing from her father. Ever-credulous, Ellen was delighted to know that he had been told and appeared to believe the story, and reassured herself that he really loved her for herself and was not after her money.

Ellen spent a lot of time in Paris with the Duchesse de Guiche, either riding in her coach or dining with her family and going to receptions given by the Duchesse de Gramont, and generally enjoying the prestige that this afforded her. Her peace of mind was shattered one morning when Mr Mackinnon asked for an audience with her mother. Ellen was terrified that she was going to be the subject of his visit and that Mr Mackinnon would repeat his warnings against the Count. She thought it might also be an attempt to concoct a marriage between her and Lord Mandeville, a suitably rich, aristocratic young man, heir to the Duke of Manchester.[1] Ellen had arranged for the Count to come to dinner, but following parental instructions she hardly spoke a word to him. Not knowing the reason, he naturally took offence, and when parting gave her a cool look and only the tips of his fingers by way of farewell. In a small aside, Ellen mentions that when she was introduced to Lord Mandeville he looked terrified and made off as quickly as possible, obviously having heard the rumour about their proposed marriage.

Mr Mackinnon was not the only matchmaker. Lady Harrington had been asked by the Prince de Monthéard to help to arrange a marriage between his son and Ellen, which would have made her one of the grandest ladies in Paris. Parisian gossip was already linking their names, but apart from the fact that he was a foreigner, Ellen would never have agreed to an arranged marriage. Lady Harrington, although refusing to act as go-between, told her the young man's mother was a royal princess, that he was half-brother to the King of Sardinia and first cousin to the Emperor of Austria, and strongly advised Ellen to accept – but to no effect. There were other more agreeable distractions. Introduced by the Duc de Guiche, Ellen went with her cousin, the Duchesse, to a very grand party given by the Comtesse de Castellane. She reported triumphantly, '*The party was most brilliant, consisting entirely of the highest French nobility with scarcely 6 English people in the whole room besides the ambassador.*'

Another important event in the Palmers' diary was an invitation to the French President's ball. This was the first time that Ellen would meet Louis Napoleon since she had danced with him at her ball while he was in exile in London. Thanks to the generosity of Harriet Howard, whom he had met at a party given by Lady Blessington, Louis Napoleon had been able to mix with a certain smart set in London and be given royal precedence in the dining room.[2] Harriet Howard, born Elisabeth Anne Haryett, was the daughter of the respectable owner of the Castle Hotel in Brighton but, determined to go her own way, had first eloped with a jockey and then become the mistress of Major Martyn, who had placed his large fortune at her disposal. Described as strikingly handsome in a chiselled style of beauty, she was intelligent and discreet. In love with Louis Napoleon, she had in part bankrolled his successful coup in 1848. The future emperor had danced with Ellen at her first coming out ball, the Palmers delighted to have him on their guest list. Having used what fortune he had on two abortive coups, the political upheavals that swept Europe in 1848 gave Louis Napoleon another opportunity to try his luck. The rise in nationalism had reinvigorated the Bonapartiste party and the dissatisfaction of the middle classes with the political leadership gave Louis Napoleon the opportunity he was seeking. Financially secure thanks to the generosity of Harriet Howard, this time Louis Napoleon realised his ambition. He was elected President of France in 1848 by popular vote.

It was with a certain sense of occasion that Ellen describes the first Presidential ball to which they were invited.

Mama and I proceeded to the ball at the President's and were ushered in to the room where all the English assemble for presentation as it is the rule now that they must be presented every year. We found the Lister Kayes and the O'Dowds in the room and after a short delay we went into the adjoining salon and were severally presented to the President. He was very gracious to us and said he remembered all our kind hospitality in England.[3]

With the aim of restoring the dignity of the presidency, the occasion was formal and the Palmers, having found a place to sit, had to remain where they were for three hours until they were released by the President's departure. Ellen did not complain, as she would have done in normal circumstances, because she was then able to have a long conversation with the Count unseen by her Mama. He urged her not to return his ring as he did not see it as binding in the sense of an engagement, but merely as a token that she loved him. He also told her that he knew from Roger that she was not an heiress, making it easier for him to prove he loved her for herself alone, and Ellen was once more able to believe that she was truly loved.

Three days later all her old misgivings returned when he called to tell her that he was returning to London. She could not imagine why he would leave Paris where they had so many chances to meet. Before he left, he managed to get the Palmers tickets for the Hôtel de Ville ball, and arranged matters so cleverly that he was asked to dinner and to accompany them to the ball. As a sop to Ellen, the Count put off his journey to London so as to be able to attend a party at the Lister Kayes to which they were both invited, although on their way in the carriage Ellen was cautioned about the Count by her mother: '*She said he was quite determined to have me if possible but that she hoped that I should never marry and still less one such as he. I reminded her that she had imagined the same thing two years ago and she said, yes she had, and he was just the same now.*'[4]

At the numerous balls she attended, Ellen continued to find herself surrounded by partners wanting to dance with her and was constantly being told what a success she was having. On his return to Paris, de Bark told her he had taken a room overlooking their street and implored her to allow him to walk with her when she went out. He said '*that if I did but know how long the hours were he spent watching at his window then I should take pity on him [...] I have doubted and doubted this man's love but I think after the most rigid scrutiny I can doubt no longer. If ever there was breath in man, he loves.*'[5] But he also became frustrated by her refusal to walk with him and jealous of her success at the balls they attended, although she was often able to dance as many as three times with him.

However much Ellen pretended to herself that her love affair with the Count was a private matter, it was clear that it was still a subject of current gossip. At a dinner party at the de Guiches, to Ellen's dismay she overheard the Duke saying that he had heard a report from London that she was to marry the Count, which meant the whole company learned of it. As a result, when they did meet they didn't dare spend much time talking for fear of adding to the gossip. Ellen, however, could be very capricious, and at a party at Mrs Gould's where she was the centre of a circle of '*adorateurs*' as she called her partners, she took malicious pleasure in tormenting him by rattling on with them and not acknowledging his presence. By way of excuse she said,

> *I thought he was jealous and am determined to cure him of that failing. He was standing close behind me talking to Miss Kaye and watching my proceedings, but at last said to her, 'I can bear it no longer' and took up his hat and quitted the house without even looking at me. I must say my conscience smote me when he was gone.*[6]

Not long after, Ellen had a real cause for alarm concerning his behaviour. She overheard the Duchesse de Guiche asking M. de Toulongeon, a cousin of the Guiches, if it was true that the Count de Bark was as much a friend of the President's as he pretended to be. According to Ellen,

> *M. de Toulongeon answered immediately that the President did not even know the Count, or if he did, he added, when the duchesse pressed the question, it was only by meeting him through* [the President's mistress] *Mrs Howard. He then, on being further questioned, proceeded to insinuate that the Count was very good friends indeed with the lady and that he was perpetually at her house.*[7]

It then transpired that the Count never rode the President's horses and that he used only those belonging to Mrs Howard. '*Someone asked how the President liked these goings on and he answered with a sneer (or something approaching one) that the President was very glad to see Mrs Howard so much amused.*'

Harriet had followed Louis Napoleon to Paris and, although cosily ensconced in the rue du Cirque with a garden door giving on to the Tuileries, she was growing tired of being kept in the background and had begun to make demands. Dissatisfied with her situation and fearing for her future, there probably was some truth in the story of her enjoying the company of the Count. However, Ellen could not accept the idea and wrote,

> *This however is a very improbable feeling on the part of a person so strongly attached to another as the President is to Mrs Howard and this consideration joined to the falsity of M de Toulongeon's assertion about the President not knowing the Count de Bark is the only ray of comfort which consoled me at all whilst listening to this horrid story.*

She sought advice from the Lister Kayes and was relieved to be told that they thought part of the story untrue; however, she made no comment on Lady Kayes' remark '*that she did not doubt that he did go to Mrs Howard's as she said no young men were saintly enough to abstain from going to such places altogether*', but was comforted by Lady Kaye quickly adding '*that I might rest assured that there was nothing more than common acquaintance between the parties and the count's friendship with the President proved the fact beyond doubt.*'[8] The rumours of the Count's involvement with Mrs Howard would not go away, and Ellen suspected the de Guiches of purposely trying to undermine the Count as she thought they probably wanted her to marry their cousin, M. de Toulongeon.

When she wanted to, Ellen could always find ways of meeting and talking with the Count and, taking her maid, she walked along the other side of the Seine to the Champs de Mars to hear what he had to say on the subject of Mrs Howard. As with his involvement with Lola Montez, de Bark had a wonderfully ingenious explanation:

> *He told me that the affair in which he was engaged (which he explained fully to me in the strictest confidence) rendered it necessary that he should be master of the latest political news, and that no place afforded such facilities for that purpose as the salon of Mrs Howard where all*

> *the ministers and friends of the government congregated and where the President himself could talk and converse with so much more freedom than when the eyes of the world were upon him.*[9]

It is true that Harriet did discreetly entertain for Louis Napoleon in the house in the rue du Cirque, and no doubt the Count was a guest on such occasions. He admitted that he did ride Mrs Howard's horses, but had not realised that that could be construed in such a malicious way, and would give it up if Ellen wished.

The de Guiches were obviously set on undermining the Count's hold on Ellen's affections and during the course of a social visit with her mother the Duchesse said

> *she thought it right to tell us that the Count de Bark had been giving out that our marriage was a settled thing. It appears that he had told Mrs Howard this, she had repeated it to the President, he had told M. Fleury and a fourth person had repeated it to the duc de Guiche. I feel quite sure this unknown person was M de Toulongeon, and now the whole scheme is plain at a glance, viz: the de Guiches want me to marry their cousin [...] Then they told us what great friends the count was with Mrs Howard but afterwards they did confess that they knew nothing against his character further than that went. However Mama was in a tremendous rage as one might naturally expect she would be and fulminated threat of forbidding him the house and I really never went through such a painful scene in my life, and when at the acme of it the duchesse suggested that perhaps I did care about the count, it was almost more than I could do to clear away in an instant all traces of emotion and turn a careless and laughing countenance to the manifold glances of enquiry turned towards me.*[10]

Out riding with the Duchesse a few days later, Ellen confessed to her that she did love the Count and did not want to marry anyone else. The Count, well aware of Ellen's feelings, must have thought that this was the time to get her to break her resolve.

> *He has been latterly pressing me very much to put an end to the present state of constraint in which we live by frankly avowing everything. He says the present position of affairs is intolerable and certainly it cannot go on forever, but still what can I do? I know the sort of reception which an avowal of the truth would meet and what course to take I know not.*

While in Paris, Ellen had persuaded Bordighini, the singing master, to take her on as his pupil. She recounts with pride that he was perfectly delighted with her performance and seemed astonished at the extent of her powers. After she had sung 'Come e bello' at her second lesson, he said,

> *I sang it quite like an artiste and that I had the style, finish and chic of the best professionals [...] he assured me this was not flattery and I might ask anybody if he was not famous for telling the truth [...] he had been unwilling to take an additional pupil but now he would do anything for me and said I have an 'intelligence extraordinaire' and shall astonish the world in a short time.*

She continues, '*I feel myself that I possess the "feu sacré" for I comprehend instantly the most delicate shades of feeling in the music I am singing and I identify myself so completely with the subject that I actually feel every sentiment and every passion which the words express.*'[11] She describes herself as a passionate being, but it was only through her singing that she was able to give true expression to all the pent-up emotions that she was forced to conceal, and it was her ability to use her feelings, together with her natural talent and her determination to succeed, that so obviously impressed Bordighini. She was given Desdemona's song in *Otello* to study and after she sang it to him he shook her hand and said '*it was "superbe" and that there were not three artistes in all Paris who could have sung so well.*'[12] Bordighini's genuine appreciation of her talent, at this time of emotional turmoil, was balm to her spirit.

Ellen was surprised that Emma de Guiche never broached the subject of the Count again and was also surprised by a change in M. de

Toulongeon's manner towards her. Returning from a party at St Germain, Emma de Guiche had invited them all in to take tea.

> *We finished the evening by a game of blind man's bluff during which the fun was fast and furious! M de Toulongeon was quite cool in his conduct today which is a most remarkable change from the last time we met, indeed he seemed to make a point of avoiding me as civilly as he could. However I enjoyed myself extremely and we did not get home till 3 in the morning.*[13]

Ellen seems never to have realised that her affair with the Count was now so well known. As she had been indiscreet enough to tell Emma that she would never marry anyone but him, she should not have been surprised by M. de Toulongeon's changed attitude towards her. She might also have wondered at her mother's inconsistent behaviour. Much as she disapproved of the Count, Lady Palmer nonetheless invited him to dinner when he called to say goodbye before leaving Paris, and they all played cards in the evening. Not only that, but she asked the Count to put off his journey for a day so that he could accompany Roger to England. But Ellen knew that her mother was not about to change her mind insofar as marriage was concerned.

To great public acclaim, Queen Victoria opened the Great Exhibition of the Works of Industry, to give the exhibition its full name, on 1 May in Hyde Park. Organised by Prince Albert and Henry Cole,[14] and housed in the spectacular glass Crystal Palace designed by Joseph Paxman,[15] the exhibition was primarily to make clear Great Britain's role as an industrial leader. It was a huge success: more than 6 million people had been through the doors when they closed in October and it made a substantial profit. Apart from its role as a showcase for British industry, it had also become a centre for social intercourse. A week after the Palmers returned to London on 6 May, they visited the Great Exhibition.

> *In the afternoon we made our first visit to the Crystal Palace which is certainly a wondrous sight. Every production of nature and indeed from every clime and in the highest state of perfection was assembled in*

> *this dazzling structure, but if I were to describe it for an hour I should never succeed in conveying the faintest idea of the reality. It must be seen to be appreciated. There were numbers of people in the building and we met several that we knew.*

In reality Ellen was more interested in the people she met at the Exhibition than in the objects. On 24 May the family visited the exhibition for the third time and Ellen commented, '*Went to the Exhibition, but saw nobody there and after all it is the* <u>*people*</u> *not the* <u>*things*</u> *one goes to see.*'

Later on in July, Ellen and her friends amused themselves by planning a party at Soyer's. Alexis Soyer, the most successful chef of the day, had resigned from the Reform Club in 1850 and set up his Universal Symposium of All Nations opposite the gates of the Great Exhibition, hoping to attract fashionable society to his establishment. It was housed in Gore House, the erstwhile home of Lady Blessington. On the appointed day a large party sat down to dinner, but as three of the guests, all young men, failed to turn up, the party was something of a disappointment. They walked in the gardens and returned for coffee, but still no sign of the young men. They then went on to Vauxhall where Ellen casually remarked, '*the last thing we did was to look at a Moorish family just imported and after this we all went home to supper [...] but altogether there was a damp thrown upon our party by our disappointments, some of the people were slow and on the whole the thing was a failure.*' Alexis Soyer's establishment also failed and he closed on 14 October, three days after the Great Exhibition ended, making a loss of £7,000.

When an invitation to a fancy dress ball at Buckingham Palace arrived, directing the guests to come dressed as they would have been at the court of Charles II, 10 years after the Restoration, the Palmer ladies drove down to Hampton Court to examine the portraits for ideas. As the sitters themselves were mainly in fancy dress this proved of no use and left Ellen free to devise an outfit she expected would be different and sensational. She decided to go as a 'bourgeoise' in the reign of Louis XIV. Much time was spent driving round town for fittings with the dressmaker Mme Camille, finding the right lace for the sleeves, trying on shoes and finally choosing a wig. With her innate sense of fashion, Ellen usually knew how to dress to attract admiration. But, arriving at the palace dressed in a white satin petticoat embroidered with gold, rather short, teamed with a matching blue velvet bodice faced with pomegranate velvet, Ellen knew immediately that she had got it wrong.

> *Almost everybody else however had long trains and I was so ashamed of my short petticoats that I sat in the second throne room and never moved except at the very end of the evening although I was frequently asked to dance. There were six fancy quadrilles […] After this the Queen led a polonaise and trotted about the rooms unceasingly all night. Count Suminski was very civil to us, he took us to the supper room and fed us. We saw a great many acquaintances, but there were few young men there excepting the Corps Diplomatique and foreigners of distinction. Sir Watkin was there, he came up to speak to me and looked such a beauty in his wig that I could scarcely help laughing. I think Lady Clementine Villiers looked better than anyone I saw. The Queen left the ball at 2 and all the company broke up immediately after. Altogether it was a very stupid ball and I did not enjoy it a bit.*'[16]

Social failures were offset by occasions when Ellen enjoyed great success, with more partners than she could dance with at a succession of balls, including her own. She continued to win praise for her singing and playing, and visits to the opera continued to please, but over everything hung the question of her future relationship with the Count. Almost as soon as she was back in London she started to see him secretly, walking with her maid in Regent's Park. A cross against an entry in her diary indicated a meeting with de Bark, although she seldom related what was discussed when they met. Primrose Hill was a favourite destination where they would sit down under the trees and enjoy the view. The only occasion she wrote about was when the Count told her he had to go to Sweden in order to lay the foundations of a new home and to oversee the planting of the park, and asked her to accept a miniature he had had painted for her.

> *I thought I was not justified in accepting it and accordingly refused to do so which grieved him very much and he said plaintively, Oh if you knew how joyfully I had this done, with expression of heart and then to find it all so thrown back in such an icy manner. I was sorry to do it but my conscience told me it was right.*[17]

By the time he returned from Sweden, Ellen had once again made up her mind to break off their relationship. '*I felt it was my duty for both our sakes to put an end to the uncertain state of mind in which we had existed so long and make a resolution never to think more on one another as I was satisfied that our case was perfectly hopeless.*' The Count tried hard to find out if anything had been said to his discredit, but Ellen would only say that her parents' prejudices against foreigners were insurmountable and that their ambition was also a factor. She forbore to tell him that they believed him to be a wild and dissipated character. He for his part swore that it was no use breaking off altogether as his love could not be greater than it was and that the feeling could never change, and so they parted. A week later they met briefly by chance when the Count had his handsome young brother, Joachim, with him. At a fête at Mr Lumley's villa on the Thames, Ellen saw de Bark parading about with Lady Poulett and Mrs Dodd in an ostentatious manner because he '[knows that] *she and her sister are my abomination.*' They could not avoid seeing each other briefly at balls and the Count had time to ask Ellen if she still loved him, to which she answered he must not ask that question. Despite parental disapproval, both the de Bark brothers were invited to her own ball and she was delighted to discover that Joachim thought well of her, as she was more anxious about his opinion than anybody else's.

In this unsettled state of mind Ellen was upset to discover that Lady Yarde Buller had cautioned her mother about letting Roger become too friendly with the Count, who she said was a gambler and a dangerous companion for a young man. '*These warnings distress me terribly because I cannot help thinking that what everyone says must be true, at least in some degree, and yet the horror of believing he is <u>unprincipled</u> is more than I can bear. Would to God I had never seen him.*'[18] The following day, the de Guiches came round to say goodbye as they were leaving for France.

They were still discussing a possible marriage between Ellen and Prince Monthéard, a cousin of the de Guiches, saying what a superb match this would be, giving Ellen the highest social position, related to most of the royal families of Europe. In her confused state Ellen wrote, *If the count loves me well and truly there is no fear of my being led away by ambition.'* But doubt crept in: '*But were I once convinced that he is deceiving me with pretended affection, then I must grasp something to fill the void of disappointed love. I can understand love in a cottage, but failing that let me have ambition in a palace. No middle course could I endure for a moment.*'

Why did Lady Palmer, who wanted to prevent both Ellen marrying the Count and Roger being led astray by him, continue to invite him and his brother to Portland Place when she considered him 'wild and dissipated'? Ellen simply recorded the fact in her diary, with no comment, that when they called they stayed a long time and that on 5 August they dined with the Palmers. Did Ellen override her weak mother, unable to bear the thought of not seeing him again as they were about to leave town? The day before, walking in Regent's Park, Ellen had come across the brothers, the Count apparently pointing out to his brother a seat where they had sat and talked. Ellen considered this romantic vision of the Count showing his brother places where he had met her sufficient excuse to agree to yet another secret meeting on Friday, 8 August. Although he was late arriving at their rendezvous, they walked to Primrose Hill and Ellen confessed that she did love him '*a little bit and at the time I was saying it I felt I could have given the world for him*'; however, not enough, it seems, to give up her parents' world. But Ellen was beginning to count the cost of her attachment to de Bark. When Colonel Taylor told her that his cousin was to marry Miss Lenore Conyngham on the 25th, she commented, '*There was another chance I threw away for the count's sake and a chance that few would have spurned, viz. to be a viscountess with £40,000 a year.*'

The end came suddenly. Having agreed with Roger to go out riding with the Count on Saturday, Roger casually informed her that the Count wanted to change the day to Monday, the day before they were due to leave. Ellen discovered from Joachim de Bark that the change of plan was occasioned by their wish to go sightseeing and inspect Windsor Castle.

Plate 1 Eleanor Ambrose (1718–1816), celebrated Irish beauty, by Francis Cope. She married Roger Palmer of Castle Lackin in 1752.

Plate 2 Ruins of Castle Lackin, Co. Mayo.

Plate 3 Portrait of Sir Roger Palmer.

Plate 4 Portrait of Lady Palmer.

Plate 5 The small anvil given to Roger Palmer and Eleanora Matthews after their wedding in Gretna Green in 1828 as a memento of their marriage.

Plate 6 Portrait of Ellen Palmer writing, date and artist unknown.

Plate 7 Portrait of Ellen Palmer by Sir Francis Grant, 1853.

Plate 8 Sample of Ellen Palmer's handwriting reproduced from her small travel diary.

Plate 9 Portrait of Ellen Palmer, date and artist unknown.

Plate 10 Portrait of Ellen Palmer's brother, Roger Palmer, in the uniform of the 11th Hussars.

Plate 11 Cefn Park, after the fire of 1830, possibly late 1840s.

Plate 12 Kenure Park.

Plate 13 Vice Regal Ball at Dublin Castle circa 1848 by F.J Davis.

Plate 14 Portrait of Nils de Barck, known to Ellen as Count de Bark; Swedish adventurer.

Plate 15 Lola Montez, by Joseph Karl Stieler, Irish dancer, mistress of King Ludwig of Bavaria, became Countess of Landsfeld and was rumoured to have had an association with Nils de Barck.

Plate 16 Painting of the Star and Garter, Richmond, 1812, artist unknown; often visited by Ellen Palmer and friends, and the family stayed there after the death of Lady Palmer.

Plate 17 Alexis Benoit Soyer, renowned chef and entrepreneur. Ellen hosted a party at his restaurant in 1851.

Plate 18 View of Constantinople, taken from the road leading to Buyukderch, 1818, where the Palmer family stayed after arriving in Constantinople.

Plate 19 Charge of the Light Brigade, 25 October 1854. Roger Palmer took part in the charge. Painting by William Simpson.

Plate 20 Lord Raglan's HQ at Khutor Karagatch, where Ellen was entertained by him on her arrival in Balaclava. Painting by William Simpson.

Plate 21 The monastery of St George and Cape Fiolente looking east; often visited by Ellen and friends. Painting by William Simpson.

Plate 22 Sevastopol from behind the English batteries; Ellen visited the batteries with William Peel, despite the danger from incoming fire. Painting by William Simpson.

Plate 23 Captain Sir William Peel, VC, by John Lucas.

Plate 24 Defence of Sevastopol, first day of Anglo-French attack, 18 June 1855, showing the city aflame.

Plate 25 Sir Jonathan Peel, by Benjamin West, date unknown.

Plate 26 Lady Alice Peel, by Sir Francis Grant, date unknown.

Plate 27 Sculpture in St Giles's Parish Church, Wrexham, by Thomas Woolner, RA. It commemorates the death of Mary Ellen Peel *née* Palmer, aged 33, and her first-born son, Archibald, who died aged 18 months.

Plate 28 Kenure Church, built by Sir Roger Palmer in 1866.

Plate 29 Rose memorial window, Kenure Church, with Mary Ellen Peel's entwined initials in the centre of the window.

Plate 30 Altar memorial window, Kenure Church, with Mary Ellen Palmer's name below.

Plate 31 Kenure Park, showing badly damaged interior staircase, September 1976.

Plate 32 The Portico, Kenure Park – all that remains of a once-great house.

Plate 34 Archie Peel on horseback.

Plate 35 Spy cartoon, 'Roger', Men of the Day Series, *Vanity Fair* 216. Sir Roger William Henry Palmer, Bt.

She poured out her anguished realisation of what this implied as far as she was concerned.

> *How does this proceeding accord with the violent love! he pretends to. The misery when absent, the intense and eager desire to see me, the torture of waiting (even one day) and all the other jargon which I have so often listened to and while doubtless he laughed at me for believing. And after all this he could voluntarily postpone seeing me two whole days for the sake of a temporary pleasure excursion to Windsor, sacrifice a ride with us for the sake of seeing the Castle (which would have done any other day) and unconcernedly trust our last meeting to the chance uncertainty of the day before our departure (for he knows we leave town on Tuesday). Suppose for instance Monday were a wet day, then we could not meet at all before our departure, but probably that would have been a relief to the count, for he evidently considers the whole thing a bore and only does as much as he is obliged by the duty of keeping up appearances.*

The scales had fallen from her eyes and the diary reflected her misery. '*How often has he told me what extreme happiness it was for him to see me for a minute, how he has expatiated upon the misery of suspense and the torments of absence.*'

What was even worse, that Saturday Ellen spotted him sitting opposite them at the opera with Mrs Dodd and Miss Saunders, although he tried to remain hidden knowing that she could not bear seeing him in the company of those two women. Roger, who had gone to say goodbye to the Count on Tuesday, told Ellen how upset the Count appeared to be and how he had asked Roger to beg her to come out and see him. To add insult to injury, Roger further told Ellen that the Count had meant to come to the opera on Monday to see her for the last time, but had stayed too long at the Cremorne and the opera house was closed when he got there.

> *I think his conduct last night showed pretty plainly how much he cared about seeing me again and when Roger told me about his arriving too*

> *late at the opera I cannot express what I suffered inwardly. And then that he should think I could overlook all this and condescend to go out and actually seek him; No! I would rather die first, and much as it may cost me I will think no more about one who is even weary of pretending to care for me, and tear up by the roots every particle of that absorbing love I once felt for him.*[19]

This time Ellen stuck to her resolution and returned to Cefn without seeing the Count again. To assuage, in part, the agonies of unrequited love, almost the first thing she did was to write him a long letter explaining why she was going to break from him entirely, and intending, when he had replied, to follow up by returning his ring. She wrote that she told him only a very small part of what she was feeling, '*as I could not condescend to reproaches and would bear anything sooner than appearing to make an appeal to his compassion by describing the misery his conduct occasioned me.*'[20] She comforted herself by believing that he would reply by return of post with an explanation.

Poor Ellen, the days went by and no letter came. '*No letter today and it is exactly a week since I sent mine.*' She invented excuses for him. '*I now think the count must have left town before he received it, in which case it may be a few days longer until it can be forwarded to him and this idea will tranquillise me for a short time.*' Finally Ellen could deceive herself no longer and on 31 August recorded in her diary her realisation that there would be no letter. In one long cry of anguish she wrote,

> *I could not have believed this, I could not have thought he would treat me with such utter contempt. And to think that this is the reward of all I have sacrificed for his sake, the wealth, the titles and splendour I might so often have grasped, and more far more than this the misery I have had to suffer all through my unhappy love; the necessity of concealment, the long hours of dejection, the endurance of all the watchfulness and annoyance I am subject to at home, the intense fear of our good understanding being discovered, the constant alarm caused by every letter or visitor whose errand was not manifest, and worse than all the torture which I have undergone at listening to the reports against his character which almost*

> *every day brought forth, and the acute anguish of those doubts which such stories as those of Lola Montes and Mrs Howard could not fail to suggest. It required no common love to withstand all this, but I have withstood it. I have resisted temptation, I have endured everything and refused to believe the voice of the world against him, sacrificed rank and wealth and even peace of mind and duty for four long years for him. And after that what was my reward?*

Reviewing the past year, as was her custom, Ellen made one last comment on her disastrous love affair. '*I can now see him in his true colours undazzled by that delusive radiance to which love casts around its objects. I have summoned Pride to my aid & have at length resolved to cast off one in every way unworthy of my love and to regard the past as a dream from which I have mercifully awakened in time.*'

CHAPTER 9

Music Her Only Solace

Once Ellen accepted that she had been abandoned by the Count and was forced to recognise that all she had been told about him was unfortunately true, and as she slowly came to terms with the pain and grief his behaviour had caused, she threw herself with renewed energy into her music, and sang and played even longer hours. Unable to sever all links with him, she continued to study Swedish, defending her action to herself by writing that once she had started something she would not give up. She did still have his ring, having meant to return it with her reply to the letter that never came. However, the Count was not quite finished with Ellen. He had commissioned a friend to paint the portrait of Rollo, the much-loved dog given to Ellen by a former rejected lover, Mr Lane Fox. De Bark now demanded that Roger pay him £40 for the painting and continued to harangue him until at last he sent the money together with the ring Ellen had secretly treasured for so long.

The dull routine at Cefn was briefly interrupted in September by a visit to Oteley Park[1] near Ellesmere in Shropshire, home of the Mainwarings.[2] The occasion was a concert at which the Duncombe's daughter, nicknamed 'Jenny Lind', was to perform. Since Ellen's musical prowess was well known, it was obvious that the main focus of the evening's entertainment would be a contest between the two girls to decide which of them was the better musician. Ellen could not help gloating as she wrote,

In the evening the musical campaign began with duets for the concertina and piano by Mrs Duncombe and Miss Duncombe. Then came the singing, for which we adjourned to the hall and as may be imagined I was very anxious to hear how the much vaunted Jenny Lind would turn out. The first three bars however convinced me that she was far enough below me in the art, the case did not admit of a comparison. When she had sung two Italian airs I was summoned to the instrument and I sang 'O Luce' and afterward 'In Questo Simplice' and although I was rather frightened and hoarse still I performed very well and delighted them exceptionally. The faces of 'Jenny Lind' and her mother fell very low indeed and they actually managed that I should not be asked to sing anymore [...] In fact Mrs Duncombe walked her daughter off to the next room and thus put an effectual stop to the music.[3]

The following day, despite the Duncombes' manoeuvres to prevent there being any music at all after dinner, the company insisted upon it and they all moved into the great hall where the new piano had been installed. Ellen again sang after the unfortunate Miss Duncombe, despite her mother calling out, '*Pray to not ask Miss Palmer it will make your cold worse*'. She then requested, so that Ellen would not be able to show off too much, that she should only sing a simple English ballad.

Accordingly I chose 'We met and we parted' which delighted everyone [...] and I next sang 'Come e Bello' better than ever I did in my life and it obtained the most brilliant success and was interrupted with frequent murmurs of applause. The Duncombes looked perfectly crestfallen and Miss D. evinced the greatest reluctance to sing after me but she was obliged either to do it, or confess herself beaten, accordingly she performed two French songs, and miserable enough they sounded. Never was defeat more signal and they really were so ill natured and envious that I was not sorry for their mortification [...] I certainly succeeded brilliantly this evening and they were all perfectly delighted with what they called my 'beautiful voice'.

There was a hidden audience: news of the singing contest was keenly followed backstairs and the servants had assembled in the gallery to listen. Ellen's maid, Emma, told her that they were all agreed that she sang much better and that '*Miss Duncombe's voice sounded nothing after mine*'. Such a success must have helped restore some of Ellen's self-confidence after the bruising end of her relationship with the Count.

The Chester and Wrexham races and balls were an excuse for a house party. Roger had invited two of his friends to stay at Cefn: Spencer Lucy,[4] who had inherited Charlecote Park near Stratford-upon-Avon following the death of his elder brother, and Sir Henry Vane.[5] Both young men were clearly fascinated by Ellen. Lord St Lawrence,[6] a possible suitor, Lady Delamere,[7] née Williams-Wynn, and her daughter, Miss Cholmondeley, were also among the guests staying at Cefn for the occasion. Ellen was invited by Godfrey Fitzhugh, a neighbour, to be patroness of the Wrexham ball and chose to open it with Lord St Lawrence, but she had rightly summed up her partner, commenting that he '*would just as soon make love to my mother as to me*', and indeed he died unmarried. Ellen danced all evening, and among her partners was Mr Peel, the rich young owner of nearby Bryn y Pys[8] who had been much talked about in the neighbourhood. Ellen found him very civil but rather shy. Miss Cholmondeley had a bad headache and did not come to the ball, and did not appear to join in much of the rest of the entertainment. Henry Vane coped with Ellen by constantly teasing her, and discovered if he shouted 'Count' this immediately silenced her. Spencer Lucy on the other hand was really smitten by Ellen, and when he discovered that she was only 22 and not 26 as he had thought, he became serious. Her mother warned her not to encourage him as the Taylors, friends from Ireland who were staying, had observed '*that they were sure Mr Lucy adored the ground I trod on and that it was certainly his intention to propose*'.[9]

Ellen had not taken him seriously, but as he never missed an opportunity to walk and talk with her, when he told her he never walked or rode with his sister or his mother this caused her to write with some amusement that the young man had fallen in love with her. But remembering what it was like to be in love, she backtracked and wrote that amusing was not the word she should have used for it was refreshing to see something natural as a contrast to the sickening deceit and hypocrisy of the world. She thought he was afraid of going too far in speaking, '*for he has the idea that I have so many admirers that I should not deign to cast a glance at him and he has often hinted that he knows how I can snub people*'. Mr Lucy, as Ellen always called him, prolonged his stay at Cefn for as long as he could, and although Lady Palmer was fearful that he would propose, Ellen was confident that she could deal with the situation. She wrote that '*it would be a tremendous bore just now*', probably meaning that she was not yet ready for another love affair. Although he asked her repeatedly to come to Charlecote for his 21st birthday celebrations in December, no invitation arrived and there was no mention of any special celebrations in the memoirs of his mother,[10] who was still grieving for her husband and eldest son. Roger, who often stayed at Charlecote, wrote and confirmed that no celebrations had been planned.

It was mid-January when Lady Palmer and Ellen set off for their long-anticipated visit to Vale Royal,[11] in return for the hospitality Lady Delamere and her daughter had enjoyed at Cefn. Port Vale, built on the ruins of a Cistercian abbey, was a large, rambling building and had been the home of the Cholmondeleys since 1615. The ladies of Vale Royal certainly knew how to make visitors feel themselves to be outsiders. When the Palmers arrived, a large house party was busy with rehearsals for theatricals and they were virtually ignored until dinner, when Ellen was taken in by Sir Watkin. He hardly spoke to her, perhaps because his engagement to his cousin, Miss Marie Wynn, was about to be announced.

> *My other neighbour, Mr Bromley, was a most disagreeable individual so that I had nothing to amuse me and was bored to death. The minute dinner was over they all began rehearsing the play and songs, and this lasted uninterruptedly until 12 o'clock at night when we retired to bed. I must say I was rather bored for I had nothing to do except look on for hours.*[12]

The following day was no better as the guests practised their songs all day and there was nothing for Ellen to do except read amid all the bustle and confusion around her. In the afternoon, she and her mother twice went out for a little stroll in the grounds to pass the time. Although some of the gentlemen in the party had come to ask if she would sing, as they had heard of her prowess, she was not even asked to join the choruses. Ellen guessed that the Delameres had not said a word about her musical ability, '*as they did not want any competition as they were anxious to catch Sir Michael Shaw Stuart for Miss Cholmondeley and he happens to be most passionately fond of music*'.

The play, *Whittington and His Cat*, was, Ellen had to admit, very clever and amusing for an amateur production, but '*the worst part of all was the singing for the altos and the chorus's songs were very good indeed but yet they were most imperfectly executed, added to which none of the people except Sir John Harrington and Sir Michael knew how to sing at all and the ladies' voices were so weak that they could not be heard*'. For the participants the main object was to have fun, and the fact that the singing was not up to much would not have bothered them, but for Ellen music was too serious a subject to be treated so light-heartedly; had she been included she would have found it difficult to fit in with the happy-go-lucky atmosphere that prevailed. In fact, unable to cope with the situation she retreated to bed with a bad headache and was forced to swallow a dose of mustard and water rather than face a 'galomic battery', the choices given her by Lady Delamere.

The Palmers had never experienced the kind of informal, jolly relationships that could exist between the county families who had known each other for generations, so were astonished at the goings-on at dinner. Lady Palmer appeared in full evening dress wearing a blaze of diamonds, while the rest of the party were dressed in the most absurd costumes they could think of.

> *Lady Sarah Cholmondeley was an admiral and Miss Cholmondeley was an old general [...] Capt. Cholmonedeley was his wife dressed in a mob cap, petticoat and bed gown looking so absurd that he was enough to kill one with laughing [...] Sir John and Lady Harrington were charity school children [...] it would be impossible to give an idea of the merriment which prevailed at dinner, the jokes which resulted from keeping up one's character [...] I was rather out of the fire of chaff which*

> *was going on much to my relief [...] directly dinner was over we all rushed to change our dresses [...] everyone now appeared in splendid fancy costumes and magnificence instead of absurdity was the order of the night.*

Nothing could have underlined more effectively the status of those in the inner circle in contrast to that of the Palmers than their response to the absurdities of the dinner party.

At the ball that followed dinner, Ellen came into her own. She had been working on the spangles for her Ondine costume for several days beforehand, and when she entered the ball room with her hair flowing wild as it had been in Dublin and Paris,

> *there was quite a murmur of applause, everyone turned round to stare and to enquire who I was. The encomiums upon it were most rapturous and my hair especially excited a wonderful sensation. Everyone told me it was something magnificent and quite extraordinary and even old Lord Delamere himself came up and complimented me as admiringly as if he had been twenty.*

Ellen's enjoyment of praise, and indeed her need for it to bolster her self-confidence, which was so often being undermined by her aunts and mother, is evident throughout her diaries, but perhaps was even more welcome on this occasion when the Palmers had been made to feel they did not quite belong. On leaving the following morning they were waylaid by Sir Michael Shaw Stewart, who tried to make them postpone their departure, but since Miss Chomondeley, who was present, said nothing there was no way they could stay. While they were waiting for the carriage, there was, however, such an insistent demand from the gentlemen that Ellen should sing that she complied with an aria from 'The Barber of Seville' and '*delighted the audience immensely*'. She did think that Miss Cholmondeley, who had overheard all the conversation, '*never actually even asked in the faintest murmur to prolong my stay with them which after their week's invitation to us was somewhat shabby*'. While Miss Cholmondeley was staying at Cefn, she too had developed such a bad headache that she took to her bed and as a result was unable to go to the ball, at which Ellen was patroness and had all the young men clamouring to dance with her, a fact perhaps not unrelated to her reluctance to have Ellen around any longer once she had achieved her object – returning the visit and snubbing the Palmers.

Early 1852 saw significant changes at Westminster and at the Castle in Dublin. Lord John Russell, the Whig prime minister, had been succeeded by the Conservative Lord Derby, who had been invited to form a minority government in February. Lord and Lady Clarenden were leaving Dublin, he having filled the role of Lieutenant Governor of Ireland for five years, and their farewell reception was a date not to be missed. Sir Roger did not attend, but the other three Palmers, now at Kenure, were keen to be seen. Although the instruction was for less formal dress, nevertheless the ceremonial was the same as a 'Drawing Room', the term for a royal morning reception, and it was all over in five minutes. Ellen had the satisfaction of recording that the Clarendens shook hands with them most kindly. Had they been at St James's Palace, Ellen would have kissed the Queen's hand.

With the change of government in London, Ellen felt very strongly that this should be reflected in the way the ADCs and other vice-regal appointments were distributed. She noted that no less than seven or eight Whig households held these appointments to the Irish court, to the exclusion of good Conservatives, and wrote to the papers expressing her dissatisfaction with the present situation. The Palmers continued to be given their usual place on the platform at the various entertainments at the Castle, but at the end of March, after attending a concert, '*Captain Bernard, the ADC in waiting, handed us up to a place near the platform but not on it, the very first time we have ever been excluded even under Whig governments. Accordingly we were excessively indignant at it and Mama expressed her dissatisfaction very forcibly to Mr L'Estrange when she met him.*'[13] Could it be that this was the ADC's response to Ellen's letter to the papers? If so, it backfired spectacularly. The Palmers were invited to dine the following day at the Castle, but would not accept until they had been assured that such a slight would never again be allowed to happen. They received a written apology and so agreed to go to a private ball for

600 at the Castle that evening. Col. Knox Gore told Ellen that the Castle had been in quite an uproar about their note. It certainly had the desired effect. This seemingly small incident was yet another indication of how seriously social distinctions mattered, with the smallest slight noted, remembered and avenged if possible.

Sir Roger and Lady Palmer had twice been to visit their extensive estates in Mayo at election time to 'encourage' their tenants to vote in favour of the Conservative interest, both times unsuccessfully. However, they felt their efforts merited a reward and so Ellen was commissioned to write to Lord Derby to apply for a peerage in Papa's name, '*a judiciously composed mixture of appeals to the gratitude of Government & promises for the future, just flavoured with a soupcon of threats rather understood rather than expressed [...] The letter was pronounced a masterpiece of diplomacy when I had finished it.*'[14] A short letter of refusal came the following month. Unfortunately there is no record of either letter in Lord Derby's papers.[15]

Ellen's small ventures into the world of politics had awakened in her a new interest: '*I devour all the leading articles and debates and catch myself trying to master the great corn question in every detail, weighing the pros and cons on each side, and arguing the pour et contre in my own mind [...] just as if I had to speak on the great question in the House of Commons.*' But no sooner had she written this than she showed how deeply she was imbued with the culture of the times and the impossibility of using her abilities because she was a woman, and a young woman at that.

> *All this is not because I wish to show off for I dislike nothing more than to hear a woman, (more especially a young one) giving her opinions upon subjects generally supposed to be out of her province, but I am irresistibly impelled by my nature either to leave a thing alone altogether, or if I do take an interest in it to master the subject in every detail [...] I must think and reflect until I have thoroughly mastered every detail, till in truth I feel that I have understood it. If I had been a man I should not have been contented with mediocrity and as it is I often feel a sort of discouragement at the almost impossibilities of a woman really becoming great. I know I am capable of better things and sometimes I actually burn with consciousness of intellect wasted and powers of no*

> *avail. But it is of no use to murmur tho the icy barrier of custom does sometimes press heavily on a mind panting for distinction [...] I believe it is this all absorbing wish of being pre eminent in something which has led me to devote all my energies to music, I must strive for something quite as much as my love of the art itself, I must distinguish myself in something, and circumscribed as a woman's choice must be I can see no object which she can pursue with more propriety (that's the conventional word) than an art which requires the greatest concentrated effort.*[16]

Ellen seldom indulged in such self-analysis, but, no longer bound by her love for the Count, she had the freedom to consider her own situation and the honesty to face her frustrations and to understand that her wish to excel in music was not only on account of her love of the art, but also because of her need to distinguish herself in the only possible way she saw open to her. With so much natural ability, born at a later date Ellen would surely have made a name for herself, perhaps in the political arena. However, bound by conventions she dared not breach, perhaps on account of her family's social insecurities and their ambition for her, she was trapped – with music her only saving grace.

Although marriage and family seemed far from her thoughts, the weddings of her contemporaries now figured more frequently in her diaries. She notes that Lord Grosvenor married Lady Constance Lewson Gower on 28 April at the Chapel Royal; and that Sir Watkin married his cousin Miss Marie Williams-Wynn at St James's Church and that the bells rang and cannon were fired all day in Wrexham, and the High Street looked very gay with flowers and evergreens in honour of the occasion. Three days later she learned that Sir John Lister Kaye's son was to marry Lady Caroline Rhys. Ellen had now had five London seasons, but her long and public entanglement with the Count, her parents' well-known ambitions on her behalf, as well as Ellen being perceived an heiress and perhaps also her wish for musical renown, had all militated against her chances of finding a suitable husband.

Established once again in Portland House, Ellen recorded with less and less enthusiasm the parties and balls she attended, and noted with increasing waspishness any slights or lack of expected civility.

> *Mama and I went to the Queen's ball which was exceedingly crowded and was as stupid as usual. There were scarcely any young men there and the few I knew happened to be my enemies; the two Ponsonbys, Lord Otho Fitzgerald etc., who would scarcely look at me at all. Capt. Seymour gave me a very cool 'how do you do' and passed on […] As we were going away we met Sir Michael Shaw Stewart for the first time since we saw him at Vale Royal. He spoke to us in a very friendly way but did not take us downstairs to the carriage as he might have done, added to which he has never called at our house.*[17]

The Palmers continued to give large dinner parties at Portland House, but this year there was no ball for Ellen. No reason was given in the diaries as to why, but perhaps Ellen herself was no longer interested in the idea. The balls she did go to were less and less enjoyable, and she often complained of feeling tired; she may well have been suffering from depression as a result of her broken romance. Roger had brought Spencer Lucy to stay, but even his company brought no joy.

> *Mr Lucy and I had a tiff at dinner time, he was very saucy and I put him down which he much wants occasionally. He is quite changed towards me since his visit to Cefn for instead of the almost adoring way in which he used to watch my every word ad followed every movement, he now scarcely takes the slightest notice of me and when he does it is only with a view of being rude and snappish.*[18]

It seems more likely that his behaviour was a reaction to what he believed the situation to be, and was said to have replied when asked about his intentions, 'Miss Palmer wouldn't look at me, she must have a coronet and neither all my money or my house would satisfy her.' Ellen continued, *'I am sure the odious reports of <u>my great pretentions</u> make numbers of gentlemen who would otherwise be very agreeable quite afraid of even approaching me'*. Spencer Lucy waited another 12 years before marrying Tina Campbell. He was the last Lucy to enjoy the traditional 'vie de château' with all its extravagances; financial pressures forced him to sell the grouse moor and his father's pictures. He had no sons and his daughter Ada married

Henry Fairfax, whose attempt to save Charlecote for the family by selling land and farms and practising the strictest economy was finally unsuccessful. The times were against him and in 1946 Charlecote passed into the hands of the National Trust.

It was while she was gossiping with the daughters of Lord Hastings, with whom she had become friendly, that Ellen was again brought face-to-face with the problem of her relationships with young men.

> *They told me that several gentlemen had told them I was a very nice girl, but they had quite given up asking me to dance (because although they liked me very much still they would not approach me under existing circumstances for fear of being thought fortune hunters). Really it is no wonder I have so often remarked how oddly many young men behaved to me. It is certainly a curious fact, that although I am never in want of beaux or partners, still they are always changing about 'adorateurs' and they are quite a class apart.*[19]

Now that she was free to make relationships with the opposite sex, Ellen's overzealous family had only succeeded in restricting any matrimonial opportunities the season was designed to create by talking up their expectations.

All was not gloom. An invitation from Lady Glasgow to join a farewell dinner for Lord Fredrick Fitzclarence,[20] prior to his departure for India, turned into a hugely successful event in so far as Ellen was concerned. A piano had been specially ordered for the occasion and she performed her old favourite, 'O luce', to rapturous applause and went on to sing 'Ernani involormi', which was interrupted by frequent bursts of applause.

> *Lord Frederick was in perfect extasies, Mr Macdonald, an old blind gentleman begged that I might be taken up to him on purpose to express his delight at my performance which he did most rapturously. Lady Hopetoun also had me brought up to her on purpose to tell me she had scarcely ever enjoyed such a treat or heard such beautiful singing [...] when most of the party were gone and we were standing in the hall with Miss Sinclair and Lord Frederick, they suddenly proposed I should*

> *sing another song [...] Miss Sinclair told me I had enchanted everybody and indeed I was made quite the lion for the evening [...] enjoyed my evening exceedingly.*[21]

Ellen learned later that Lady Hopetoun had an ulterior motive for wishing to talk to her, as she wanted to see if she would be a suitable bride for her son.[22] There was no further mention of the matter, unlike Lady Chichester who was doing all she could to promote the chances of her son, Edward, as a possible husband, much to Ellen's disgust.

Another pleasure was a visit to a fête at Holland House, chaperoned by Lady Talbot, her mother not being grand enough to merit an invitation. Ellen wrote triumphantly that they went '*not as the public but as visitors to Lady Holland*'.[23] After an exhibition of ancient sports and games there was a supper party for 300 of Lady Holland's guests followed by dancing in beautifully illuminated gardens. For Ellen, possibly the most rewarding part of the evening was meeting Luigi Lablache, the famous opera singer[24] whom Ellen had long admired. Whether she knew it or not, through meeting with him she could, by association, link back to some of the greatest musicians of the time. As a young man he had sung the solo part in Mozart's requiem at the funeral of Haydn and taken part in the same requiem for both Beethoven and Chopin. However, she may have been more interested in his son who had introduced her to his father. She was quickly made to understand that he would not become a professional but was '*intended for a private gentleman*' and asked her if he might call with some Neapolitan songs and if she would sing with him. '*Mr Lablache handed me to the carriage and we left the fête at about 11 o'clock, quite delighted with our day.*'

Instead of returning to Cefn at the end of the season, the family decided to go to Baden perhaps in the hope that it might provide some distraction for Ellen. If so, the idea was not a success. Baden, a spa town in south-west Germany, always attracted a large number of English visitors. Fashionable European society went to drink the waters and to amuse themselves by dancing at the balls, gambling in the Kursaal and occasionally driving into the mountains to admire the dramatic surrounding scenery. There was a reason for Ellen's lack of enthusiasm for

Baden. Lady O'Dowd, with her unmarried daughter Rose, was already in residence and having tried to persuade the Palmers not to come, made sure that when they did, Ellen was not introduced to any young man if they could help it and was excluded from parties and picnics.

Their journey out was unremarkable except for an encounter at Homburg with 'Uncle John', presumably a brother of Sir Roger's from whom he was estranged. His name does not appear in any known family tree. Sir Roger was the youngest of the Palmer brothers and was made heir to Kenure at the time of his sudden marriage to Eleanora Matthews. The eldest of the Palmer brothers had died of dropsy,[25] and any other known brothers had died without issue at the time of the marriage. Did John Palmer, whoever he was, believe he had a claim to Kenure and was that the reason for the estrangement? He had written begging to be allowed to see Sir Roger, who had refused the request,

> *but Roger and I thinking it a pity to indulge in rancour for so long resolved to make amends as far as we could, so Doddy* [her brother's nickname] *called upon him and was very kindly received. I should like to have spoken to him also, but it could not be managed, however I did see him whilst we were all standing around the door of the post house. He approached us but Papa received him so badly that he walked away directly.*[26]

Who he was will never be known.

Going to the Kuursaal with Roger to look in on the ball on their second day, Ellen notes that it was a very poor one and the only people they knew were the Gores. She went on,

> *I believe the O'Dowds stayed away from the ball on purpose to avoid introducing us to people, for their frantic jealousy is apparent in every look and although the two great nobs of Baden, Lord Belfast and Lord Edward Thynne have joined them repeatedly whilst Mama was walking with them still they have scrupulously avoided introducing them although it could not be done without positive rudeness.*

And so it went on. On 24 August she recorded,

> *Took the waters before breakfast and in our walk were joined by Lady O'Dowd who spoke to sundry grandees but who took care not to introduce us. Finished my walk with Granger* [her maid]. *Went to sing with Miss Gore at 12 and afterwards went to call on our old friend the Duchesse de Valentinois*[27] *who has just arrived in Baden.*

The arrival of the Duchess was a godsend to Ellen. She was young and the Duke was not particularly loving or attentive so she was delighted to have Ellen as a companion and Ellen, cold-shouldered by the O'Dowds, was grateful for her company. The Valentinois marriage had been an arranged one and, as the Duke explained to an astonished Ellen, the normal French plan was of one or two interviews before the irrevocable took place. Furthermore, he told her he believed in '*amitié*' between men and women, and in reply to a question as to why he was so seldom with the Duchess, replied, '*husbands and wives ought not to be seen together for the "adoration" of the honeymoon soon passed and people were content to "s'aimer tranquillement".*' Ellen continues, '*really I should by no means relish the picture of conjugal happiness which he paints*'.

While Ellen was listening to the band playing with the Duchesse de Valentinois, they were joined by friends of hers, among whom was Prince Frederick of Prussia[28] and his attaché, as well as the Comte de la Rochefoucault. Introductions such as these were some compensation for the snubs the Palmers had received from the O'Dowds. It was even more gratifying to go with the Valentinois to a ball where

> *the Prince of Prussia danced with the Duchess, the first time he had stood up in Baden and the Duc de V. and I were their vis-à-vis, much to the discomfiture of the English ambassadress who looked stubbornly to fill that post herself. We walked back from the ball quite a party. I had my hair done in a new style tonight, namely in curls falling over the comb behind. The duc admired them very much and both he and Prince Frederick were in raptures with my little red cloak; the latter christened me 'petit chaperon rouge'.*[29]

But despite all her success with the foreign nobility, when the time came to leave, Ellen wrote, '*I cannot say I much regret leaving for the whole place has been stupid enough and the whole society so poor that it was very dull in consequence.*'[30]

CHAPTER 10

Joy and Despair

After leaving Baden, the Palmers stopped in Paris so that Ellen might have the benefit of a few more lessons from Bordighini, the noted singing master who only took on those he thought would benefit from his teaching. They found lodgings in the Champs Elysées but discovered, to Ellen's great disappointment, that Bordighini was still away in Italy. However, the Valentinois were also in Paris, so the two families continued to spend time together. Returning from a shopping expedition, the Palmers found they had missed a call from the Prince Monthéard, an old acquaintance and possible suitor, but he came again the following day. To Ellen's surprise he knew all about their time in Baden because a friend of his, M. de la Garde, had been so struck by Ellen's appearance that he had kept a diary and noted how she was followed and stared at while she was in Baden. Without being aware that the Prince knew Ellen, he had been entertaining him with his account of her activities. The Duchess told Ellen that he was '*à très beau parti, another I refused in the time of my delusions for the Count de Bark.*' Another legacy from Baden was a secret her mother bravely kept until their return to London.

Paris was in a state of political uncertainty. Louis Napoleon, unable to secure a two-thirds majority which would have allowed him to stand as president for a second term, had launched a coup in 1851 and won a plebiscite to sanction the extension of the Prince President's authority. Playing again on the magic of the Napoleonic name, he promised peace, order and reconciliation in a carefully orchestrated campaign. He had been 40 in 1848 when he won the election by an overwhelming majority and became President of France. Now the electorate responded, but with far less enthusiasm, to his wish to return to past glories and have himself made Emperor of the French. The alternatives, broadly speaking, seemed to be civilisation as against a return to chaos. Plans were being made for his triumphant return to the capital and the Palmers had decided to stay to witness the event.

Bordighini finally returned and Ellen went for her first lesson. '*I walked home with Granger in a state of wild excitement after Bordighini's praise, every pulse beating with ardour and ambition and feeling the life of an artiste was one which my every impulse would lead me to embrace.*'[1] Bordighini had told her that there were very few who sang like her and said he wished she was an artiste and could go on stage because her voice inspired him. She took lessons every day and he told her she learnt as much in one lesson as others did in four. He told her the part of Desdemona would suit her beautifully. Her London singing master, Crivelli, had also told her that more dramatic music would be her forte. To have her talent recognised and appreciated in this way was music to her soul and fed her ambition to excel.

> *I think the genre is the one that would suit me best. I know I am capable of entering into and expressing all the passions which can find utterance in song and knowing that I possess the 'Feu Sacré' necessary for this it seems to me to be almost beneath one's talent to employ it loosely in warbling nearly mechanical music of Barbiere* [The Barber of Seville] *which requires no genius, no soul but simply the musical box kind of facility which constant practice gives.*

She was given a new song from the opera by Rossini, *An Italian in Algerie*, called 'Pensa a la Patria', to learn. She had read it over with Bordighini on Saturday and with a little practice on Saturday and some more on Monday before she went for her lesson she was able to sing it perfectly. As she said, it is very difficult with a very long recitative and *andante* before it, yet she was able to sing it perfectly with all the changes and embellishments that Bordighini had put in. She reports that he was perfectly amazed by this *tour de force*: '*no artiste could have learnt it better, I sang beautifully and he only wished he had a dozen pupils like me. I had grande intelligence and he was très content.*'

Ellen continued to please and astonish Bordighini, not only by singing the aria from *Donna del lago* and the 'Casta diva' from *Norma*, but also by doing some very difficult vocalisations at first sight which he said was quite extraordinary – there were not two people in Paris who could have done them. Ellen recognised that she had the rare gift of being able to sing the most puzzling music and the most difficult passages at first sight correctly, without the slightest assistance from the piano. Bordighini told her mother, who had come to collect her, that '*when people sing like that they need not be afraid of anybody*' and that she possessed '*a real belle voix to Mezzo Soprano*'.[2]

There is no way of corroborating Ellen's account of her final lesson with Bordighini, but considering the hundreds of hours she spent practising and given her obvious natural talent and her known determination to excel, there is no reason to disbelieve her. It was almost certainly the apogee of her singing career, because tragedy was to strike and never again would she have an opportunity such as she had enjoyed over the past two weeks in Paris, which so clearly brought her great fulfilment and joy. She savoured the phrases Bordighini had used, that she had done '*des choses étonnantes*', that she had made '*the most astonishing progress*' and that she had '*an intelligence extraordinaire*'. She reassured herself that this was not just flattery by the fact that Bordighoni was

> *celebrated for not flattering his pupils and being terribly severe and hard to please. I know he very often refused to teach unpromising people, so I may believe what he does say. Besides I feel I deserve his praises for in addition to my natural talent (which nobody ever disputed) I have given my very soul to the art and it has been my day and my dreams by night to attain excellence in singing and it is no exaggeration to say this is the great passion of my life, the one all engrossing object of my existence.*

Who knows what might have been in store for Ellen had she not been constrained by her family and social background from using her talent to greater public effect. Most of Ellen's contemporaries had but one single objective, to find a suitable husband, but Ellen, feeling betrayed by the Count, had now substituted music as the great passion of her life.

A conversation she had with the Prince Monthéard about women's role in marriage shows how much her new-found self-confidence had grown. Perhaps with Bordighini's words that 'she need not fear anyone' ringing in her ears, she argued against the propriety of women being blind slaves to their husband's will and defended her point of view with such high and heroic spirit that the Prince said she '*should be the woman to rule, to command a troop of Arabs in the desert like Lady Hester Stanhope*[3] *but that I had far too much the instinct of power and domination, too much consciousness of superior intellect, in short ever to be happy in the quiet subjection demanded of women in domestic life.*' The comparison with Lady Hester Stanhope, a socialite and traveller whose adventures scandalised London society, was not altogether unfair. Ellen was 10 when Lady Hester died in 1839; they were both strong-minded and passionate women, but Ellen unlike Lady Hester was unable to throw off the restrictive conventions of the time. Ellen thought the Prince might well be right, '*indeed I almost think he is; for my spirit certainly does rebel at the thought of ever being required to yield like the blind, unresisting, unreasoning submission of an animal to any fellow creature simply because he happens to be a man and despite the possibility of his intellect being far inferior to my own.*'[4] Holding such strong views was certainly going to complicate her search for a husband. But she held to her convictions and when she finally did get married she made it plain she would never be dictated to.

The Palmers had rented a room in the Boulevard de Temple to witness the entry of Louis Napoleon as virtual emperor. He had prepared his entry well.

> *Most of the balconies on the Boulevard were decorated with banners and triumphal arches every few yards and loyal inscriptions to 'Louis Napoleon, Empereur', and 'L'empereur, c'est la Paix' etc., etc., were put up in every direction […] The street gradually filled with people and was lined with a double row of soldiers, deputations from all the trades and from the different provinces, bands of young girls dressed in white*

with flower and laurel crowns, old soldiers of the empire, all marching to one common goal, the statue of the Emperor where they were to meet Louis Napoleon on his entry into Paris.

This was all carefully orchestrated to underline the link with past Napoleonic glories and bolster the legitimacy of an undistinguished mediocrity with an historic name who had known how to play on the nation's desire for a return to the glory days of their last emperor.

Between ½ past 2 and 3 o'clock the procession at last appeared in sight, and after a tiresome procession of the cavalry had rushed past in a very disorderly manner, Prince Louis Napoleon's personal staff became visible. The Prince himself showed great courage, for inspite of the general fear that an attack would be made he rode quite conspicuously and alone on a magnificent horse all caparaisoned with gold.

Ellen noted the lack of enthusiasm in the applause and hinted at how dangerous it might prove to voice any opposition. '*I did not think the shouts which welcomed him were very enthusiastic and afterwards heard that the people were cool in other places where he passed, but of course it is treason even to hint at such a thing in the present state of affairs in general.*'[5]

The family arrived back to a grey and foggy London on 19 October and to make matters worse there was only a decrepit old piano in the house, so the following day Ellen could only play for half an hour; but she sang for four hours. That Sunday came the first hint that all was not well with Lady Palmer. She had a bad cold, and told Ellen that she needed extra advice about her throat and might have to have a trifling operation. This was said to conceal the fact that she was aware that she might well have cancer of the breast and was only waiting to have the diagnosis confirmed before telling Ellen the truth. When she knew, Ellen reported the fact with horror. There are relatively few overt mentions of breast cancer in a non-medical context because it remained an embarrassing and taboo subject until the 1960s. When her aunt had died two years earlier, although the family knew the cause, the word 'cancer' was never mentioned. Remembering the long months of distress Aunt Abbey had suffered, Ellen leapt to the conclusion that it meant her mother was doomed to months or even years of pain.

Although aspects of the present-day operation to cure breast cancer had been tried, the practice of mastectomy was still in its infancy in the 1850s. Mr Fraser, an eminent surgeon, who had been called in to join the family doctors Mr Travers and Mr Bullock, was very reassuring and thought that an operation could save her. The doctors all emphasised that: '*Immediate danger there is none and nobody ever heard of the operation itself having any serious consequences.*' Ellen's room was quickly prepared for the operation, which took place the next day. Chloroform was to be administered by Dr Snow, although it had only been in use for 10 years as an anaesthetic and it was a year before it was administered to Queen Victoria to help with the birth of her eighth child. The publicity generated by the royal connection helped to allay the fear of this still controversial method of pain-relief. Mr Ferguson, the surgeon, performed the operation assisted by four doctors, while the Palmers' resident medical man, Mr Roberts, had been sent out with Sir Roger to keep him out of the way. He had seemingly not been told about his wife's condition, for fear of upsetting him.

The operation took only 20 minutes. Ellen was allowed in to see her mother afterwards and found her free from pain, faint and exhausted. A nurse was employed to care for the invalid and total quiet was imposed. By the third day Roger and Ellen were allowed to talk to her, and the doctors were so pleased with her progress that they said there was no need for any uneasiness. Ten days after the operation Lady Palmer had been able to walk back to her own room, the wound almost healed, and the doctors said they had never heard of a more favourable case. They do not seem to have taken account of her complaints of pain in the shoulders, which they dismissed as caused by lying down too much. However, the next day the pain had increased so much that she could scarcely move her jaw or swallow her dinner. The doctors called again and seemed to be in denial, saying that perhaps Mama was suffering from a cold rather than the symptoms of lockjaw; it was left to Mr Roberts to spell it out to Ellen and to say that he believed she had lockjaw (tetanus). None of the medical men had ever heard of lockjaw coming on after an operation on the breast but when they called again that evening they could no longer pretend it was anything other than lockjaw. However, as she was still to some extent able to swallow they continued to say that the case was not hopeless.

Still unable to believe there could be a link with the operation, their confidence was bolstered by the arrival of Sir Benjamin Brodie,[6] the most eminent doctor of the time, who had attended her sister.

> *He does not take such a bad view of the case as the other medical men, he says, as yet the symptoms are not so very dangerous and he gives us great hope that by supporting her with brandy every two hours her strength may be kept up until the violence of the spasm is exhausted and the jaw will relax itself. He says that in all his practice he has never known a similar case.*

He had never considered a contaminated wound or one containing dead tissue as the cause of an infection, or that bacteria could exist in house dust and enter the body through a break in the skin.[7] It is inevitable that Ellen's bedroom, where the operation took place, was far from sterile. It would be several years later that Louis Pasteur[8] put forward his radical views suggesting that microbes could produce putrefaction, and his remarkable breakthroughs in the causes and prevention of diseases were still in the future. Likewise, the pioneering work of Joseph Lister,[9] who recognised the dangers of infection and how the use of carbolic acid to cleanse wounds and to sterilise surgical instruments would dramatically decrease the number of post-operative deaths, also lay in the future. And it was not until 1924 that the tetanus vaccine was discovered and widely used during World War II to prevent the disease. It was almost, in Lady Palmer's case, as if the doctors were in denial as to the gravity of her illness since they had never known a case like it before and wanted to reassure the family. When her surgeon, Mr Fraser, called, he was shocked and said that in all the course of his practice and even in his literary researches he had never once heard of such a case.

It seems that Lady Palmer had a foreboding about her illness and was very well aware of the danger she was in, whatever the doctors said. She continued to give directions to her two children and her sisters as to what should be done in the case of her death, although she never referred to it in so many words so as not to upset her children. Ellen read prayers night and morning, and when she suggested that Mr Russell, the clergyman they knew, should come her mother welcomed the suggestion. He arrived just as Lady Palmer was recovering from one of the spasms which Ellen vividly described: '*Good God, what a fearful sight awaited me! Supported on the nurse's lap lay my beloved mother her head thrown back, her arms stretched out in agony, her chest heaving with the most frightful struggles for breath and her hoarse gasps sound through the house.*' What Ellen witnessed is typical of the symptoms associated with lockjaw. Although those around her thought her last hour had come, Lady Palmer rallied, was comforted by the clergyman and able to speak. Her thoughts were for her husband, and she begged her children to take care of '*poor Papa*'. Both at that time and later, after the death of his wife, Ellen could not help being surprised at the lack of emotion shown by '*poor Papa*'.

The spasms continued and hopes rose and fell. On the Sunday, five days after the first symptoms appeared,

> *poor dear Mama, who had previously been a little better cried out that her teeth were tightening. Alas, alas, they had long been as fast clenched as it was possible to be. An hour afterwards she wished to take some nourishment so I called Mr Bullock up and we awaited the experiment with fearful anxiety; but our last hope failed as she almost choked attempting to swallow half a spoonful of arrowroot, and God alone knows the anguish with which I saw her sink back on the pillow after the spasm was over and said that she would try no more but die in peace 'although it was awful to starve to death' [...] Oh how dreadful to think that all the resources of science, all the secrets of art had been exhausted and yet nothing, nothing could be done to save her.*

A slight improvement in the patient's condition led to false hopes that the remedy the doctors had last tried might have saved her life and they even resolved to try another remedy. '*The joy, the rapture with which we received even this glimmer of consolation; it seemed as if we were lifted with one bound from the darkest abyss of despair to the glad hope that yet, even yet, our dear dear mother might be restored to us.*' An hour later, as another lighter spasm abated, Mr Roberts let go of her pulse and the nurse called out, '*Sir she is going*', and Eleanora Palmer's life was over.[10]

It seemed that all along Lady Palmer had had a presentiment that she would not survive the operation and her children discovered that she had written letters of instruction which she had given to Mr Roberts to keep. Anxious that her husband should be shielded from the aftermath of her death, she had arranged for them all to leave the house and go to stay in Richmond at the Star and Garter Hotel. But far from being upset, Ellen records that while they were all as miserable as possible, '*Dear Papa is wonderfully well, he bears his heavy trial with more fortitude than we had ventured to hope for.*' Ellen, who had been so critical of her mother when alive, quickly became aware of the burden her mother had carried in managing the estates and the household, and besides her natural grief at the death of her parent, realised with a sense of shock that all that responsibility was likely to devolve on her. It is difficult, with so little to go by, to assess the state of Sir Roger Palmer's relationship with his wife, but it would seem that Lady Palmer was more of a loving, protective parent than wife. His lack of emotion at the news of her death and his apparent detachment with regard to the events taking place around him puzzled and saddened Ellen. On the day of her mother's funeral Ellen wrote,

> *the delicate health of my father is a sad aggravation to our horrible bereavement, for it now appears like almost losing <u>both parents</u> at once. Poor Mama, our guide, our support, in short she was everything to us and God alone knows how we grieve her loss. Papa bears his heavy trial wonderfully well, but still we cannot venture to intrude our sorrow upon him and she that we turned to in all our troubles can no longer comfort us.*[11]

Perhaps Ellen was also feeling a sense of guilt at the way she had continually complained about her mother in her diaries, never giving her any credit for the skill with which she managed the family and their estates. Now the sudden realisation of the difficulties she would face without the steady and reassuring presence of Mama only served to increase her sense of despair and exacerbate the grief she naturally felt. As the memories of all the love and support she had received from her mother came flooding back, so her sense of desolation increased and with it an even greater appreciation of the extent of her loss. If she did feel regret at her lack of appreciation of the weight of the burden her mother had carried for so long, a competing emotion was one of self-pity for the situation in which she now found herself.

Sir Roger did not go to the funeral at Kensal Green, which was performed as quietly as possible, with only Roger, Dr Twiss, General Jackson, Mr Alexander Mackinnon and Capt. Mackinnon among the mourners. Mr Russell performed the service. Lady Palmer was interred in the vault at Kensal Green cemetery by the side of her little daughter.[12] By way of contrast, the previous day, 18 November, had seen London packed with crowds, said to be a million and a half strong, to watch the spectacular funeral cortège of the Duke of Wellington pass by on the way to St Paul's Cathedral. His state funeral of unsurpassed pageantry and unparalleled magnificence had been planned during the two months following his death at Walmer Castle. The huge and costly funeral car, specially built for the occasion, was drawn by 12 black horses caparisoned with feathers, and the streets were lined with soldiers, some of whom Roger met returning from duty. When the coffin was lowered into the cathedral burial crypt the bells of all the parish churches of England rang out. For those who witnessed the scene it was an unforgettable occasion. It is likely that Lady Palmer had taken tickets for seats along the route to watch the cortège pass, as Ellen wrote sorrowfully: '*How little did we think only a few days ago that the interment of one so dear to us would follow so closely that great pageant which she herself has so often anticipated.*'

A sad little party arrived back at Cefn a few days later, without having returned to Portland Place. Beside her natural grief, Ellen's despair at the situation in which she found herself was amply recorded in her diaries in the days that followed. She still found it difficult to understand her father's seeming lack of any emotion at the death of his wife.

Strange to say the association of ideas which was so exquisitely painful to me did not seem to affect Papa at all. His equanimity was wonderful, nay I had almost to say painful, to behold but we must not murmur at this for it is such a merciful dispensation of providence and the medical men tell us to do all in our power to promote his cheerfulness.[13]

The only change in his behaviour noted by Ellen was his increased irritability and his liability to become so cross if he was losing at cards that the game had to be abandoned.

Acutely aware of how vulnerable she was without her mother to lean on, the behaviour of her Aunt Mary and of her brother Roger also contributed to her distress. With her younger sister now dead, Mary Matthews thought she was the one who should now be in charge and running the household. Ellen knew that if she allowed any such a thing to happen it would spell disaster.

I am sorry to say Aunt Mary increases our troubles by her ridiculous assumptions of authority. She took possession of poor Mama's keys immediately, ransacked all her papers and actually fought hard with Roger to keep the cheque book in her own hands. How I dislike these contentions, but they are absolutely necessary unless we submit to see my aunt usurp my poor Mama's place and rule us with a rod of iron.[14]

Ellen tried hard to keep the peace, allowing Aunt Mary to run the household up to a point, but keeping the engagement and dismissal of the servants in her own hands.

This morning I engaged a cook for Kenure, my first essay in housekeeping affairs. In fact engaging and dismissing servants is the only part of the domestic economy that I keep in my own hands and <u>even</u> this Aunt Mary will not let me do in peace, for she sat by the whole time, took every word out of my mouth, kept the whole conversation to herself and in short made me look like a <u>perfect idiot</u>.[15]

But Aunt Mary was no match for Ellen who, despite initial difficulties, managed to get the reins firmly back into her own hands.

After their return to London it was only following a visit from Mr Mackinnon a month after the funeral that Ellen truly spelled out the situation that confronted her and laid out the true extent of her father's disability and weaknesses and how it affected her.

> *This morning had a long walk with Mr Mackinnon and talked over all our affairs. He says and truly says that ours is the most delicate position possible to conceive; being perfectly inexperienced in the management of business and yet having everything pertaining to Papa's vast estates to manage ourselves, having difficulties besetting us on every side, having to guard Papa from the inroads of his own relations (who would ruin us quickly), having likewise to guard against the danger of having a step mother (which Papa's propensity for falling in love renders all too probable) and which his easy temper would render an absolute destruction of our interests; then having to manage Papa himself, tho' absolutely necessary, though for his own children rather difficult to do, and lastly with all these complicated interests to reconcile, being left entirely to our own devices and having no relation in whom we could apply for advice and assistance. As for me individually, I have nobody to look to for Papa's delicate health prevents his advising me, supporting me, chaperoning me as he would else. Losing Mama is like losing both parents at once, and whichever way we look the prospect of the future is a bleak one.*[16]

This sudden and astonishingly sharp analysis of her father's failings, which she had until now kept silent about out of filial duty, throws a new light on the family relationships. It also poses many questions. Who were the relatives who would ruin them given half a chance? Although Ellen did not then know it, the Mackinnons believed that they had the right to part of the Kenure inheritance through the female line. It is true that the decision was taken very quickly to make her father, who was the youngest son, the inheritor of Kenure, following her parents' sudden marriage. Were there others who felt they also had rights? How did she know about her father's propensity for '*falling in love*' as she puts it? Were the medical men who lived with the family, latterly Mr Roberts, engaged as much to guard against his running after the ladies as to deal with her father's epileptic fits? Was his propensity for '*falling in love*' the reason behind the hasty and unlikely marriage of her parents? It was all very well for his wife to try to manage him, but, as Ellen surmised, it would be very awkward for his children to do the same. Never again does Ellen refer to her father's weaknesses so openly, except to record the embarrassment caused when he had a fit in public.

Roger solved the problem as far as he was concerned abruptly and very selfishly. Just after Christmas,

> *a letter arrived this morning offering Roger a commission in the 11th Hussars. I had imagined that this military fancy was at rest for ever since the recent sad loss we had sustained renders Roger's presence so necessary at home and we were all horror struck when he announced his intention of going up to London to see about it.*[17]

On New Year's Eve Ellen wrote to her brother imploring him not to go into the army, '*as it would be ruinous to his own interests and those of everyone else; and to our comfort at home it would be the final death blow*'. Roger took the easy way out; lazy and spoilt, he was not going to be bothered with the management of the estates or the care of his father and nothing Ellen could say would alter his determination to join the army.

CHAPTER 11

A Parting of the Ways

Ellen had had a bad year. Her first diary entry for the year 1853 reviews the sad events that had befallen her during the past 12 months, beginning with the deaths of Aunt Abbey, then her mother, and the aching void left by her reluctant acceptance that the love of her life had betrayed her trust. Although time had softened the first bitter anguish, she wrote that '*the blighting influence of such a disappointment can never be wholly eradicated and nothing can restore to me that first freshness of heart which has been so cruelly and so treacherously withered*'. She became increasingly suspicious of any man attracted by her personality and beauty, afraid they were more interested in her fortune than in her. There was yet another sorrow to be added to the list: Ellen's beloved brother was still determined to join the army and by 2 January had accepted a commission in the 11th Hussars. For Roger this was an escape from the constrictions of family life and its attendant responsibilities. Ellen saw it as '*tacitly condemning her to a melancholy life of constant dutifulness at home and of wearisome devotion to business which Papa's health will not allow him to attend to himself and which therefore ought to fall to my brother's lot*'. Nevertheless, Ellen permitted herself to hope '*that the future would have brighter joys*'.

Ellen did all she could to dissuade Roger from joining the army, but by 14 January he had passed his exam and was congratulated on his proficiency; by the 23rd his appointment had been gazetted. Such was Ellen's devotion to her brother that she successfully coaxed her father to pay the £840 for his commission and was furious with Aunt Mary when she refused to back her father's bill for the £3,000 it would have cost to accept the offer of a transfer to the 2nd Life Guards, as Roger, being underage, needed a second guarantor. When Roger finally left to join his regiment on 9 April Ellen sorrowfully accepted that her close relationship with her brother had come to an end and she could not help crying. '*It was a very sad parting from dear Doddy, he has now entered the world fairly on his own and he will never be the same to me more. I dread his absence for it will leave me very lonely.*'

She was right. Lacking female friends, her unhappy love affair with de Bark had left her mistrustful of men, her relationship with her father being of necessity more that of a parent towards a child, she was more than ever in need of the emotional support that Roger had always provided. But Roger had clearly had enough of home life dominated by quarrelsome aunts and a father who was a liability. Spoilt, as he had always been, he was unwilling to take on the responsibility, not to mention the work that running the family estates entailed. Shortly before he left for the army, Miss Celia Gore (who was later to marry Edward Thynne) had come to stay at Cefn at Roger's request. While Ellen contented herself with a mild flirtation with Captain Cotton, a neighbour, who knew that as a penniless captain, although a long-time admirer, he had no chance, Roger was conducting a passionate flirtation with Miss Celia Gore. Ellen thoroughly disapproved of the amorous Miss Gore and suspected that she was leading Roger astray. She decided to keep watch and saw Miss Gore leaving Roger's room at 5.30 in the morning, confirming her worst suspicions. '*I cannot describe the disgust and horror I felt at this proof of her depravity, for bad though her manner of going on, still I could scarcely believe her to be so utterly lost,*'[1] she wrote, although there was no word of blame for her beloved brother. It didn't take Ellen long to decide how to bring an end to this affair without creating a scandal. She cleverly arranged to leave the house, accompanied by Lord and Lady Edward Chichester, who had been staying, to visit Lord and Lady Ferrers at Chartley Castle.[2] Lord Ferrers had sent his carriage to Stafford to meet them and they were welcomed in the most kindly manner. With the lady of the house absenting herself, etiquette demanded that Miss Gore leave at the same time, despite Roger's pressing Ellen to allow Miss Gore to stay on. This little episode can only have strengthened Roger's desire to free himself from what must have seemed to him petticoat government by a dominating and judgemental sister, although, as before, no word of blame is attributed to his behaviour by her.

Ellen's prediction that with Roger's departure her life would be one of wearisome devotion to business was borne out by the daily diary entries. There was no longer time to sing and play the piano: '*I have scarcely any time to devote to music and that to me is the greatest deprivation as business and the writing of letters takes so much time*,' and she notes that her diary entries were always being written up in arrears. But life had to continue and in preparation for the family's return to London, the first since her mother's death, she stayed with her cousins, the Mackinnons, to make the return to the house in Portland Place less painful. Ellen, and indeed the whole family, had always relied on the Mackinnons for advice and help over family matters, so it came as a considerable shock to Ellen to learn from Louisa Cochran, the Mackinnons' second daughter, in a burst of confidential friendship that she should '*beware of her own father*'. She told Ellen that Mr Mackinnon '*had always had a grudge against us for being possessed of the Palmer estates instead of his wife and has utopian ideas that if neither Roger or I marry they must eventually return to what he considers the right line, viz his own family*' and that she had heard her father '*deprecating and pooh-poohing my reputation before a number of people*'. Ellen was left feeling not only shocked but betrayed and even more vulnerable and friendless. She wrote that she saw herself as an '*imprisoned girl, left unassisted with a clever and wary man of the world*'. But she also wrote defiantly, '*my courage does not fail, though I plainly see what hard cards I shall have to play*',[3] a reference to the entail that she was working to have altered in her favour.

Before leaving Cefn for the usual migration to London for the season, Ellen had to ensure that things were left in '*working trim*' and wrote: '*It is very hard work certainly, and to think that it should devolve on me, who until lately never knew what the word "business" meant. I have actually to look after every single thing, property, agents, servants, household matters and business of every description and dealing with very crusty tempers [...] indeed a very fagging life.*' Notwithstanding all the business she had to attend to,

Ellen still aspired to make her mark in London society and to do that she needed a chaperone of suitably sufficient standing. To this end, as her father was totally unable to help and despite all she had heard about the Mackinnons, she must have sought their help. Her aunts were tacitly deemed socially inadequate for the role. She picked on Lady Tankerville[4] as someone who had the required social standing. Lady Tankerville had been born a De Gramont, and was a relative of her cousin Emma, so with the backing of the Mackinnons, Ellen approached her to ask if she would act as her chaperone for the coming London season.

Ellen was elated when her request was received with interest. Corisande Armandine Tankerville was the daughter of the Duc de Gramont and de Guiche; she was very well connected and moved in the best society circles. Her husband, the Earl of Tankerville,[5] had succeeded to the title in 1822, and was the owner of Chillingham Castle. He had been an MP and a great supporter of Charles James Fox[6] until partial blindness caused him to retire from public life. Married by special licence at Devonshire House, the young Lady Tankerville had been dismissed by Lord Melbourne as 'a frivolous little girl who doesn't know what she is about', but Lord Esher was more generous, writing that she 'possessed undoubted charm and wrote delightful letters in the purest French'.[7] From Ellen's point of view she had all the right connections and would get her the entrée to the grandest balls and open doors which poor Lady Palmer had been unable to unlatch. Perhaps Lady Tankerville was attracted by the idea of chaperoning a beautiful and wealthy young girl and going out in society again, as a change from her whist parties, but for whatever reason, she accepted Ellen's request. If there was any financial arrangement it was not disclosed in the diary, so Ellen and Lady Té, as Ellen called her, must have come to some mutual understanding as to what this entailed. There were disadvantages to this loose arrangement: Lady Tankerville would have had the use of the Palmer carriage, but it left Ellen with no means of exerting any kind of pressure when she later felt that Lady Té was not looking after her interests in the way she had hoped.

For now, Ellen was elated at her success in attracting such a '*grande dame*' as her chaperone, and her friends were duly impressed when she told them. Although Ellen did not then know it, her first ball chaperoned by Lady Té was to lay down an unwelcome pattern for the future. Their first appearance together was at the Breadalbanes' ball, Lord Breadalbane[8] being then Lord Chamberlain to the Royal Household. There was the usual tremendous crush getting in, but once in, to Ellen's dismay, Lady Tankerville promptly sat herself down in a retired corner of an ante-room and stayed there all night. From her point of view this was hopeless as scarcely any young men came her way and she found the ball more like a palace ball, '*all official people and old fogies, the number of grandees quite tremendous*,' she wrote. However, she appears to have enjoyed the evening tolerably well, despite the lack of dancing partners.

It did not take Ellen long to discover the disadvantages of being chaperoned by the ageing Lady Té. At the Austrian Ambassador's Ball the pleasure of being seen with Lady Té was beginning to pall. According to Ellen, she created quite a sensation when she arrived in her black and white ball dress with diamonds in her hair, and was greeted by the Ambassador saying, '*Ah! Quelle apparition, vraiment très jolie*'. But Lady Té could not stand and insisted on sitting on a sofa, where they were both immediately half buried alive by a mob of dowagers and chaperones standing in rows three or four deep. Even when Lady Té moved, it was to a corner in the next room, which was almost a worse place for finding partners. Added to that, Lady Té insisted on going home at one o'clock, just as the ball was beginning to be pleasant, which Ellen found very tiresome. On another occasion, Lady Té took Ellen to a concert and she sat with her and Lady Jersey on the sofa of honour. Ellen was totally unimpressed at finding herself in the company of the accepted leader of London fashion, a patroness of Almack's but now a faded beauty, and thought the occasion '*fearsomely stupid*'. She may have wondered if the price she had to pay for her desire to move in more elevated circles was worth the tedium, but what alternative did she have?

Despite her complaints, the fact that Ellen was now going out with Lady Té was beginning to have an effect. Ellen noted with satisfaction that the Lister Kayes, whom she had previously consulted about her family's lack of social success, were making up to Lady Té '*amazingly*' and that Lady Lucan had given her quite a friendly greeting. She commented sardonically, '*I suppose she thinks that now I am purified by Lady*

Tankerville's chaperonage she may venture to be gracious without derogating from her dignity'.[9] Even Gerald Ponsonby, the erstwhile ADC to Lord Clarenden, '*who has all but cut me at every ball where we have met, came up with outstretched hand tonight*'. After going with Lady Harrington to a morning party at Lady Hall's she wrote, '*strange to relate and actually (wonders will never cease) Lady Agnes Duff whom we have not spoken to for years greeted me quite kindly, put out her hand and said she was afraid I had forgotten her. Everybody seems growing wondrous civil*'.[10] Ellen's newfound social acceptance, and the pleasure she felt in noting the changed attitude towards her, reveal how much she had minded the slights and snubs she had too often had to endure.

As the season wore on, Ellen began to notice that Lady Té was arranging fewer balls, and thought it would be a terrible lookout for her if this continued. By 25 June, she had asked Mrs Mackinnon to go '*and rub up Lady Te who is slackening in her attentions to me*'. There were other little niggles. Lady Té refused to go to the Lister Kayes' ball '*despite their making up to her*', presumably because it was not grand enough for her, so Ellen was reduced to asking for a ticket for Aunt Mary, one of the few times noted in the diaries that her aunt was allowed to accompany her to a social occasion. This was Ellen's sixth season, she was rich, beautiful and unmarried; offers of marriage began to be made to Lady Tankerville to transmit to Ellen. Lady Tankerville indeed felt the idea of finding a suitable husband for Ellen was part of her role. She had once discussed the matter with Ellen, asking in particular what sort of husband would suit her. After all, matchmaking was the main *raison d'être* of the London season and Lady Té very much approved of the French way of parents arranging marriages for their offspring. She had told Ellen that she would not scruple to do such a thing on her behalf. When she started to push the idea of a match with a Mr H. Howard, Ellen gave no clue as to who the gentleman was, except to say that he was fat, and the very thought of such a match made her sick. Lady Té was vexed by Ellen's refusal even to contemplate such a proposal.

The mother of one prospective suitor, Lady Edward Chichester, was pressing the claims of her son George on Ellen as a suitable husband. He was the heir of the Marquis of Donegal, would have £24,000 a year and was good-looking to boot. On an occasion when Ellen called, Lady Chichester actually made a formal proposal of marriage on behalf of George. Ellen commented that '*it was embarrassing enough, but she would not take any answer now, but merely told me to think about it*'. Ellen makes it abundantly clear in her diaries that she had no intention of marrying for money or rank without love. She, who had been so passionately in love with the Count de Bark, knew what love meant and although two years had now elapsed since she had broken off the relationship, she was far from forgetting him. She still reverts from time to time in her diary to the bitterness of his betrayal and writes of how hard she found it to accept his gradual indifference to her and how he had '*withered her brightest dreams of happiness*'. So far, among her multitude of admirers there was no one who in any way came near to inspiring such feelings of love and devotion.

Matters were only made worse at a ball given by the Marchioness of Claricade when, sitting in a back room as usual, she was discovered by the Comte de Saux, the brother of the French ambassadress, Madame Waleska. He took it upon himself to talk frankly to her, telling her what people were saying:

> *Everyone agreed she was jolie et charmante, that I have the name of being so rich that it made everybody afraid of speaking to me. It was a bad reputation, he said, for a girl to get. He told me that he could not stay talking to me, for everyone would think he had been making up to me for my money.*[11]

He was not telling her anything that she didn't already know, but it didn't make it any easier for her to have it spelled out so directly. And there was even worse to come. She had heard it said that Lady Té had a regular plan to sell her for £5,000. She wrote in her diary that some gentleman had heard it discussed at a club that she (Lady Té) had a young lady to dispose of, and a handsome girl, to Mr Goodlake, that innocent youth, if he gave her £5,000. Although Ellen took it to be nothing more than a horrid intrigue, nonetheless she would not be able entirely to dismiss from her mind a suspicion that Lady Té might have an ulterior motive for pressing the claims of any potential suitor for her hand.

Although we have only her own account to go by, there is no reason to doubt that she was making an impression on London society. On one occasion she wrote: '*I had a new black dress from Camille trimmed beautifully with violets and wreath of violets in my hair. I believe I looked exceedingly well, for everyone turned round to look at me as I passed through the rooms in a way no woman could mistake.*' This knowledge gave her the confidence to stand up to Lady Té, to get what she wanted. They were together at Lady Ashburton's ball, sitting in a back room as usual, when Ellen noticed that Lord Cardigan was present and she very much wanted to go to his ball. But Lady Té, perhaps because of his reputation or for reasons of her own, wanted to avoid being near him so as to prevent Ellen getting the coveted invitation. Ellen, not to be thwarted, took advantage of Lady Lucan's recent graciousness towards her and the fact that she was Cardigan's sister, approached the Lucans and managed to get a card through their good offices. Lady Té was obliged to take her and Ellen wrote triumphantly: '*I was determined not to be done in this instance*'.[12] Lord Cardigan was also Roger's commanding officer, probably the reason she so much wanted the invitation, but even she could not have imagined that summer how useful the contact would be a few months later when plans for war against Russia made her fear for her brother's future.

Although Ellen continued to complain about all the business she had to attend to and the large number of letters she had to write, it was the hours she used to spend practising her piano playing and singing that suffered rather than her social life, which continued unabated despite Lady Té's tepid commitment to her duties as chaperone. Ellen had made friends with Lady Harrington,[13] a colourful character who had married Lord Harrington in 1831 and was a widow when Ellen met her. The Earl of Harrington, an eccentric leader of fashion during the reign of George IV, was the model for Disraeli's character, Lord Fitzbooby, in his novel *Coningsby*. He married late in life a much younger woman who had once been an actress and who had had several affairs before becoming Lady Harrington. Ellen found her much more fun than Lady Té and often used her as a chaperone, enjoying being able to stay on late at the balls under her protection. She often went round to breakfasts, where she had fun and met the nicest people of her set, rather than boring '*grandees*'.

Ellen either did not know about the lady's past, or did not care. But there were evenings when she could find no one to accompany her and she had to remain quietly at home, although her social successes seem to more than make up for the occasional missed party.

It was at the Lister Kayes' ball at the end of June, with Aunt Mary as her chaperone, when Ellen danced without intermission from two in the morning till past four, where she first met Prince Dentice.[14] According to Ellen, he asked her if she was going to the two other balls being held that night and when she said she was not, he said '*that he had both invitations in his pocket and would burn them and stay where he was all evening*'. Ellen noted approvingly that he remained all night but scarcely danced at all and, although he kept his eyes on her all the time, he was not at all pointed in his attentions. The following evening Ellen went with Lady Té to another of Lady Ashburton's balls and it was there that she met and danced with the Prince de Salm,[15] who was also very attentive. The following day Ellen, with her aunt, went to Lady Harrington's breakfast[16] where she danced the whole time with, among others, her two princely admirers. When she went with the Harringtons to the Queen's ball, the Prince de Salm was again there and, she says, followed her about the whole evening, refusing to go to the Queen's private supper on purpose to dance with her. Prince Dentice, not to be outdone, took her into supper and tried to steal a flower from her bouquet. When she said no, he returned it without a word, doing himself a power of good because Ellen wrote afterwards that it was '*exactly as Count de Bark would have done; he is very like him in point of sensitiveness*' – the first time she had ever compared any of her admirers to her erstwhile lover.

The season was coming to an end and Prince Dentice was lamenting the fact that he had to return to Naples. Ellen writes that she '*is really sorry he is going for he is so nice*', another sign that she might be recovering from her ill-fated love affair. In the meantime, Ellen had not only turned down two more proposals of marriage passed on by Lady Té, one from M. de Saux and one from Count Bentivoglio, but had had to deal with a renewed onslaught by Lady Chichester with regard to her son, George. Despite his brilliant prospects, she writes that she couldn't like the man and wouldn't agree to seeing a little more of him, ending her account of the meeting with his mother with the words '*disagreeable interview*'. Ellen recognised that she was being made a tremendous fuss of and had '*flattery and admiration enough to turn anybody's head*', but where was it leading?

On 14 July at Lady Harrington's Ellen was informed that the Prince de Salm had made a proposal of marriage; he owned one-third of the principality of Westphalia, had the right of precedence over all the German nobility, and if she married him Ellen would acquire the title of Serene Highness. He was said to be desperately in love with her and would sell his estates and wait any length of time. Lady Harrington thought it was an amazing match and that such a position might never be attainable again. Ellen was unimpressed by the offer and all she wanted was that her friend should get her out of it civilly, for she said she didn't care about him a bit. Lady Té, when she heard about it, was '*quite amazed, thunderstruck, said it was an immense match, recommended that I should take it*'. Felix de Salm was in fact a second son, an officer in the Prussian cavalry, a short, stocky man whose wild act of bravado in the Prussian War of 1849 had left him wounded and for a while a prisoner of the Danes. It was probably just as well that Ellen turned him down for shortly afterwards he joined the Austrian Imperial Army, where he ran up huge gambling debts leading to his dismissal for conduct unbecoming to an officer. He subsequently sailed to America, arriving in time for the Civil War, joined the Union Army and distinguished himself by obtaining the rank of Brigadier General.

It was little wonder that Lady Té was thunderstruck at the news of Salm's proposal, as she had just heard from her friend Madame Waleska that Prince Dentice was also desperately in love and had begged her to ask Lady Té if he could continue his attentions to Ellen. He presumed that, as was the custom on the Continent, marriages were arranged by the relations or, in Ellen's case, by friends. In two days Ellen had received definite proposals from two princes, one of whom she rejected out of hand, the other she was prepared to consider. Lady Té told Madame Waleska to inform Dentice that things were not done that way in England; that he had to '*make himself agreeable to me if he wished to succeed and in the meantime I am to act as if I know nothing about it*'.[17] Lady Té repeated what she had been told and said it was an excellent match: he had 100,000 francs a year and came from a very high family. Ellen could not rid herself of her suspicions, writing, '*I can't help being suspicious of everyone spoken of by Té, but* [the rumours of selling Ellen for £5,000] *probably ill natured, exaggerated things, she has never pressed anyone on me as she might have done*'.

It was agreed that Ellen should be allowed time to get to know Dentice better before she had to give an answer. This was easier said than done – it was soon common knowledge in the circles in which they both moved that Dentice had proposed to Ellen. Dentice found the situation inhibiting, particularly if she was surrounded with admirers, as she often was at the various social functions they both attended, making it difficult for him to approach her. Ellen, for her part, acting on the advice to pretend that she knew nothing of his proposal, often appeared cold and unresponsive to him. Ellen was as puzzled and perplexed by his behaviour as he was by hers, but she did think him a pleasant prospect and it is noticeable that when Dentice was not among the guests at some of the social occasions she attended, she wrote them off as '*stupid*'. The Duke de Guiche was consulted and made enquiries about Dentice. He told Ellen that he had heard only favourable reports on all sides. Dentice belonged to one of the finest old families in Italy and was a most amiable young man. He was very well off now and would be rich eventually. Moreover, the Duke had told him about Ellen's position *vis-à-vis* her father, and the young man offered to spend nine months of the year in England, as well as saying Ellen could invite not only her father but his medical man and her aunt to Naples. But Ellen still hesitated. When Aunt Mary was informed of the proposal, to Ellen's surprise she took it quite calmly and said it must be considered.

At the end of July, at a dinner at the Mackinnons', Ellen complained to her diary that everyone seemed bent on giving her advice.

> *Really wherever I go my affairs seem to be the all absorbing topic of conversation and I cannot show my face at a party but what everyone begins talking about me. Unenviable notoriety, everyone thinks it necessary to give me advice, or advises me to mistrust what the others*

> *have told me – my head is in a whirl. Lady Harrington declares that Lady Té is to have £5,000 for selling me to Dentice, enough to make one's blood run cold. Who can I trust? Not one person in the world to give me disinterested advice and everybody watching to pounce on me for some purpose or other. Sad abandoned position for so young a person and totally abandoned to my own guidance, not a soul to counsel me and everyone interested in deceiving me. Lady Harrington said in a note to Mr M*[ackinnon] *that with all my fortune and beauty I was in a very dangerous position and heaven knows she is right.*[18]

Ellen in the past had always been able to confide in Roger, but with him now unavailable she felt very much alone and very sorry for herself.

Opportunities for getting to know Dentice went on proving difficult to find. At a very grand party at Holland House, although Dentice was seated next to her he couldn't say much as his other neighbour, the Duke of Inverness, '*took up his conversation a great deal and could hear everything he said to me*'. At a concert at Madame Waleska's they couldn't say a word to each other; at another party at Holland House, while they were walking in the gardens, Dentice was just about to propose when Lady Té came up and interrupted them, so all they could do was dance a quadrille together. A plan to go to Spithead to see the naval review was abruptly cancelled by Aunt Mary. If Lady Té did really want Ellen to marry Dentice, it seems strange that she gave her so little opportunity of getting to know him. Even during a pleasant walk at the zoo in Regent's Park they were unable to talk because Lady Té was always listening.

It was now well into August, the season was over and Dentice had to return to Naples. He was a passionate young Italian, very much in love and driven to distraction by what he took to be Ellen's coldness, but what was in fact partly her natural instinct to hide her feelings, and partly that she did not know her own mind. He wrote her a note demanding to know whether, if she became his wife, she could love him as he loved her. Feeling that he deserved a proper answer, in a move that recalled her clandestine meetings with the Count de Bark, she arranged to meet him out riding in the park and they talked seriously. Again,

Ellen used her father's health as the reason she could not commit to marriage, even though the young man had told her of his plans to live partly in England and his willingness to welcome her father to Naples. Ellen wrote,

> *He told me no-one could love me as he did and feeling had grown to such a point that he would sacrifice friends, family, country, interests, everything for me. Nothing in the world he would not do for me. Told me his history. He had had a grande passion for his cousin for six years. She died three years ago and his heart was quite desséché* [dried up] *ever since, never meant to marry though his mother had begged him on her knees to do so. Several magnifiques marriages possible but he could scarcely bear to look at a woman. The first time he saw me he placed on me the same affection he had for her. I told him I would ask Papa about it but thought the answer would be negative.*[19]

The fact that they went on to discuss whether Dentice should come to Ireland shows that Ellen was really interested, but she also knew her father's probable reaction and she felt bound to tell him that there was a great risk of refusal, '*which he seemed to dread, but still I saw it as the most likely plan. He embraced it gladly even contemplating the possibility of a no, he said even in this case if I would let him, he would come back next year and take a chance*'.

Here the diary for 1853 ends; even the notes she had made recording the events of the last weeks were not transcribed. It was the first time for six years that Ellen had not written up the daily account of her life. She would not pick up her pen to write again for eight months, and when she did she gave no hint as to why she had kept silent during that time. Having had such a successful season in London, with perhaps the possibility of finding a new life with a man she clearly liked, she may have felt depressed at the thought of returning to Ireland with little hope of anything changing for the better, with the inward knowledge that her father was bound to object to any engagement, and particularly one to a foreigner. She must have really been attracted to Dentice or she would never even have gone along with the possibility of his coming to Ireland.

Because there is no record, we do not know if he ever visited Kenure, but the likelihood is that he went back to Naples promising to return next year in the hope that he would be more successful in his courtship. Ellen was resilient, but perhaps the long months in Ireland, followed by the dreary time in Wales without even her brother to keep her company, with thoughts of the life she might have had were it not for the family responsibilities that weighed so heavily on her mind, sapped any desire to record this period of her life.

During the months that she remained silent, events overseas were taking place which would in effect change her life. While the Turkish Ambassador in London gave glittering parties that Ellen had often attended over the years, the enfeebled state of his country, dubbed the 'sick man of Europe', was giving cause for concern to Britain and France who feared that Russia would take advantage of Turkish weakness to strengthen their influence in Constantinople and threaten British and French interests. Although the diplomatic manoeuvrings as to who should have the right to protect the Holy Places in Palestine may sound trivial, with Tsar Nicholas of Russia championing the rights of the Orthodox monks and the counter-claim by Napoleon III of France in support of the rights of the Latin monks, in reality the wrangling masked a struggle for diplomatic pre-eminence in Constantinople. When Nesselrode, the Russian Chancellor, suddenly announced that Russia claimed a right to a protectorate over Orthodox Christians within the Ottoman Empire, Britain and France took fright at what they saw as a threat from Russia and ordered their fleets to sail through the Dardanelles. This action so emboldened the Turks that they issued an ultimatum to Russia on 4 October, demanding the withdrawal of Russian troops from Moldova and Wallachia, two Ottoman principalities south of the Danube. This was tantamount to a declaration of war and shocked Britain and France. The British Ambassador to Constantinople, Sir Stratford de Redcliffe, attempted to broker a truce, but when the Russian fleet intercepted a Turkish flotilla taking supplies across the Black Sea to their forces and destroyed and sank all the Turkish ships at Sinope on 30 November, a war became inevitable. Britain was in a bellicose mood and there was pressure on Lord Aberdeen the Prime Minister from Palmerston and Lord John

Russell, both in cabinet, to take action to prevent Russia from gaining control of the Black Sea and threatening the supremacy of Britain and France in the East.

The Government had already decided to send 10,000 troops to Malta on 8 February. A joint ultimatum was sent to the Russians by the British and French demanding that the Russians withdraw their troops from Wallachia and Moldova on 27 February 1854 and that they confine their fleet to their only naval base, Sevastopol. A month later, no answer having been received, war was declared on 28 March.

Ellen must have been becoming increasingly worried as it became obvious that there was going to be a war in which Roger would be involved, and in all probability sent overseas. The date of Ellen's letter to Lord Cardigan is not known, but it was written, without the knowledge of her brother, before the official declaration of war, appealing to him to allow Roger to remain at the depot instead of going abroad. She based her plea on the grounds that without his support she would have to manage the family estates in Ireland and Wales as her father's frail state of health made it impossible for him to take on the administrative burden, and that as a motherless girl it was not a task she should be asked to undertake. Despite the fact that she had contrived to meet him socially, she admitted that it had needed a lot of courage to write the letter.

Ellen recommenced writing her diary on 1 April, two days after war had been declared. She knew that Cardigan was a stickler for discipline and would in all probability turn down her request. Looking to the future, she could see that there would be new and difficult challenges ahead which would be worth recording. The other important decision Ellen had taken at some time during this period of diary silence was to write to Dentice definitely declining his proposal. Away from his beguiling presence she was able calmly and coolly to evaluate all the difficulties that such a union would throw up, not to mention the certainty that her father would oppose it. The idea that Dentice would spend nine months in England was unrealistic and, whatever her private feelings, duty dictated that she could not leave her father. This cannot have been an easy decision, when she had agonised for so long over the possibility of marriage and a new life, but she may well have felt relief at having written decisively so as to leave no room for further discussion.

While waiting for the reply from Cardigan and in a heightened state of anxiety, Ellen nonetheless continued to organise house parties at Kenure and to enjoy herself. In a description of a picnic to Lambay Island, she noted that '*although poor Doddy was obliged to remain in Dublin*', the party had a '*delightful scramble around the rocks in which I distinguished myself greatly and far outstripped everyone else. About half past two we had our lunch and as it was a lovely warm day we spread it on the grass and were exceedingly merry*'. The parties and picnics were the highlights; the day after the guests left Ellen spent eight hours going over the accounts, '*wading through Mr Chapman's (the agent) accounts and searching into every particular. It is most laborious work and very necessary to be done as I fear great roguery has been going on and it requires extraordinary sharpness and great investigation to detect it.*' As with everything Ellen did, she was exceedingly thorough and by going into every detail did indeed discover that the trusted agent had been systematically defrauding the family. The next day she was ready to confront Mr Chapman. She awoke with a palpitating heart but determined to have it out with him. Mr Norman, Mr Chapman's superior, would not help although he saw the justice of Ellen's case and, after '*the most painful scene I ever recollect*' she accused him of '*gross neglect and extravagance and worst of all fraud and dishonesty*'.[20] Immediate changes were put in train, but Ellen was merciful and when Mr Chapman succumbed to illness she delayed his sacking.

The reply from Lord Cardigan came on 7 April and '*the sum total of it was that he could not grant my request to allow my brother to stay with the depot instead of Mr Maddock as the officers remaining were chosen by rule and it was impossible to make any deviation from the usual routine*' – a not unexpected reply. However, that was not the end of the story because surprisingly Cardigan did have a change of heart. On 19 April, while in Dublin, Ellen wrote: '*Doddy called and told me the other day he had received (through Major Douglas) a formal offer from Lord Cardigan to allow him to stay at the depot instead of proceeding on foreign service with his regiment.*' Ellen's delight was short-lived for Roger immediately told her '*that he thought it would not be consistent with his honour to accept such a proposal and had therefore written to Lord Cardigan by return of post that he preferred proceeding with the regiment to the seat of war [...] It is too bad,*' wrote Ellen, '*to find all my toil and trouble has been in ruins. Oh it is too bad.*'

It was almost certainly at about this time that Ellen began to think about taking her father and her Aunt Mary on a journey to the East to be near Roger. She had little to look forward to. She had just turned down the offer of marriage from Prince Dentice and the idea of a seventh London season, chaperoned by Lady Tankerville, cannot have held much interest for her. Although Ellen acknowledged with a certain cynicism that her social status had benefited from the association, she didn't trust Lady Tankerville's motives; she had been unsettled by the malicious gossip that Lady Té stood to make £5,000 if she could marry off Ellen to a suitable *partie*. This thought, along with her constant fear of being courted for her wealth rather than herself, added to the attraction of foreign travel where she would be relatively free from the pressure to find a husband. Although she had sent an unequivocal refusal to Prince Dentice, she suspected that Lady Té might be '*bottling her up*' in order to press Dentice's suit again this summer and travel would give her the respite she needed.

The family were at Kenure as was usual in the springtime when the Cardigan correspondence took place. But Ellen had been rushed to Dublin the week before because she had suffered a horrendous accident. Out in the jaunting cart with Aunt Mary and Eliza (the former Miss Ward),

> *the horses shied up against a tree, the car was smashed, the shafts broken and ourselves hurled in different directions. My companions were scarcely hurt at all, but I was thrown with tremendous violence right over the front of the car, falling with all my weight upon my cheek and being dragged at the horses' heels for several yards upon my face over the gravel.*

She was so terribly bruised and cut that Mr Roberts advised going straight to Dublin to put herself under the care of Sir Philip Crampton.[21] Ellen accomplished the journey to Dublin without complaint, never flurried or fidgeting and she suggested that she kept off both fever and inflammation owing to the

> *extreme tranquillity of my mind. Not a feature could be recognised, one side of my face was swelled to a perfectly incredible extent making my head as large as two; the eye was thoroughly closed up and hidden under the protruding of the flesh, my nose nearly two inches broad and my mouth drawn entirely to one side of the frightful swelling and my cheek was bruised to a perfect jelly, a great part of the skin torn entirely off and five deep cuts staring wide open in different places.*[22]

The remedy was cold applications to her face every 10 minutes the whole night through, and leeches applied to her shoulder which '*very much hurt*'. Sir Philip Crampton declared he had never seen such a face in the whole of his practice. Indeed, Ellen's self-control was remarkable, for she might well have been left disfigured, and for someone so proud of her universally acknowledged beauty, this would have been hard to bear. As it was, she was unable to eat anything solid for several days and had to continue having her dressings changed all through the night at 10-minute intervals. Her only complaint, apart from the inconvenience, was that the wounds were '*terribly sore*', but she rightly prided herself on her resolute composure throughout her ordeal and noted with satisfaction that Sir Philip was amazed at the way she bore her misfortune: '*he never saw a lady make so little fuss*'.

Only 11 days after her accident Ellen organised a house party at Kenure and appeared with '*one side of my face bandaged up with green ribbon and it looks quite decent, my cheek and eye are still too dreadful to go uncovered*'. However, '*Roger would have been disappointed if the party had been postponed any longer*', such was her devotion to her brother. As she herself noted with some pride, everyone was amazed at her agreeing to it as it showed such an absence of personal vanity. The guest list included Miss Blenerhassett, Lady O'Dowd, Mr and Miss Yelverton, Capt. and Mrs Creswell (Mrs Creswell was to join her husband in the Crimea and would be left a widow), Mr Bland, Capt. Paynter and Capt. Sandes (with both of whom Ellen was enjoying a mild flirtation), Col. and Miss Taylor, and Lord St Lawrence.

On 5 May the family took the train to Dublin because they had heard a rumour that the 11th Hussars were about to depart. The rumour proved unfounded, but it gave Ellen and Roger time to plan a party before embarkation on the following Monday, 8 May. They had wanted to picnic at Dalkey but the weather was so bad that they had lunch on the *Asia* – the ship in which Capt. Cook's troop would sail on Wednesday. Capt. Wombwell and Capt. Creswell were the only officers of the 11th Hussars mentioned by Ellen, but she noted that Miss Yelverton, Miss Blenerhassett, Lady O'Dowd and Miss O'Hara were among the guests as well as Capt. Sandes and Capt. Poynter, her two admirers. Crowds of people from Dublin came out to watch the business of embarkation, which went on all day. There was one more twist to this bittersweet occasion. Ellen noted that '*Major Douglas came up and complimented me highly upon Roger's gallant behaviour in refusing Lord Cardigan's offer of remaining at home. He said that not one young man in ten would have behaved as Roger did. Alas! He has purchased these praises dearly.*'

While the 11th Hussars were embarking on the *Paramatta* at Kingstown, the *Shooting Star*, with a party of the 8th Royal Irish Hussars, another light cavalry regiment, was anchoring in the harbour in Malta, having set off 10 days earlier from Plymouth. On board was the redoubtable Mrs Duberly, wife of Henry Duberly, Quartermaster-General to the regiment. Fanny Duberly, tiring of peacetime army life, childless, bored, not wishing to be parted from her husband, was looking for adventure. Although she denied it at the time, she was nursing a secret ambition. She would keep a daily journal of all she saw, but she was also writing it with an eye to publication in due course, and perhaps making a little money, always a consideration with Fanny. When her book, *Mrs Duberly's War*, was published in 1856 it was first received with a storm of interest and critical acclaim, but this later changed to mockery. Victorian society found it difficult to accept that a gentlewoman, an officer's wife, could be taken seriously as a writer. The fact that she had witnessed and described so candidly such terrible scenes of suffering and distress, not as a nurse but as a spectator, and that for practical reasons she had dispensed with petticoats and worn trousers under her dress, all counted against her. She herself was aware that she might have committed an 'indiscretion' and wondered how she might be received by polite society once back home. Although reviews in both the *Examiner* and *Punch* made fun of her and caused her much distress, nevertheless her journal continues to provide one of the most vivid and important accounts of daily life during the Crimean War.

While horses and supplies continued to be loaded on board the *Parramatta*, a violent storm in the Mediterranean Sea hit the *Shooting Star*. Mrs Duberly wrote: 'a hurricane of wind thundered in our rigging […] today has been a day of much suffering […] the ship had heeled over till her deck was under water […] every horse was down' – a foretaste of the hardships to come. While Ellen was making her last scramble in her long skirts up the side of the *Parramatta* to say a final farewell to Roger, Mrs Duberly was recovering from the havoc caused by the storm. Brother and sister breakfasted together and Roger gave her his last directions, probably to pay his debts. At 1 o'clock, the visitors were told they must leave the ship. '*Oh the agony I felt at this moment! A hurried farewell, one close embrace and we were gone […] I shed a few tears, for my grief was too deep to find relief in weeping.*'

Ellen's despair at the departure of her brother was profound, but her sadness had an element of self-pity as her analysis of their relationship demonstrates:

> *To me this parting feels as if I were bidding farewell to the last hope in this world, and indeed if my brother were taken away what more would remain to me on earth. Nothing excepting two aunts, both upward of 70 and an invalid father whose health prevents him taking his own position in the world […] I have actually no other relation to look to, no-one to guide and sympathise with me in youth and comfort me in old age. I might marry but that is always a lottery […] Mine is indeed a dark and dreary prospect with only one hope to cling to, that hope is centred on my brother, he is friend, companion, all in all to me and if I lose him I should not wish to live. We are not like other brothers and sisters, we were brought up together in childhood with no other*

> *companions to divide our affections, amusements, instruction, joys and sorrows and we were never separated till Roger went to school. Even then we used to pass the time in counting the days until his return.*[23]

At Eton, Roger had been making new friends, living a different life apart from Ellen. It was not so long after leaving school that he decided to break the tie with home and join the army, to Ellen's intense distress. Now the worst had happened: he was being sent overseas and could be facing real danger. At the end of the pier they watched the vessel being towed out of the harbour: they could see Roger within a few yards as it passed, not knowing when they would see him again.

CHAPTER 12

To Constantinople

After Roger's departure the family left Kenure for London. Stopping briefly at Cefn, they arrived back at Portland Place at the end of May. Ellen set about trying to re-ignite her social life. She immediately drove out to leave cards and went to see Lady Tankerville, who didn't seem put out by the letter she had written to Dentice ending any possibility of marriage. However, she soon discovered that Lady Té was tiring of her role as chaperone, finding a game of whist with friends less taxing and more enjoyable. Ellen wondered if Lady Té had give up on her because she had refused Prince Dentice's offer of marriage or if she was '*bottling her up*' in the hope that Ellen would change her mind.

In any case invitations to the best balls had started to dwindle. When she did go, Ellen was often forced to ask Lady Harrington or Lady Talbot as well as the Kayes to stand in for Lady Tankerville, who always insisted on leaving early. When no one was available she was at risk of being snubbed if she asked for a ticket for Aunt Mary. The true awkwardness of her situation was made clear to her when she went to Lady Listowel's ball. Feeling seedy, she was reduced to promenading with Lord Ranelagh; but worse than this, after Lady Té had left, Ellen had to wait two hours before she could get a cab. No one helped her and she records that she never felt so distressed in her life.

Now out of mourning, she had ordered herself a new set of ball gowns, but because of the risk of inflaming her face, which was still slightly swollen and red, she could only dance quadrilles and had to sit out the waltzes and polkas she so much enjoyed. Although she wrote that she hated formal dinner parties, they were one way of getting to know people who might be useful. They must have been something of an ordeal for her because she could never be sure her father would not have an attack in public, as he did on one occasion:

> *Had a large dinner party at home, the first large one I have had to preside over, Mr Kinglake*[1] *among the guests. Just as the company were assembled poor Papa had an attack. It nearly unnerved me for it was a most distressing occurrence, however he got well enough to make his appearance in the evening which was some compensation.*[2]

There were highlights like Ascot, where she was surrounded by beaux, but she noted she did not see so many friends as in the past. The expectation for her to marry was unrelenting, but when Lady Talbot tried her hand at matchmaking and pressed the claims of Lord George Beauclerk, heir to the Duke of St Albans, Ellen dismissed him as '*too old, too poor and too stupid*'. The music parties she attended were more often than not categorised as '*stupid*' or '*boring*'. She went to the opera and saw Grisi in a farewell performance of *Norma*, commenting sharply, '*She should quit the stage, her voice is quite gone*'.[3]

It is no wonder that the idea of going East became an increasingly attractive proposition, a welcome alternative to her life as it had become. Always one to enjoy a challenge, she found consolation in planning her projected tour to Constantinople, '*where I have set my heart on going*'. She may have convinced herself that the journey was entirely on Roger's account, but running the estates, caring for her father, trying to make a success of the London season and warding off unwanted proposals of marriage was an unattractive alternative. She was also pinning her hopes on being able to persuade Roger to leave the Army. Ellen made no secret of her plans and was unsurprised by the almost universal condemnation of the enterprise: '*of course everyone is against our going, to be singular is enough to condemn anyone*'. She had some supporters in the shape of M. de Saux and Capt. Paynter, who both wanted to accompany her as secretary, and both entertained hopes of marriage. But by far her most important ally was Alexander Kinglake, whom she had first met at Elvaston Castle in Derbyshire while staying with the Harringtons and met again at Lady Bray's musical party. Kinglake, a successful solicitor, had earlier travelled to Syria, Palestine and Egypt and the published account of his journey, *Eothen: Or Traces of Travel Brought Home from the East,* had been an instant success. Ellen knew of his intention of going out to the Crimea and when he declared himself all in favour of her making the trip, she took advantage of his friendship and invited him on more than one occasion to dinner at Portland Place. He not only encouraged her but gave practical advice on the best route to take and how to obtain the necessary visas. Ellen clearly used her feminine wiles to get all the information she could from him, noting '*that the way to make Mr. Kinglake do anything is to look as pretty as one can for he is a great admirer of beauty*'.[4] Although there was much talk of a meeting in Constantinople, it never took place as Kinglake returned to England in October, before Ellen and her party arrived, to write up his account of the war in the Crimea; however, they continued to correspond.

Unfortunately there is no record of the correspondence between brother and sister, apart from Ellen's diary entries, after Roger's departure. Roger's first letter was from Gibraltar on 30 May, and Ellen didn't hear from him until 22 July, when he wrote from Varna more than a month after the French and British armies had passed through the Dardanelles, disembarked and set up camp. Varna, a Bulgarian city on the Black Sea coast, would serve as the headquarters and principal naval base for the British and French armies while they waited for orders. Mrs Duberly gives a graphic account of the disembarkation of the horses, frightened and restive as they were lowered into rowing boats, kicking, screaming and plunging as they came ashore. She describes the quayside crowded with Turks, Greeks, infantry, artillery, Hussars, and piles of cannonballs and shells, and riding to the camp nearly a mile away. But despite all the hardships, being bitten by fleas and ants and with little by way of food, Mrs Duberly writes, 'we are all in good heart and have plenty of pluck'.[5] What Roger did not say in his letter was that cholera had broken out, that the city was overcrowded and drunken fighting between the men was a daily problem. In an attempt to escape the disease, several regiments, the light cavalry included, moved further inland, first to Devna and later to Jeni Bazaar, in the hope that away from the overcrowded port the troops would escape the ravages of the disease, but deaths from cholera continued. The last letter Ellen had from Roger was written from Jeni Bazaar, saying that though life was hard he was well. In all probability both he and his sister escaped the cholera epidemic as they had both had the disease in a mild form in Ireland. Roger also reported some camp gossip concerning Lord Cardigan's unreasonable behaviour, while Mrs Duberly wrote complaining about him to her sister. The Duberlys had just arrived at Jeni Bazaar and were resting under some trees, before marking out the ground for their tent. 'We had not been there five minutes, hot tired and grateful when my Lord Cardigan sent his aide de camp to deliver the following message, "Lord Cardigan desires I will say you must not *pitch your tent* under these trees as he is going to put his there". Of course I spread the story all over the camp.'[6]

In April, the allied fleets had bombarded Odessa, an important Black Sea port. In retaliation, the Russian army had crossed the Danube and occupied the Danubian islands opposite the town of Silestria. On the direct orders of the Tsar, who was furious that his commander was not being sufficiently proactive, General Pasevitch laid siege to the town. The attack began in earnest with the bombardment of the Turkish forts which formed a defensive ring a little way from Silestria. The large Turkish force under the leadership of Omar Pasha,[7] the Commander-in-Chief of the Ottoman forces, proved much more difficult to dislodge than expected. The defence of the key redoubt called Arab Tabia was led by two experienced British artillery officers, Captain James Butler of the Ceylon Rifles and Lieutenant Charles Naysmith of the Bombay Artillery, both of whom lost their lives. Had Silestria fallen, the way would have been opened for the Russian armies to threaten Constantinople itself. The French and British armies had expected to be deployed to assist the Turkish army, which had shown unexpected courage and determination defending the town. But before the allied armies could march to the assistance of the Turks, the Russians suddenly withdrew their forces on the very eve of their expected attack. Much to everyone's surprise, on 22 June news came through that the Russians had suddenly abandoned the siege of Silestria and had withdrawn across the Danube.

Because the fall of the city had been so widely predicted, its sudden evacuation gave rise to much speculation. The Russian withdrawal was so unexpected that some doubted the truth of the report, resulting in Lord Cardigan being ordered with 200 men from the Light Brigade to make quite sure that the Russians had indeed crossed back over the Danube. Mrs Duberly writes scathingly, 'At last we had the satisfaction of seeing the poor old creature (pitiable Lord Cardigan) ride away at the head of a squadron of 8th and 13th without having, as I believe, the smallest idea of where he was going or what he was going for.'[8] Roger escaped what must have been a very gruelling few days as he did not take part in the patrol. Forced to ride in the broiling heat, with no water for the horses and with no clear destination in view, the squadron returned several days later, never having reached Silestria, with an araba[9] full of injured men and 75 horses unfit to work for months, if ever again, according to Mrs Duberly.

It was while the 11th Hussars were camped at Jeni Bazaar that Roger, with some fellow officers, rode over to Shulma, where Omar Pasha had his headquarters. On 10 August Mrs Duberly records that she also rode over to Shulma accompanied by her husband and Capt. Tomkinson, Capt. Chetwode and Mr Mussenden. She had risen at half past three, was in the saddle by five and took two hours and five minutes to reach Shulma, a distance of 15 miles. There they met Capt. Saltmarche, Mr Trevelyan and Mr Palmer of the 11th. Mrs Duberly and her party, and Roger with his companions, had a very nasty breakfast together at the Locanda, an establishment belonging to some Turks.[10] That meeting, curiously enough, is the only recorded meeting between a member of the Palmer family and the Duberlys. Later on, when Ellen reached the Crimea and she and Fanny Duberly lived on ships almost side-by-side in the crowded harbour in Balaclava, they never met or spoke.

Back in London, before she was able to start on the much-anticipated expedition, Ellen had just finished fighting her own war with Aunt Mary. Her father was all in favour of the trip, but every time Ellen thought she had persuaded her aunt, fresh rows broke out. Once, having rowed all evening, Ellen woke early the next morning to find Aunt Mary sitting beside her bed ready to continue the argument. A visit to see the Diorama of Constantinople was a success, and encouraged by Kinglake's support for the expedition, Mary finally gave in and agreed to go. Lady Tankerville did Ellen one more favour and introduced her to Lady Stratford de Redcliffe, the wife of the British Ambassador to Turkey. Despite the introduction, during Ellen's time in Constantinople, Lady Stratford seems to have delighted in withholding longed-for invitations till the last minute, causing Ellen much anguish.

By the end of July, Ellen's plans were almost complete: she had taken her complaisant father to the city to arrange about finance for the trip; she had decided to go via Vienna and had found out about the sailing of the Austrian Lloyd steamers down the Danube; she had bought a travelling bonnet and trunks and had checked the repairs to the house; her portrait by Francis Grant was finished to her great satisfaction and she had been seen by Sir Philip Crampton, who said there was no reason not to go and that time would heal her face. Ellen had been following Roger's progress and knew he had moved from Varna, where an epidemic of cholera was raging, to Devna and then to Jeni Bazaar where it was hoped that the troops could escape from the ravages of the disease. Roger wrote on 7 August of the possibility of an expedition to the Crimea, but on 20 August Ellen received a letter mentioning the pleasing possibility of the army being quartered in Constantinople for the winter. Roger's letters reflect the lack of a clear military strategy at that time, with Lord Raglan,[11] the inexperienced Commander-in-Chief, uncertain how to carry out the Government's instructions to prosecute the war whilst also having to manage a fraught relationship with his ambitious French counterpart, Marshal St Arnaud,[12] who had been given command of the French armies by Louis Napoleon as a reward for his support.

At last, the great day arrived and the party of seven left London on 31 August. Ellen, Papa, Aunt Mary and Mr Roberts with their carpet bags, Ellen's maid Therese, the valet Bevan and another male servant caught the train, crossed the Channel and, after many changes, arrived at Cologne the following day. Ellen in her snobbish way notes that '*the Rhine is utterly ruined by all the shopkeepers who go a pleasuring there as they used to go to Margate*'. The party journeyed on to Hanover, a town containing nothing of interest as far as Ellen was concerned, then to Berlin. Perhaps scarred by the memories of her intensive sightseeing undertaken as a young girl,

Ellen wrote: '*Sight-seeing! It is a horrid bore to see the sights, but there it is, a sort of duty to oneself, museum, royal palace, picture gallery.*'[13] Ellen found Berlin one of the noblest cities she had ever seen, with a sort of grandeur in the aspect of its public palaces, yet she thought little of its citizens: '*I have never seen a plainer or more ill-dressed set of people.*' Every evening Ellen had to settle all the accounts, find couriers and generally oversee all the arrangements for the following day.

Ellen did not care much for Dresden despite its beauty, perhaps because it had a museum, a royal palace and a picture gallery which needed to be visited. '*I hate sightseeing for my own part, but then everyone seems to undergo it from a high sense of moral duty – the same sort of feeling that induces people to sit out* Fidelio *at the opera, or take mineral water when in perfect health.*'[14] Leaving Dresden, they then sailed down the Elbe to Prague, where there was a further bout of sightseeing. There had been tensions between the Czech population and the Austrian Government since the 1848 revolutions and Ellen, who was very observant, commented: '*It must be really terrible to live in a country so ground down by an absolute government that they can only speak in whispers.*'

From Prague they travelled for 14 hours to Vienna, where they found a letter from Mr Kinglake advising them not to sail from Trieste because the Greek boat was now in quarantine in Corfu due to an outbreak of cholera. This put Ellen in a quandary, as the only alternative was to sail down the Danube. An old friend, Captain Maxwell, told them that this entailed a certain amount of risk – they would be passing through bandit territory – but despite the terrible inconveniences they were assured there was no real danger. Weighing up the situation she wrote,

> *We can always carry enough accommodations with us to make Papa and Aunt Mary comfortable, the rest of the party can endure anything. I feel quite delighted at the prospect of a scramble, it will be quite off the beaten track of railroads and steamboats by which all the world moves about [...] I really do not think there is any fear of going by the Danube, at any rate we can go part of the way and return again if everything is not favourable.*[15]

Captain Taylor,[16] their Irish neighbour, had heard of Ellen's plans and wrote in a letter to his mother, 'Ellen Palmer's expedition is the most hair brained undertaking and with people such as her father and Aunt Mary to look after it would be madness to think of her working her way through the Balkans and Bulgaria all the way to Constantinople. Roger will be in the Crimea, the 11th are lying in a steamer not far from us at the moment. I trust some judicious friend will turn her back at Vienna.'[17] But there was no judicious friend and it is easy to see why Ellen was so taken with the idea of the journey down the Danube; there was nothing she liked more than to be different from other people and to show off her ability to overcome obstacles that to others would seem insurmountable. There is no record of Aunt Mary's opinion as to the feasibility of the expedition. Perhaps if Ellen had fully realised the hardships the party would be subjected to, even she might have hesitated. As it was they were all glad to leave Vienna, '*for it is one of the dullest capitals – everyone seems afraid to speak, the streets are narrow and gloomy [...] I only saw one metropolis duller than this and that was Wrexham.*'[18]

Before leaving Vienna, Ellen had ordered a hot bath and she left an amusing description of the consternation caused by this unusual request.

> *This unprecedented demand threw the whole household into a state of commotion – the housemaid worried herself into a nervous fever, the head waiter was so agitated that he kept popping his head round the door and actually forgot to fold the dinner napkins from pure distress of mind. When the dreaded moment arrived, every servant in the house was assembled to watch my progress to the bathroom and when I did get in I bolted the door very fast indeed for I was not at all certain where the investigation might lead. As this was the first hotel in Vienna what on earth happens in the others?*[19]

On 21 September, Ellen heard that the troops had landed at Sevastopol; this put her in a fever of anxiety about the danger to Roger. In fact the British and French armies had landed at Kalamita Bay, north of Sevastopol, and by 24 September, as the Palmers started their voyage down the Danube, the Battle of the Alma had been fought and won.

Their first stop was Pesth. Ellen, who had changed their notes into gold ducats for this part of the journey, now took the courier off on a marathon shopping expedition. She listed all her purchases:

> *rugs, sheets, mosquito curtains, flannel belts, towels, medicines of every description, tea, coffee, flour, rice, arrowroot, sugar, salt, mustard, ham, tongues, preserved soup, sardines, butter, sherry, brandy, beer, pistols, a compass, sacking (to fill with straw for our beds), travelling baskets, plated cups, tea urn, plated dishes and plates (unbreakable), knives, forks, spoons, tea urn, coffee and egg pots, lamps, candles, salt cellars, whips (to drive the Turkish horses), spirits of wine, string and rope, saucepans, jar for water, insect powder, olive oil, cold cream, dishes and a pie dish to wash in. We have prepared ourselves for everything. We don't expect to find more than four walls and a roof.*[20]

She was to be proved right.

At Pesth they boarded the *Hildegarde*, but it was not long before it ran aground and they were forced to change steamers, to little effect as low water in the Danube had stopped all navigation and they were forced to disembark and travel overland. They joined a train of 18 to 20 open wagons, their party with all their baggage occupying three of them. They sat on rough sorts of seats, which were set over straw with some matting spread overhead to protect them from the sun and the rain. When they stopped at Drancova, everyone rushed to the inn and grabbed whatever they could before continuing on in their unsprung wagons, then boarding yet another steamer. Ellen, who had always enjoyed wild scenery, let herself go with a rare purple passage: '*Vast and grand the majestic scenes, they conveyed a sense of utter solitude which I have never yet experienced and one felt it almost profanation to raise one's voice except in awe and reverence in these wild regions, fresh from the hands of the creator.*' What really pleased her was that she could look at '*and wonder at the grandest scenery without the drawback of hundreds of cockneys looking and wondering at your side*'.[21]

Eventually they arrived at Orsova, a city port on the Danube which had changed hands many times and was then part of the Kingdom of Hungary on the border with Moldavia. The steamer they were hoping to take did not arrive so they had to stay on board another 24 hours. Ellen confided her frustrations to her diary:

> *The management of the Danube boats is certainly scandalous, it would never happen in a civilized country. It rained and after dinner at 8 we had to go to bed because the gentlemen composed themselves to sleep in the saloon. Paddles had a comfortable cabin, I slept on the floor. Everyone cheats you of money, our courier is a goose so I have to do everything as before.*[22]

This included deciding to join the caravan of wagons that was going overland as the next day no steamer had materialised. Ellen notes that the neat little towns of Moldavia changed as they crossed into Wallachia: '*the villages were composed of wretched wattled huts, dirty, filthy looking; in short they appeared about ten degrees worse than any Irish cabin I ever saw*'.[23]

In Wallachia they passed the celebrated Town Gates of Severus, marking the spot where there are dangerous whirlpools. Once past the whirlpools they found a large, handsome boat awaiting them. Taking a stroll in the evening they saw the Tower of Severus on a small hill surrounded by a moat, but fearing to stay out late after dark in such a '*barbarous country*' they returned to the relative comfort of the steamer.

The French consul gave them a letter to the Pacha of Silestria and they found other agreeable company on board: '*Papa enjoys it thoroughly and even Aunt Mary shares in the general enthusiasm.*' They stopped off for a short while at Rustchuck before they arrived at Silestria and '*were accompanied into the town by a crowd of inhabitants who had scarcely seen a civilized European and certainly not a European lady*'. Ellen was indeed breaking new ground and must have been the first European lady to walk around the town since the siege that had ended on 22 June. '*The houses were mostly what we should call hovels with tiled roofs, but my previous experience of Irish cabins had prepared me for the squalid misery of the interior and taught me not to be particular.*'[24] These references to the misery of Irish cabins are particularly interesting, for in her earlier diaries Ellen never makes any reference to visiting the poor or even seeming to be aware of the squalid conditions in which the starving and impoverished Irish were living.

When they eventually found the Pasha's house, they were directed to their lodgings: two small rooms in a cottage. Although they could not stand upright in them, they were so delighted to have somewhere clean they hugged themselves with joy. After a walk with their guide, an Italian medical man attached to the Turkish regiment, they returned with a doctor, who told them he had not seen a single European except for a few officers visiting the place. Ellen described their evening together:

> *There were our own provisions to eat, our own cups and saucers that wouldn't break, excellent milk and eggs from the village, 3 legged stools to sit upon and above that a keen sense of novelty and adventure which gives zest to everything and caused us to feel pleasure in all contrivances and even inconveniences inescapable from our position. I think I never enjoyed a meal so much as I did in this tea in the Turkish cottage, in wild regions thousands of miles from home and amongst a set of barbarians who scarcely ever set eyes on a Christian before.*

The barbarians, so called, kindly turned out of the house to make room for the party and slept in the garden. Ellen goes on to describe the fun they had making preparations for bed. She was in her element. Her diary entries during the journey down the Danube are longer than usual; she had little else to distract her during the evenings, and for her this was the adventure of a lifetime. The evening before, they had already walked outside the town along the fortifications, '*which appeared wonderfully strong and bristling with batteries on every side. The ground was strewed with pieces of bombs and shells which the Russians had thrown into the town. Only a few hundred yards distant lay a small village in ruins which the Turks had destroyed for fear of its falling into the hand of the enemy.*'[25]

The next morning they set out to explore the town. Ellen's description of Silestria after three months of siege painted a vivid picture of life for the inhabitants at that time. To her great disappointment, Omar Pasha had left the day before they arrived. They made a pilgrimage to the tomb of Captain James Butler of the Ceylon Rifles who, together with

Lieutenant Charles Naismith of the Bombay Artillery, had volunteered to act as advisers to Mustapha Pasha and were partly responsible for the robust defence of the town.

> *We walked to see the tomb of poor Captain Butler who is buried in a small cemetery in the middle of the town. The Hero's grave is surrounded by a rude wooden paling and marked by a simple black cross bearing the inscription 'Captain James Amar Butler, died June 21st 1854'.*[26] *Poor fellow it was sad fate to die in such a far away land with scarcely even a comrade's hand to close his eyes and cheer his last moment.*

It was particularly sad as Captain Butler had died the day before the sudden departure of the Russians. There was no mention of a grave for Charles Naismith. They visited the Greek church, built underground according to Ellen, and a Russian church where many families had sought refuge from the shelling. Most families had lived in their cellars during the 45 days that the siege lasted, and although the whole town bore witness to the effects of the enemy fire, the part near the large mosques was almost in ruins. They passed the house where Mustapha Pasha had been killed; Ellen was told that a bomb entered the room where he was sitting and actually cut him in half. She noted the price of food:

> *Before the fighting began one might buy eggs at 40 a penny, fowls a half penny and turkeys for 4 and everything in proportion, but now the prices are almost doubled [...] there is nothing but black bread to be had in the town, and as for the meat it is nearly inedible and a piece of scrag which one would use for soup at home would have been beautiful compared to it. The tough old bullock which furnished the beef was alive and well this morning and Bevan actually saw him killed before our door about an hour before a lump was cut off him for our dinner.*

Owing to Ellen's foresight they had brought their own supplies of rice, bread and cheese; the novelty of having to wash their plates between every dish and managing everything in a rather primitive way appealed to Ellen – '*it was all great fun and we enjoyed it amazingly*'.[27]

Later that afternoon they decided to visit the fortifications and were forced to walk as there was no other means of transport.

> *The forts are situated on eminences some little distance from the town, and are, I think seven in number. We visited the Forts des Moulins, Fort des Serpents, and the celebrated Arab Tabir which is the key to the whole position and point which the Russians were most desirous of getting into their hands. They advanced quite close to the base of the fortifications and I ran down and examined the lines which they had dug and which had almost progressed under the feet of the besieged. One of these mines blew up in the wrong place and instead of injuring the Turks it did considerable damage to its unwary constructors. The Russian engineers worked very hard and there are the remains of covered roads running in every direction [...] The enemy crossed over the Danube by means of these little islands, on the last of which they established a battery which did a great deal of damage. From the projecting point on this island they threw a bridge on the opposite shore and landed quietly on a sloping hill not many hundred yards' distance from the fort of Arab Pasha himself. A few more days and Silistria must have given in.*

Ellen could have known nothing of the letter that Tolstoy, who had arrived as an ordinance officer, wrote to his brother saying he also believed that Silestria could not have held out for more than two or three days.[28] The Russian withdrawal back across the Danube had taken everyone by surprise, as already noted that Cardigan had been despatched to verify the fact that it had actually happened. But the Tsar knew that Austria had massed 100,000 troops along the Serbian border and British and French troops had arrived at Varna, not far away. If the enemy had attacked and captured Silestria it would have left the Russian army dangerously exposed, so he had ordered a withdrawal on the very eve of a proposed assault on the town. Like any tourist Ellen picked up some pieces of bomb to keep as souvenirs of their visit to Arab Tabir, commenting that they must have been the first travellers to have ever been there.

The party then travelled on in three bullock carts and Ellen thought that even the manure carts she had seen in Ireland were elegant in comparison. There was a piece of coarse matting to keep off the sun and they jolted over rough roads, driven by wild-looking Turks with daggers in their belts. They were guarded by two mounted police provided by the Pasha. Despite the hardship of the journey, when they stopped to rest the horses they made a very good meal of preserved soup, ham, tongue, potatoes, bread, rice, cheese and beer. '*This was a picnic in real earnest, and there we were, servants and ourselves, Turks and Arabs sitting altogether and making a very curious group with the wagons and horses disposed around.*'[29] It must, indeed, have been an unusual spectacle – wealthy European travellers sitting with their servants and natives sharing such a luxurious picnic in such inhospitable surroundings. That night they stopped at a village, no more than an assemblage of mud cabins, '*many degrees worse than the one of last night, in short it was the very picture of Irish huts we have so often seen and wondered how people could live in them*'. Here again Ellen revealed her knowledge of how the poor lived in Ireland, but writing in such a detached way, as though it had no connection with the rents they received from their estates in Mayo that she was now managing. She was proud of the fact that none of them minded actually sleeping in a mud hut, with no understanding that although for them this might be an adventure, for the Irish poor it was a way of life.

The next day they travelled for nine hours

> *and when we got out of the araba every bone in our body was aching from the terrible jolting we had experienced all day. When the wagons go at a walking pace the shaking is bad enough, but when the horses trot or canter over the rough road the motion is really too awful to think of. We are packed so closely so that we have no room to stretch a limb.*[30]

As they approached Shumla, Ellen noticed the guides had cocked their pistols and were looking around cautiously. Afterwards, Ellen learnt that because of the lawless nature of the land it was always dangerous and after nightfall totally impossible. She describes Shumla as a large town, prettily situated in a semi-circular valley surrounded by steep hills crowned with forts. Having just endured several days being jolted over rough roads, Ellen reverts again to her astonishment that the army was supposedly unable to go to the aid of the Turks because of the state of the roads, which, she noted, were no worse than many in England. They found a good-sized house to stay in, but as usual without a stick of furniture, so they lay on the floor to sleep. It is unlikely that Ellen saw the Locanda, where two months ago, almost to the day, her brother had breakfasted with Mrs Duberly; or that she even knew about the meeting as he most probably never mentioned it.

The French doctor with whom they had made friends arranged for them to call on a Bulgarian family, but since neither of them could speak the other's language, '*the visit passed off in dumb show, and there we sat grinning at each other and looking amiable with all our might*'. Ellen noted that the Bulgarians were Christians and considered themselves distinct from, and indeed superior to, their Turkish neighbours who were Muslim. Although Shumla was beautifully situated it must have been something of a disappointment as a centre of civilisation. '*The streets were perfectly horrid, being a mass of mud without any attempt at road making, full of deep holes and nothing in the way of paving, except a few large rough stones stuck in every now and them and of no possible use unless it is to tumble over.*'[31]

Even Ellen was beginning to find the going tough, let alone her father and her aunt and the servants. '*I am nearly worn out with the ill tempers of our party individually and collectively; the servants do nothing but quarrel all day and then appeal to me to settle their disputes and Aunt Mary has taken it into her head to be as cross as two sticks.*' Who can blame her? She didn't want to come in the first place and, being considerably older than Ellen, it is no wonder that Mary found the journey extremely trying. Ellen made no comment as to how her father was standing up to the rigours of the journey except that she made sure that he always had the best room and the best bed.

The following morning they set off for another uncomfortable journey to Ennisgroi, a small village where they were to spend the night. As soon as they arrived, Ellen was eager to set off on foot for Jeni Bazaar which she particularly wanted to visit as Roger's last letter had been sent from there.

> *Jeni Bazaar is a very pretty village, lying in a valley surrounded by mountains and our troops were encamped on a plain situated between the villages and a range of hills. We saw the marks of the tents, the fireplaces, horses' feet etc., and strewed about were pieces of English newspapers, pipes, playing cards, letters and other objects showing that the ground had only been freshly abandoned by our troops. How little did Doddy think when he left this place three weeks ago that we should so soon visit the places where his footsteps still lingered.*

In fact the cavalry had left more than a month ago and were about to disembark at Kalamita Bay in the Crimea, from where they had been expected to march on to Sevastopol; but Ellen knew nothing of that.

> *I could hardly believe that this silent and desolate plain has so lately been rife with bustle and movement and that the barren looking turf all round us had formed the hearth and homes of thousands of our brave countrymen. The General's tent (Lord Cardigan I suppose) was pitched under the shadow of three fine trees and we broke off a branch to commemorate our visit to Jeni Bazaar.*[32]

Roger had evidently told his sister of Lord Cardigan's behaviour as recounted by Mrs Duberly. Ellen continued, '*We did not leave without paying tribute to the lonely little burial place where some freshly made graves mark the last earthly home of some of these gallant spirits who left their native shores but a few short months ago in health and happiness.*' The dead soldiers were victims of the cholera epidemic that continued to ravage the camp despite the move from Varna. It was indeed a strange turn of fate that Ellen and her party should have visited the place where her brother had been so recently encamped. She ends her account of the visit by hoping that they would find Roger at Varna, not knowing he was already in the Crimea and soon to take part in the Battle of the Alma, calling him '*beloved truant*'. That was how she thought of him, but it was very far from his own perception of himself; he was enjoying army life and had no intention of resigning. It would be another two months before Ellen saw her brother and by then he would have taken part in the Charge of the Light Brigade.

On the road from Jeni Bazaar to Devna they came close to being in real danger. Some French gentlemen had been robbed and murdered in broad daylight the previous week so it was fortunate that they were travelling in a convoy with two other wagons full of Bulgarian merchants. They met two brigands looking like cut-throats and had seen others who disappeared into the brushwood and did not dare molest them.

> *Our drivers and guards were exceedingly apprehensive during the whole morning. The gend'armes made all the wagons keep in a close line and told us all to have our pistols loaded and ready to use at a moment's warning. The mounted men rode forward and examined every clump of brushwood and at several parts of the road they caused us to hurry on as much as possible and made our clumsy wagons gallop at a furious pace. I never saw such scene of alarm and confusion as it was; for some drivers seemed nearly mad with fright driving in every direction in the most reckless manner [...] all morning (I sat in the most exposed seat ready to see the fun) we were on tiptoe of expectation, but towards afternoon the danger diminished for there was more traffic on the road and bullock carts were passing backward and forwards.*[33]

Ellen sounded almost disappointed that they arrived safely at half past four without having being ambushed. There was no time to explore the town that night.

Ellen was determined to see the site of the English camp at Devna, which she described as a '*low marshy unhealthy looking valley, intersected with streams and containing a large lake, the exhalations of which are most pernicious to health. Alongside the banks of this lake the cavalry were encamped and the infantry was posted on the other side*'. It was no wonder that the men, hoping to escape the cholera epidemic at Varna, continued to succumb and Ellen notes that the rough burial ground consisted of large pits, rather than graves, where the bodies of hundreds of men were thrown. She learnt that the Turks call Devna the 'Valley of the Shadow of Death'. Again Ellen looked for traces of the tents and tried to imagine to herself how Roger would have felt. '*Perhaps in the very spaces where we unthinkingly trod dear Doddles had sat thinking of his home in utter desolation of spirit, heartsick at the misery that surrounded him. Dear, dear boy, he shall suffer no more from feelings of loneliness and isolation from country and kindred.*' From all accounts, Roger was a popular officer, enjoyed military life and was only too glad to escape the tyranny of his female-dominated home. Ellen, with her sentimental vision of bringing succour and comfort, as well as persuading him to leave the army, was setting herself up for a disappointment.

It took six hours to travel from Devna to Varna on one of the worst roads they had yet encountered, but Ellen, although not much given to feeling sentimental about her country, nonetheless, after their long journey '*did feel a thrill of pleasure at the sight of the wooden walls of old England lying in Varna bay and the red coats and familiar accents of dear military old John Bull*'.[34] They were escorted into town by a whole posse of officers and Ellen had the satisfaction of seeing their astonishment that anyone could have possibly reached Varna by road. They called on the British Consul and were at length installed in a house formerly used by the Quartermaster General, perhaps Henry Duberly's office, where they spent the night. The following morning they went to get their tickets for the packet to Constantinople. The French were still embarking troops for the Crimea and the beach was crowded with soldiers, sailors and government officials. There were no English troops apart from depots for each regiment. They had not heard from Roger for a long time and sought out Captain Ennis who was in charge of the depot for the 11th Hussars. Corporal Royal, the soldier who took their note to the Captain, was '*enthusiastic in his praise of Roger and said he was beloved by the whole regiment*'. Although this was pleasing for Ellen to hear, it again reinforces Roger's enjoyment of and aptitude for military life.

Ellen thought Varna far less wretched than described by the newspaper, but after the miserable little villages they had passed through and Silestria and Shulma, Varna must have seemed positively civilised with quite respectable-looking shops. The French and English soldiers had renamed some streets to make themselves feel more at home and Ellen noted that they lived in Cadogan Square and that Belgrave Street was close by. Ellen was amused at Papa being constantly mistaken for a general and people kept enquiring whether his orderly knew the way about. She also learned that Captain Creswell had died of cholera. The Palmers had last seen the Creswells at Kingstown during the embarkation of the 11th Hussars. They were old friends and had been entertained at Kenure. Mrs Creswell was one of the few officers' wives to have accompanied their husbands to the Crimea and Ellen would have liked to visit her on board the *War Cloud*, but she was too ill and feverish.

They left Varna on 14 October on the French packet belonging to the captain of the *War Cloud*. The sea was rough, but the next morning when they emerged on deck Ellen was overwhelmed:

> *We had entered the Golden Horn and Constantinople lay before us. Words cannot do justice to the wondrous beauty of the panorama which now burst upon our astonished gaze. On either side of the harbour rose towering hills crowned with buildings each overtopping the other in picturesque confusion until they formed a perfect amphitheatre of loveliness, palaces, domes, minarets, intermixed with cyprus groves climbing up to the very crest of the mountains and mirroring themselves in the blue waters of the Bospherus.*

Landing at Topkapi they made their way under the searing sun through the narrow streets, to the Hôtel d'Angleterre, commonly known as Misseri's. They were welcomed by Mr Misseri, the Greek owner, who had been forewarned of their arrival by Kinglake.[35] '*Misseris Hotel is very nice house and quite full of English comforts. When I looked round and saw myself surrounded with all the signs and appurtenances of European luxury I could not help laughing at the apprehensions of our cautious friends in England who fancied we were venturing into savage regions where we should be torn to pieces, starved to death or come to some other equally tragical end*,' wrote Ellen in triumph.

CHAPTER 13

The Crimea, So Near and Yet So Far

Having brought her party safely to Constantinople, Ellen expected that she would be able to meet up with Roger and they could spend some time together. This was not to be. Had Raglan been able to press on and attack Sevastopol immediately after the Battle of the Alma, the fighting might have been over much sooner, but he was frustrated by the French General, Marshal St Arnaud, who, though terminally ill, had vetoed the idea of any such rapid advance. This fatal mistake cost the allied armies dearly: they lost the advantage the victory at Alma had given them and with that the possibility of capturing Sevastopol while it was still relatively undefended. It was not only the French who disagreed with Raglan, but General Burgoyne of the Royal Engineers also argued that a rapid assault would result in the loss of too many lives. The allied armies had no option but to lay siege to a city which was rapidly building up its defences owing to the work of the brilliant engineer, Colonel Eduard Todleben. The whole population, only recently so vulnerable to a determined assault, started working with frenzied energy to fortify their city under the inspiring command of Admiral Kornilov, Vice-Admiral Nakhimov, the victor of Sinope and Colonel Todleben. Working with astonishing speed, they rapidly made it more difficult by the day for the allies to take Sevastopol by bombardment and assault. A long, tedious siege, the only alternative, meant the armies were tied down in the Crimea and there was certainly no hope of Roger coming to Constantinople for Christmas.

Safely installed at Misseri's Hotel with a courier to advise them, the Palmers had time to explore Constantinople and make plans. They found letters from Roger awaiting them, giving an account of his part in the Battle of the Alma. Ellen was delighted that he was so grateful to them for coming out. Having seen the condition of the sick and wounded sent from the Crimea, and noted that many of them were dying of pure neglect, she was even more convinced she had been right to insist on coming because they could at least care for him if necessary.

> *The very chance of being of such use to him, indeed the actual comfort he experiences in thinking we are so near is worth all the toil and trouble of our joining him ten times over; and as I have said before I can never feel thankful enough that my obstinacy prevailed and that I was the means of bringing the party here. Even Aunt Mary now rejoices that we have come.*

Apart from the annoyance at having to breakfast at the public table, '*a very great nuisance*', Ellen was enchanted by the novel sights and sounds of the city and wrote enthusiastically of the view from the Galata Bridge.

> *It stands in the midst of a forest of little caiques darting about on the sparkling waves, Constantinople arising on either side, terrace upon terrace, in all its loveliness, places of snowy whiteness overhanging the dark blue waters of the Bosphorus, earth, air and sky all radiant with sunshine. It is a picture which words cannot paint and no imagination can conceive. The streets are crowded with figures of every nation and costume, the solemn old Moslem in his turban and flowing trousers, the smart dandy Turk of modern times with his European clothes and scarlet fez, Greeks in their picturesque national habiliments, Jews, Armenians, priests, dervishes all in different getups and all looking very sinister and very dirty Bashi Bazouks[1] looking very ferocious, veiled Turkish women shuffling about in the concealing mantles and odious*

> *yellow boots [...] it was all so new and strange. I had to pinch myself to make sure I was awake.*[2]

The nearest comparison Ellen could make was in terms of the theatre; it reminded her of a ballet at the opera or a scene at the carnival. She likened the gilded arabas that jogged along to Cinderella's coach in a stage production, only now they were filled with veiled women attended by guards on their way to take the air. The streets were so tortuous, rough and ill-paved that the only way to get about was on foot. While fighting their way onwards, they were jostled out of the way by a '*fierce multitude of half-dressed men bearing aloft a curious instrument very much resembling a magnified squirt and tearing past with awful yells*'. These were firefighters on their way to put out a blaze near the Galata Bridge; it destroyed 700 of the wretched wooden houses that made up almost the whole city.

The visit to the Bazaar was a disappointment. The party was tired and hot when they returned to the hotel, where they were given a list of the killed and wounded at Alma and discovered that both Lady Wynn and Mrs Yorke of Erdigg had lost relations, which re-awakened all Ellen's anxieties about Roger. After dinner at six there was nothing to do: '*the evenings are very dull and we sleep, read and pass time away as best we can after returning to our rooms after dinner*'. It was necessary for the party to find somewhere permanent to stay and they sailed off next morning to Buyukderch on the Bosphorus and inspected the hotel there, Ellen in raptures about the beautiful scenery. She knew that Therapia across the bay from Buyukderch was the fashionable place *par excellence*, where most embassies had their summer residences. She sailed across and hoped to reserve rooms in the Hôtel d'Angleterre, but was much put out to find there were no apartments available.

The next few days were spent exploring rather than sightseeing – no visits to the great mosque of Hagia Sophia or the Blue Mosque, but a visit to Scutari by caique and then by carriage to Chalcedon overlooking the Sea of Marmara, finishing with a visit to the Convent of the Howling Dervishes. One day they lined up to watch the ceremonial progress of Sultan Abdulmecid on his way to pray at the mosque. After a procession of minor dignitaries, the Sultan came riding by slowly in the midst of the Imperial Guard. Although it was sad and melancholy, Ellen found his countenance inexpressibly interesting, only to discover later on the interesting melancholy look was caused by drink. Despite this handicap, his face pleased Ellen more than any she had seen before, which is saying quite something as she had had her pick of handsome young men in the ballrooms of London and Paris.

> *He was dressed in European style but with a fez on his head and a long cloak almost concealing his whole person. His saddle cloth was a scarlet cloth magnificently embroidered in gold and diamonds, and the collar of his coat was perfectly dazzling as the jewel flashed in the sunlight. We watched his exit from the mosque when the surrounding spectators cheered and the nearest made a motion of prostrating themselves on the ground.*[3]

This was the man who, giving in to pressure from his religious leaders, had declared war on Russia and precipitated the Crimean conflict.

A walk of nearly five miles along the banks of the Golden Horn brought them to the Valley of Sweet Waters, a pretty, sunny spot where the Sultan had his summer palace and Turkish ladies congregated under the trees and ate sweetmeats and gossiped, but unfortunately on this occasion it was too late for there to be much company, so the party consoled themselves by walking about and eating kebabs before returning to the hotel. The next day, under the aegis of Mrs Cumberbatch, the wife of the British Consul, the party went again to the Bazaar. Ellen somewhat changed her opinion of the merchants and their offerings; among the many curiosities she noticed a silver hand mirror which, after haggling in the required manner, she bought. That evening for the first time she and Aunt Mary dined out, transported by sedan to the Cumberbatches' residence. Ellen wore a green silk dress with white cambric body. Mr James, secretary to Admiral Boxer,[4] was of the party, as was Mr Doria, one of the attachés at the British Embassy, who was much impressed by Ellen. She was very gratified to find that all the company were amazed at the Palmers' courage in travelling via Silistria and Varna, and could hardly believe their ears when they recounted their adventures.

The following day, 24 October, Mr Doria came to call and told Ellen that there was no particular news from the Crimea, and that the siege was progressing steadily.

> *There are wondrous reports relative to it put about every day and people fix definitive dates for the final capture of Sevastopol according to their several ideas upon the subject. All these stories are very harassing for me and indeed I have not one moment's peace on Doddy's account. However as cavalry have really little to do in a siege, I hope and trust he is relatively safe.*

This was written the day before the battle of Balaclava and the infamous Charge of the Light Brigade.

Although they found letters and newspapers from England awaiting them on their return to the hotel, there was nothing from Roger. Mr Kinglake had written expressing great sorrow at having to miss them. There was no way he could get his account of the Battle of the Alma to England other than taking it himself, so he was on his way home. Ellen had written to Roger twice. It is possible that he didn't reply because she may again have been pressing him to leave the army. Several officers had handed in their commissions and returned home, seeing no prospect of action in the near future, only the weariness of siege life. Ellen had held high hopes of being able to persuade Roger to resign and return to England; indeed, it was the underlying reason for the whole voyage. However, it seems that Roger, although grateful for the support of his family, resented Ellen's continual urging him to leave the army, particularly as military life clearly suited him.

On 25 October, Ellen and her party, having dismissed their courier and settled their accounts, sailed down the Bosphorus to Buyukderch, a small village on the European side of the Bosphorus, one of the most beautiful neighbourhoods of Istanbul, to take up residence in the only hotel available. They had the hotel to themselves and, despite the owner's absence, were well looked after by his wife and given a good supper.

That same day, Mrs Duberly went without breakfast, summoned by her husband to 'lose no time, but come up as quickly as you can, do not wait for breakfast'. Although feeling unwell, Mrs Duberly mounted her horse and rode out of Balaclava through the narrow streets, now crowded by throngs of fleeing Turks who had bravely held off the Russians for two hours until forced to abandon the three batteries they were holding. Fanny's first port of call was the camp, where she superintended the striking of their tent and the packing of their valuables to prevent them being seized by the Russians. Then she met up with Henry to watch the battle out of range of the bullets from the safety of a vineyard. She describes how the Scots Greys and the Inniskillins stood like rocks as the Russian cavalry came charging down, only to be felled with one terrific volley when they were about 30 yards off.

When it comes to describing the 'glorious and fatal' charge, Mrs Duberly was so sick at heart that she could barely write of it, even later on: 'I only know that I saw Captain Nolan galloping, that presently the Light Brigade leaving their position, advanced by themselves, although in the face of the whole Russian force, and under fire that seemed pouring from all sides, as though every bush was a musket and every stone in the hillside a gun. Faster and faster they rode. How we watched them! They are out of sight, but presently come a few horsemen, straggling, galloping back [...] see they form up together again. Good God! It is the Light Brigade.'[5] Fanny's description in short staccato sentences vividly reflects the horror of the occasion.

Cardigan did not lack courage and rode at the head of the Light Brigade, but having reached the guns he seems to have considered he had done his duty, turned and galloped back, leaving some of the brigade who had galloped past the guns to fend for themselves. Colonel Douglas, leading the 11th Hussars, pursued the Russian cavalry beyond their guns until he suddenly discovered himself facing a formidable mass of Russian cavalry in position. He halted his men and gave the order to retire. Believing the two squadrons of Lancers in his rear were the 17th, he was aiming to rally with them. Roger Palmer, who obviously had better eyesight than his Colonel, rode up and said, 'I beg your pardon Colonel, that is not the 17th, it is the enemy'.[6] So, together, the remaining men of the 11th Hussars and the 4th Light Dragoons charged the Russians and got through with few casualties.

But Roger was not yet out of danger. Private Jowell, cantering on his way back, saw a Russian cavalry man raise his carbine to shoot Roger from behind, rode up and clove the man's skull to his chin.[7] Two days previously, Roger had found Jowell asleep on sentry duty and had let him off with a caution instead of reporting him for this lapse. So, when told of his deliverance by his fellow officer Lieutenant Dunn, Roger remarked that Jowell might not have been so inclined had he been flogged for his misdemeanour. Dunn himself won the VC for conspicuous bravery, saving the lives of Sergeant Bentley and Private Levett[8] during the retreat, the first Canadian to be so honoured.[9] Although the loss of life was considerable, it was the very large number of horses either killed outright or that had to be destroyed later that fatally undermined the fighting capacity of the 11th Hussars. Much has subsequently been written about the reasons for the charge: the confusion as to the meaning of the orders from Raglan to Lucan; the misunderstanding over which guns were to be retaken; the seeming foolish impetuosity of Captain Nolan; the desire of the men for action; and the embittered relationship between Cardigan and Lucan which inhibited any further rational discussion of the order. Nolan's part, both as messenger and in his fatal attempt to redirect the Light Brigade, has been the subject of much controversy.

Recent work in the archives has shown that Nolan came down from the Sapoune Ridge via the Col well before 10 a.m. with a first verbal order from Airey to 'retake' the British guns captured by the Russians. Lucan and Cardigan jointly refused to obey this order and Nolan went back up via the Col (possibly with a view to reporting that non-compliance to the Adjutant General) and met Higginson on the way. At about 11 a.m., after a discussion with Raglan and Airey, Nolan set off with a second verbal order. He was called back by Airey and handed the fourth order that he had written in haste in Raglan's presence. It invoked Raglan's authority as Commander-in-Chief precisely because of the failure of the verbal orders to produce action.

Nolan reportedly offered to join the cavalry advance as a guide and may have been specifically authorised and instructed to do so. He rode down the face of the Sapoune Ridge and met Lucan on a small hillock between Redoubts 4 and 5, possibly near the present location of the

British Balaclava monument. Nolan delivered the written fourth order to Lucan – apparently without clarifying the objective. He then moved before the 13th Light Dragoons and later joined Captain Morris in front of the 17th Lancers. Cardigan designated their right front squadron as the 'squadron of direction'. As the Light Brigade moved off at a steady 'Walk March', Nolan crossed at speed diagonally in front of Cardigan shouting and with his sword at 'Right Engage' (equivalent to an order) – pointing to the causeway heights. At the front of the 13th Light Dragoons he was hit by a shell fragment which smashed his chest open. His horse turned and carried him back through the squadron interval of the 13th Light Dragoons before his body fell to the ground.

Compelling evidence exists that Nolan did try to divert (not lead or command) the Light Brigade after it moved off without changing front towards the Causeway Heights. Given the immediacy of the Commander-in-Chief's demand, it appears that Nolan did not read the fourth order and that he assumed it was explicit. In fact it ordered 'an advance' rather than 'a charge', did not identify the target guns and did not suggest or require that the cavalry should change front before or while advancing. Neither Lucan nor Nolan realised that there was a misunderstanding and they did not confer. Beyond doubt, Lucan and Cardigan then took it that the direction of advance was literally 'to the front' as their brigades were then disposed, due east down the North Valley. Nolan broke ranks, wholly contrary to Queen's Regulations, and in an act of courageous desperation tried, in vain, to remedy a gross error. That single act, outrageous on the face of it, was enough for many to brand Nolan as a hothead or worse and to level heavy and persistent accusations against him. Raglan bears the ultimate responsibility for the fourth order to the cavalry, but Airey, Lucan and Nolan all compounded this disastrous error.[10]

Ellen was still blissfully unaware that her brother had nearly lost his life, or that on the following day what became known as the Battle of Little Inkerman was taking place. Colonel De Lacy Evans, whose 2nd Division was heavily outnumbered, successfully fought off 5,000 Russian troops whose aim had been to dislodge them from their outpost on Telegraph Hill. This skirmish was a dress rehearsal for the later Russian offensive. Meanwhile, Ellen was glorying in the beauties of Buyukderch and the pleasure of an invitation from the British Ambassadress, Lady Stratford de Radcliffe.

> *At night the effect of the whole is truly magical and I am never tired of sitting at the open window watching the noble ships riding at anchor and the calm waters of the Bosphorus sleeping peacefully in the moonlight, and then the plash of oars and the voices of Greek sailors singing in chorus add a new charm to the romance of the scene. The celebrated quay of Buyeckderch is a long promenade running along the edge of the water and commands the whole of the delicious view. We walked there for some time this afternoon and whilst resting ourselves on a small landing space overhanging the waves who should suddenly appear but Lady Stratford de Radcliffe.*[11]

Ellen was gratified to be immediately recognised and to find that the Ambassadress was on her way to call on them and to ask them to dine tomorrow. Tiresomely for them, they were unable to accept because they were due to meet up with the Cumberbatches at the Sweet Waters of Asia, an expedition which nearly ended in disaster.

They had hired a leaky boat and the boatman took them across to Therapia to leave cards at the embassy, but instead of taking them to the real Sweet Waters,[12] owing to a ridiculous misunderstanding they were landed further along the shore and made to walk for an hour until they came to a straggling, dirty village. '*We kept wondering where the Sweet Waters were to be found, when our perplexities were suddenly put an end to by being marched up to the town pump and told by our guide that none of the water about there was particularly good but that was the sweetest to be found in the neighbourhood!*' To add to their frustration, the boatman refused to go on as the boat had to be repaired. While they were waiting, '*all the dignitaries of the village came to stare at us and we were conducted in state to a dingy café where we spent two hours lamenting our misfortune and drinking dirty Roseglio which was brought out by a ferocious looking Turk who stood by, sword in hand to "see us take it".*' Not only did they miss their rendezvous with the Cumberbatches, they had also missed the embassy dinner.

The weather changed; it became gloomy and dismal, and the rain fell in torrents. As the Palmers watched the ships coming from the Black Sea without calling in, they felt an increasing sense of isolation, cut off from communication with the world. On Sunday the 29th, they had the first news of an engagement in the Crimea and Ellen and her father, accompanied by Bevan, set off to the British Embassy in Therapia to make enquiries. They discovered to their relief that Roger's name was not on the list of killed or wounded. Even though Roger was safe for the time being, Ellen wrote that '*I never see a stranger approach, nor receive an unexpected letter without a sickening shudder lest they bring evil tidings, nay I cannot even hear a whispered sentence without fearing that it may be the herald of misfortune.*' The beautiful scenery was no longer any comfort:

The locality does not console us, for though we are on the banks of the blue Bosphorus, it is hard to be romantic in a mackintosh and a pair of India rubber clogs. It rained furiously all day, not in drops as it does in England or in any other civilised country but in regular pailfuls as if the Heavens were emptying themselves out upon this nether world.

To make a wretched situation worse, the rain turned Ellen's room into a swamp and she had to share with Aunt Mary. By 3 November Ellen was writing, '*This dismal weather and our complete isolation from the rest of the world are really enough to make one melancholy mad.*' Their only distraction was to play billiards, and on that particular day Sir Roger was so cross they did not even do that. Ellen spent a lot of time writing, both her diary and letters to friends.

The next day at last brought a letter from Roger giving his account of the charge. Ellen copied his account into her diary: '*It was a fearful thing for the cavalry, they had to charge uphill at an enemy more than a mile off, and in numbers perfectly overwhelming. The order was a <u>most insane</u> one and everyone united in saying that it is a miracle one man escaped alive.*' Ellen continued his account:

Roger's regiment went into action 130 strong and lost 55 men killed and wounded (60 were lost I afterwards discovered). Mr Huyton, Mr

> *Trevelyan and Captain Cook were wounded and now there are actually only 3 officers left with the regiment, Col. Douglas, Mr. Dunn and Roger. Dear Doddy's life was saved by a man,*[13] *whom he had got out of a scrape two days before, who cut down a Russian who was taking deliberate aim about 2 yards off.*

Ellen knew of the fatal charge of the Light Brigade a week before the British public were even aware that the siege of Sevastopol was not proceeding according to plan or that anything was amiss. That news only reached London when Delane,[14] editor of *The Times*, reported on 11 November, 'We have received a telegraphic despatch from our correspondent which proves that the loss sustained by the allies in the encounter of 25th October on the heights above Balaclava was more serious than recent reports have lead us to believe.' William Russell's[15] full letter arrived two days later and the nation was shocked by the revelations it contained. Russell continued to send eyewitness accounts of the harsh conditions under which the British Army was living in the Crimea, alerting the nation to the mismanagement of the war, all of which were printed in *The Times* and led to the resignation of Lord Aberdeen and his government.

In a later account of the charge, at a banquet given to honour him at Wrexham in October 1855, Roger had nothing but praise for the men:

> Nothing but the coolness of the men saved the whole regiment from being destroyed, for although the ranks were awfully thinned, still the men kept their formation, and the Russians seeing this did not charge, as they might have done, but which if they had he would not be here to tell the tale. The conduct of the men was beyond all praise – there were officers in other armies who might have led such an attack, but where were the men to be found who would have followed them? Not a man of them faltered for a moment, and they obeyed their officers as coolly as if they had been on parade.[16]

In the meantime, the weather had put a stop to all social intercourse. Ellen, though, learning that Mrs Creswell was in Constantinople, went in search of her and found her on board the *Cambria*. They had a great deal to talk about and Mrs Creswell could give Ellen a first-hand account of hardships the troops had suffered, and told her how well Doddy had behaved through it all. She was invited to stay with the Palmers for a few days in Buyudkerch and arrived the following day. The Palmers began to hear rumours of another battle in the Crimea, which threw Ellen into a frenzy of anxiety. The next day they all went to Constantinople and at Stamper's shop were told by a gentleman the dreadful details of the slaughter at the Battle of Inkerman. As Ellen hurried down to Mr Grace's to look at the lists, the gentleman who had told her the news hurried after her lest the news was bad. They took her to an upper room to read the list.

> *The numbers killed and wounded is frightful, indeed several regiments have lost more than they did at Waterloo. Many friends of ours are on the fatal list, many poor souls whom we know are made widows and orphans. Generals Cathcart and Strangeways are killed, poor Capt. Pakenham has gone too. It makes one's heart bleed to think of the anguish which is in store for so many and oh! How dreadful too is the idea that our only hope and joy and pride hangs on such a thread. God preserve dear dear Roger is my ceaseless prayer.*[17]

The Battle of Inkerman was fought in dense fog, and to begin with this helped the Russians to advance unseen. It also helped the British who were outnumbered by more than six to one, by hiding the weakness of their defences from the Russians. General Paget left an account of the part played by the 11th Hussars in the battle, which amounted to very little. They were mounted and called into the line and took 20 casualties before they were ordered to retire beyond range of fire. General Paget declared it was because Cardigan did not arrive on the field of battle until 12 noon that no mention was made of the small part they played, since had it been included it would have shown up the late arrival of their commanding officer.[18] Although the Russian troops had the overwhelming advantage in terms of numbers, owing to lack of a proper command structure the Russians were heavily defeated, losing 12,000 men on the battlefield of

Inkerman in the space of four hours. British casualties amounted to 2,610 and French 1,726, all killed in the same amount of time.

The Russians had failed to dislodge the allies from the heights around Sevastopol, but it availed them little. General Canrobert, with Raglan's agreement, insisted there could be no question of an assault on Sevastopol until the spring. The decision to keep the army on the heights with little shelter from the bitter cold filled many with foreboding. In the two months after the Battle of Inkerman, with only a long, cold winter to look forward to, 225 British officers are recorded as leaving the Crimea.[19] The fact that so many officers were leaving, some known to Ellen, encouraged her to hope that Roger might be persuaded to follow their example. She felt it more than ever necessary to somehow get to see Roger and talk to him face to face.

By mid-December, Ellen was beginning to despair. '*It is a bitter disappointment not to have seen him before this, and now alas they talk of the troops hutting*[20] *themselves and remaining all the winter before Sevastopol […] it will be a cruel disappointment if dear Doddy does not come back here for the winter as it was always said they would do.*' Indeed, the family's whole expedition to the Crimea had been predicated on the expectation that Doddy would be with them over the winter, and Ellen found the present situation hard to bear. '*I cannot bring myself to believe that such will be the case, as it would be too much after all our hopes and expectations and our long, long journey from the other side of Europe.*' All she could do was to pack a box with food and clothing that she thought her brother might need, and send it with a long letter via the offices of Mrs Cumberbatch.

Added to Ellen's frustrations was the sadness that her brother did not write. She notes, '*We were much disappointed not to hear from Doddy as the mail came in yesterday from the Crimea and it is a long time since he wrote.*' Matters must have been made worse for Ellen because when her brother did write, the letter was addressed to her father's doctor, Mr Roberts. She makes no comment, but it must have been hurtful. The reason for Roger's unkind behaviour can be guessed at and perhaps the only way he felt able to counter his forceful sister's continued pressure on him to leave the army was to cease writing to her. More than a week later there still had been no letter from Roger. '*No letter from Doddy as I had hoped and expected, we must go and see him for ourselves.*' Ellen had now made up her mind. She would find a way to go to the Crimea to see Roger, if Roger either could not or would not come to them and failed even to write. A letter came at last to thank her for the box of provisions and to say how welcome it was, and that Ellen could not have done better in her choice of articles she sent.

The weather improved, Mrs Cumberbatch invited the Palmers to stay with her at the British Consulate in Pera for a few days, and Ellen had now a definite object in view. This all made for a welcome change. On their way to Misseri's before going to the Cumberbatches they met with Col. Creach, who had just returned from the Crimea and had seen Roger five days ago. From him they learned that Roger had been in command of the regiment as '*everyone of the officers except himself had been knocked up. Col. Douglas told Col. Creach that he was "an excellent officer and a very clever fellow". He rallied the 11th at Balaclava and did his duty like a man.*' They also learned of the death of their cousin Lionel Mackinnon. He had been shot in the thigh at Inkerman and did not survive the loss of his leg. '*Poor fellow, the news choked us sadly for we have known him so long and so well. Would to God this terrible war were over for every day brings forth some fresh tale of sorrow and look where one will there are scenes of distress, lamentations for the past and apprehensions for the future.*'[21]

The Cumberbatches gave a dinner party to entertain the Palmers and to Ellen's delight she discovered that the young French attaché, Mr Doria, was as passionately fond of music as she was. He was asked again the following evening and Ellen accompanied him on the piano, and appreciated his fine tenor voice. She then sang some of her old favourites, including 'Come e bello', and recorded with her usual pleasure the surprise and delight of the audience. On the first occasion she wore a pink dress trimmed with black with a plait round her head, and on the second a black dress and shawl. Whittaker, the lady's maid, must have accompanied them, packing and dressing Aunt Mary and Ellen, but though she must have been vital to Ellen, she is seldom referred to in the diary.

A visit to the military hospital in Scutari had been planned for the first day, but owing to bad weather had been postponed. Despite Mr

Cumberbatch imploring them not to go as the wind was still very high and it would be extremely dangerous, Mrs Cumberbatch would not be put off a second time:

> *We embarked in a two oared caique of the smallest and frailest description. When we rounded the Seraglio point we saw at once the danger that was before us, the waves were rolling mountainous high and our tiny skiff was tossed like a feather on their foaming crest. The boatmen showed wonderful skill for they watched the advance of each wave and manoeuvred the caique so as to cause us to catch it in the most favourable point [...] It was the most frightful thing I ever saw [...] We were nearly carried a mile into the sea of Marmara before we could turn round and when we did manage to stem the current, the risk we ran was still greater than before. We now had to cross the waves sideways instead of topping them and the billows threatened every instant to engulf our tiny barque. When we arrived at Scutari we were met by a naval captain who lifted up his hands and eyes at our escape and told us for what it was worth in the world he would not have run such a risk.*[22]

They had very little time for the visit to the hospital and visited only one ward, where Ellen reported the men seemed comfortable enough lying in little bedsteads in a row and were mostly engaged in reading books or newspapers. This is very different from the description given by the Rev. Sydney Osborne who had visited Scutari just after the arrival of Florence Nightingale. Walking down one of the long corridors thickly lined with cases of cholera and dysentery, he found himself entering a 'vast field of suffering and misery in which men lay either on the floor on this stuffed sacking or on rotten wooden divans at the side, alive with vermin and every unimaginable kind of filth'.[23] The reports in *The Times* of conditions in Scutari had brought a stream of visitors, some of whose eyewitness accounts were as damning as that of Osborne, but others reported more favourably on the conditions they found in the hospital. Ellen's rosy view may not have been entirely without foundation, but as they had so little time it is probable that they did not see the more severely wounded men. Considering the number of visitors that Florence Nightingale had to cope with, it is perhaps not surprising that the Palmer/Cumberbatch meeting with her was not a success. Ellen was already prejudiced against the idea of '*amateurs*', and called the nurses coming out to help, instead of a regular staff of hospital nurses and matrons who had been used to the business all their lives, an '*absurd idea*'. As for Florence Nightingale herself, the verdict was harsh and damning: '*She is a plain repulsive looking person with an exceeding disagreeable manner.*' Florence Nightingale had been at Scutari just under a month, and besides the many visitors, she had to deal with a mass of official business as well as overseeing the running of the hospital, so she may well have found two unimportant ladies taking up her precious time an unwelcome distraction. In terms of family background and social standing, the Nightingales were not dissimilar to the Palmers, but Ellen was obviously shocked that someone of her position in society should defy the social norms of the day to take on superintending a military hospital. Part of Ellen's adverse reaction to Florence Nightingale was obviously because Florence offended her sense of propriety, but there could also have been jealousy at her ability to successfully flout social norms and be praised for doing so. Ellen often lamented the fact that as a woman so many openings were closed to her, when she knew she had the ability to do so much more – yet here was a woman who had made her way in a man's world. Ellen's diary record of their meeting was an emotional over-reaction to a situation which did not fit in with a view of the world she may not have liked, but had accepted.

Ellen now had a new objective – to get herself and her family to the Crimea. In early December they had the good fortune to meet with Captain Fox, the captain of the *War Cloud*, while walking on the quay at Buyudkerch. Ellen plied him with questions as to the possibility of their going to the Crimea and to her delight he seemed to think that it was perfectly feasible. Ellen spent a lot of her time writing letters: she was gratified to read of her old friend Lady Harrington's delight at the account she had written of her journey to Varna, and busied herself writing a long letter to Mr Kinglake who had been so helpful to her. Her piano had come, the weather was lovely, and she was looking forward to having Mr Inglis to stay. John Inglis was a brother officer of Roger's who must have been on sick leave as he was to return to England in January for health reasons.

Ellen now thought the time had come to sound out her father about an expedition to the Crimea, but dreaded broaching the subject with Aunt Mary and felt unable to consult with Mr Roberts '*as he was in one of his sulky fits*'.[24] It was not difficult to gain her father's consent. The matter had become even more urgent as a belated letter from Roger had arrived with the news that he had no wish to leave the army. She reported that '*he cannot do so at present, but this I scarcely believe. It is really necessary for me to see him and speak of his future plans*'. Roger, too, thought that the time had come for a bit of plain speaking and wanted Ellen to come to Balaclava. He had an additional reason for wanting to see her. He not only wanted to remain in the army but to exchange his regiment for the Life Guards. This would be expensive and he would need her support to obtain the necessary finance from their father for such a move. Ellen, aware that although she had the consent of her father and aunt to go to the Crimea, it was she who would have to make all the arrangements. '*I am obliged to depend entirely upon myself, but I conceived the idea and I will bend all my energies to carrying it out.*'

The first step was to consult with the Cumberbatches, and Mr Roberts was dispatched to Constantinople to seek their advice. An immediate invitation came by return for them to come and meet with Captain Drummond of the *Retribution* who might be able to help. The streets of Constantinople were so filthy that when they arrived at the Cumberbatches', they first had to retire to their rooms to clean themselves before spending the afternoon chatting. At dinner that night their Crimean expedition was considered with wonderment and incredulity. Captain Drummond tried to dissuade them from going, but he did helpfully tell Ellen that her only hope of a passage was to gain the consent of Admiral Boxer.[25] Ellen did not enjoy the dinner party, commenting that Lord and Lady Napier, Colonel Cadogan, Captain Drummond and Mr Doria '*all knew one another very well, whilst we were strangers to the greater part of them*'. A socially handicapped father and a dull maiden aunt must have made an awkward addition to a party so at ease with one another.

However, she was determined not to be put off by the lack of encouragement from Captain Drummond and decided her only option was to '*not be discouraged, to take the bull by the horns and go boldly up to the Admiral at once*'. Rear-Admiral Boxer was in charge of all the transport ships for men and supplies, and reported directly to the Admiralty rather than to Raglan, the Commander-in-Chief. This led to continued complaints and disputes, as the Admiral was incapable of organising the necessary complicated rota and was blamed for the resulting chaos and disorganisation. In Mrs Duberly's opinion, he was '*a noisy, vulgar, swearing old ruffian and a man very easily swayed*'. Whether Ellen knew this or not, she meant to try to win him over using her feminine charms, writing: '*coaxing and charming often do wonders and I even succeeded in melting Lord Cardigan's obdurate heart on one occasion.*'[25] So, on 16 December, Ellen sallied forth with Aunt Mary to see if her powers of persuasion would suffice to get the agreement of the Admiral. His secretary, Mr James, assured them it was totally impossible to obtain a passage to the Crimea, that Ellen's only chance was to stay and plead her cause herself, as the Admiral was more susceptible to ladies. This was a hopeful sign. After a long wait, they were granted an interview. The Admiral received them politely and smilingly, and said, '*so this is the young lady who wants to go to the Crimea*'. He, too, tried to dissuade them from the enterprise. Ellen gives a graphic account of the interview:

> *He said that he was not even allowed to grant passages to ladies. Our cause seemed desperate but I was determined to try my eloquence so told the Admiral that we had come all across Europe to see my brother and that if he were so hard hearted as to refuse our request we should be obliged to return home disappointed in our hope.*

The plea, put in this form, was more than the Admiral could resist. He ended by telling her that she had only to let him know the day they wanted to go and he would manage it for them. Ellen commented rather smugly that '*when I try the effect of a little personal persuasion and coaxing I never fail*'.

When they returned in triumph they found Captain Drummond, who, despite his seeming unwillingness to help them, had succumbed to

Ellen's charms and brought with him Captain Derriman, the commander of the *Caradoc*, earlier used by Raglan as his flag ship, but now used to transport mail and supplies between Balaclava and Constantinople. To Ellen's delight he offered to take them to the Crimea the following week. Ellen wrote: '*I feel as if I were treading on air*'. With barely a week to go before Christmas they were plunged into a flurry of activity, making plum puddings, plum cakes, potted meat and anything they could think of to take with them. Ellen began ordering stores, not only for themselves and Roger, but as presents for friends in need. '*It required a great deal of exertion and management to make out lists of all the things that were required, give orders for them, settle the prices and see that they were properly packed.*' Indeed, Ellen seems to have thought of everything, for her list included:

> *4½ sheep, a whole bullock, 16 chickens, 4 turkeys, 40 loaves, 2 hams, 3 plum cakes, 6 doz. Mince pies, onions, preserves, 2 large jars of potted meat, 3 boxes of biscuits, a pot of butter, 6 lbs. salt, a loaf of sugar, box of sweetmeats, 20 lbs apples, 4 lbs tea, 8 packets of candles, a bottle of cayenne, cigars, tobacco, 3 drums of figs, 4 tongues, oranges, a bottle of brandy, 2 doz. sherry, 4 doz. beer, 1½ doz. of porter and a doz. champagne.*

By Tuesday they were packed and a note came from Captain Derriman telling them to be ready to embark the next day for a sudden departure. They left Buyudkerch the following day and, taking two caiques from the Galata Bridge, went straight on board the *Caradoc*. Captain Derriman received them very kindly and they were given a '*charming home on deck for a sitting room and two cabins down below which are most comfortable sleeping quarters. We have our own provisions on board and captain's servants make us very comfortable. The ship's boat is also at our command.*' Ellen made use of it to do some last-minute shopping at Stamper's, the local general store, and to pay a farewell visit to Mrs Cumberbatch.

Ellen's pleasure was somewhat diminished by a disagreeable incident she had to deal with. A certain Mrs Lister, accompanied by two officers, came to try to persuade her to allow this lady to join their party.

There are no more details as to who this lady was, but Ellen had been forewarned about her by Captain Derriman and refused. '*It was a very disagreeable thing to do however, and I was exceedingly glad when the interview was over.*' They did not see much of Captain Derriman that day as he was ashore most of the time. The next day they had a much more interesting visitor.

> *Lord Cardigan came on board and, finding we were here, came to our cabin and sat with us a long time, telling us about the campaign, past, present and to come. He assured us (unasked) that Roger had done his duty thoroughly well, and had displayed so much zeal, ardour and ability that he had complimented him personally upon it. This from a general officer to a cornet was indeed gratifying, and I cannot say how delighted we were to have such an account of our dear boy.*

Cardigan had been before a medical board earlier in the month which had decreed that he was 'much reduced in strength' and that owing to 'the serious character of his complaints he should be allowed to proceed to England for the recovery of his strength'.[26] However, instead of leaving for home, he decided to spend a few weeks in Constantinople recovering and that is how he came to meet the Palmers.

It was not until some time after Cardigan's eventual return to England, where he enjoyed playing the role of hero, that doubts began to circulate publicly about the truth of his account of the charge and his part in the drama. In his account, no mention was made as to why, on reaching the guns, instead of attempting to rally the men he had turned round and galloped back. Among the many witnesses and accounts of Cardigan's strange behaviour, a letter from General Paget in the *Morning Post* in June 1856 was the most damaging. Paget claimed truthfully to have rallied the 4th Light Dragoons and the 11th Hussars from behind the Russian guns and, charging through the Russians, led them to safety. Col. Douglas, only insisting that the 11th Hussars were under his command rather than under Paget's, confirmed Paget's account. This undermined the credibility of Cardigan's story of his own actions. It was his duty as

General of the Brigade to have overseen the withdrawal of his men, and if Paget and Douglas were correct, it was a duty he failed to perform. But this controversy was all in the future. Ellen, meeting him just before his return to England, would have known nothing of Cardigan's lapse. To her he was simply Roger's commanding officer. Roger himself, who must have known the truth of the accusation, is not known to have made any comment on the controversy.

The *Caradoc* was waiting for dispatches from France to take to Balaclava. Already on board were 400 of Soyer's famous patent stoves, so practical and efficient that they were not replaced by the Army until the Falklands War. Though the Palmers were very comfortable on board and soon got used to ship life and being called to meals by the sound of bells, as well as making the acquaintance of the sailors' pet bear, Ellen felt immensely frustrated by the delayed departure. She had set her heart on spending Christmas with her brother. Busy as he was, Derriman tried to spend as much time with the Palmers as he could; beautiful young girls were a rarity in that part of the world. Ellen discovered that he was quite well aware of who she was, having given up his seat to her on the steamer to Buyudkerch on one occasion; she thought him a very agreeable man.

The dispatches arrived at last and they set sail on Christmas Eve. Ellen wrote, '*Oh dear, oh dear, how sick I shall be before I open this book again.*' She was very prone to seasickness, but on this occasion she was spared and enjoyed the voyage. The entry must have been written in the expectation that she would continue to write. But, after describing Christmas Day on board, she ceased to write up her diary and the only record of her time in the Crimea is the notes that she kept in a little journal. Her penultimate diary entry reads, '*the vessel pitched and tossed a great deal and our party grew small by degrees and beautifully less, until at length only Papa and myself and the Captain remained upstairs and we remained chatting very pleasantly all evening and Captain Derriman made himself very pleasant.*' Ellen was evidently enjoying herself, glad not to have the disapproving Aunt Mary watching the growing intimacy between herself and the captain. The evident admiration of the gallant captain, who was only too pleased to be able to give her his arm as she walked on the deck during the afternoon, was gratifying. Her regret at not being with Roger over Christmas seems to have receded.

Her final entry reads:

> *We dined at 6 and a very merry time we spent, indeed I never had a jollier Christmas dinner in my life than the one we spent thousands of miles from home, tossing about on the Black Sea. It was the first entire day I ever spent on a voyage and it seemed quite curious to be from morning to night without catching a glimpse of land; nothing but sea, sea, sea in every direction.*

Then as far as her blue cloth-covered diary, the last volume of the locked diaries, is concerned, only blank white pages and silence are left.

CHAPTER 14

Balaclava

Ellen continued to make notes in her journal, a small, blue leather book. They were never transposed to the diary. Sharing a cabin with Aunt Mary meant there was little privacy, and Ellen may have meant to write up her notes back in Constantinople. But once there she found herself involved in a situation that she did not wish to share, even with the beloved diary, and it is only known by a fortunate accident. Her account of her time in Balaclava is taken from the notes in her small, blue notebook.

After a cheerful Christmas on board the *Caradoc*, Ellen recorded,

> *We were awakened this morning at 7 o'clock by the news that we were just off Cheronese point and soon afterwards we anchored close by Admiral Lyons' ship, the 'Agemmenon', and immediately in front of the harbour of Sebastopol. We could distinguish the houses in the town, the entrance to the harbour and the celebrated Fort Constantine. The French lines were just before us and we could occasionally hear the report of guns and see the flash of smoke which broke the mists of the morning.*

There was no reason for the *Caradoc* to anchor off Sevastopol so early in the morning other than for Captain Derriman to have the pleasure of giving Ellen a chance to see the town at close quarters. Very soon afterwards they sailed on past the rocky coast and the celebrated monastery, and arrived at Balaclava at 12 o'clock.

There are many accounts of the horrific state of the town and harbour. William Russell reported to *The Times* that a week after the arrival of the troops Balaclava had become a scene of desolation. Kinglake painted an equally depressing picture. Balaclava, so dramatically situated between high, rocky cliffs, must once have presented a charming aspect, with its picturesque white houses, green-domed churches, and its trellises covered with grapes in summer clustered round the waterfront. Mrs Duberly's account, written on 3 December, gives a particularly graphic description of its present horrors:

> If anybody should ever wish to erect a model of Balaclava in England I will tell them all the ingredients necessary. Take a village of ruined houses and hovels in the most extreme stage of all imaginable dirt, allow rain to pour into and outside them until the whole place is a swarm of filth ankle deep: catch about 1,000 sick Turks with the plague and cram them into houses indiscriminately; kill also about 100 a day and bury them so as to be scarcely covered with earth, leaving them to rot at leisure, taking care to keep up the supply; on one part of the beach drive all the exhausted ponies and bullocks and worn out camels and leave them to die of starvation [...] collect all together from the water of the harbour all the offal of all the animals slaughtered for the use of the occupants of about 100 ships, to say nothing of the inhabitants of the town – which together with an occasional human body, whole or parts, and the driftwood of the wrecks pretty well covers the water – stew them all up together and you will have a tolerable imitation of the real essence of Balaclava.[1]

Ellen appears to have been oblivious to all the horrors as she merely records that they anchored '*in the wonderful little harbour of Balaclava*'.

While Mrs Duberly may have been striving for effect (she was intending to publish her recollections), Ellen had a great capacity not to notice what she didn't want to see and was only too happy to have reached Balaclava, thinking only that she would soon be seeing her beloved brother.

The Crimea was a very public place and the arrival of the Palmers caused quite a stir. Immediately invited to dine with Lord Raglan and offered the use of his horses, Ellen must have been gratified to receive such a welcome. A letter from Major Taylor, the Palmers' Irish neighbour, to his mother at Ardgillan Castle on 28 December gives the only description we have of the Palmers at that time. He wrote, 'To my surprise I found Sir Roger and Miss Palmer and "suite" on board the Caradoc two days since, they came to see the Hussar, as he could not go to them. The fair Ellen, I found had made up a box of creature comforts for me, which has been a most acceptable Christmas Box. It was thoughtful and good natured of her. I dine with them tomorrow [...] She paints her eyebrows (only) heavier than ever – they all desire kindest regards to Ardgillan. Sir Roger looks well and Mathews has been done a power of service by her expedition.'[2] After his dinner with the Palmers, Taylor continued his letter and described Ellen again as having corked her eyes and eyebrows and flirted with a young officer. He did not think much of young Roger's behaviour: 'His manner towards his sister when I dined with them the other day was that of a showy schoolboy.'

Although Mrs Duberly was living at this time on board the *Star of the East*, also anchored in the small crowded harbour in Balaclava, and could not have been unaware of the arrival of the Palmers, surprisingly she makes no mention of them, or of their activities. She may well have felt more than a little jealous at the preferential treatment Ellen received. Ellen, never one to cultivate female society and always anxious to preserve her social position, most probably did not consider Mrs Duberly, the wife of a mere quartermaster, worthy of notice, though they had many friends in common. The two never met, in spite of living at such close quarters. Mrs Duberly, for her part, must have decided that a dignified silence was the best way to deal with the unspoken snub. But it would have been interesting to know what she thought of Ellen.

Almost immediately, Ellen was reunited with Roger.

Dear Roger came on deck and spent the rest of the day with us. We were instantly invaded by a horde of visitors. Capt. Lindsay, Col. Conyngham, Major Taylor, Col Brownrigg, Capt Damer and many others, all looking 'seedy' to a degree. None but Roger dined with us, both the Captains spent the night on board. Nothing but sights and sounds of war on every side.

It was a rare treat to have a beautiful unattached girl in a theatre of war, and Ellen took advantage of the fact; she hugely enjoyed the social whirl occasioned by her arrival at Balaclava and entertained lavishly on board the *Caradoc*, welcoming friends both old and new. She was, though, bitterly disappointed that she failed to achieve the real purpose of the visit, to get Roger to resign from the army.

The next day,

Colonel Poulett[3] *and Mr George Foley called, the former bearing a message from Lord Raglan to invite us to see the camp and offering to send me a horse to ride. Soon after they left Lord Burghesh*[4] *came post haste direct from Headquarters on the same errand. The offer was accepted most gratefully and I am to go tomorrow. We have had invitations to every part of the camp and offers of more escorts than we could accept in a twelvemonth.*

The invitations continued to flood in. Next day Ellen rode up to the camp.

Lord Raglan sent me one of his own chargers and it carried me beautifully. Col Somerset came down also, and showed me the greater part of the camp, so I had a delightful ride. We passed the cavalry camp and then rode into the 3rd and 4th Divisions. Then we proceeded right to the front of our lines and had two excellent views of Sevastopol both from the Quarry and another place called the 'Old Fort'. We were only about a mile from the town and saw the houses in it as plain as possible. The trenches were close to us and we saw a good deal of firing going on. Dead horses were lying about in great abundance and the living animals looked miserable to a degree. At ½ past 1 I went to Lord Raglan's headquarters and lunched with him after which Lord Somerset escorted us quietly back to Balaclava.

As usual Ellen gave no details about the lunch or what she thought of Lord Raglan. This was a war setting and not a society occasion, so she did not even list who else was present or comment on the privilege accorded to her, but described her surroundings.

The country is very hilly and picturesque but the roads are ankle deep in mud. I am to have the horses sent down whenever I like, and am to be shown the rest of the camp upon some other opportunity. The roads are perfectly alive with extraordinary figures, sailors, civilians dressed in every imaginable garb, and carts, guns, dromedaries and all sorts of strange objects meet one at every step. The tents are dotted about in the country in every direction, the Cavalry and Highlanders nearest to Balaclava.

The following day, as Roger was on duty, Ellen spent it quietly with him in his tent and was very pleased when she heard that Lord Lucan had given him a week's leave from the regiment. With Roger now living on board the *Caradoc*, and as it was Sunday, they read the service as they usually did at home when they could not go to church, before going for a walk. Ellen was exhilarated by the proximity to danger and always mentions how close she was to the range of shot. '*In the afternoon we walked up the mountains to the Genoese Castle at the entrance to Balaclava, and had an excellent view of the harbour and heights occupied by the Russians which are quite within range of shot and shell.*' The family celebrated the passing of the old year quietly, but were startled at midnight when all the ships in the harbour rang their bells to usher in the New Year.

The next day the weather was so cold and wet that it prevented Ellen from taking advantage of the horses she was offered and she and her brother took a walk up on the heights overlooking the harbour, passing through the camps of the Highlanders and the Zouaves. The following day the weather was not much better.

The morning was too doubtful for our excursion to Inkerman, but we ventured out for a trip to the monastery, and after a cold bleak rainy ride across the Crimean hills we were obliged to return without having

> *attained our object. The scenery was most magnificent, but wild and savage to a degree, and we heard the cannonading going on quite close to us. Visitors in the evening.*

On 3 January, Ellen entertained Lord Lucan, his son, Lord Bingham, Captain Peel,[5] third son of Sir Robert Peel, and his cousin, Archy, son of Sir Jonathan Peel. From now on all the entries end with '*company in the evening*', although the guests' names are not always mentioned. Among those that are frequently mentioned are those of Captain Peel and his cousin – until 16 January, when there is a sudden lull. There had been visitors during the day, so Ellen wrote that they were '*alone in the evening for a wonder*'.

The freezing winter weather had now set in, making visits and meals on the *Caradoc* even more popular. The provisions the Palmers had brought with them were soon exhausted and the resourceful Ellen was now '*obliged to send forage parties on board the different ships as they came in, and this morning we succeeded in procuring a leg of mutton, a goose, a couple of fowls and some preserves*'.

The snow prevented them leaving the ship on 4 January, but the next day they went to Inkerman, just two months after the battle in which so many thousands of men had lost their lives. In all probability some of the dead Russians may not have even have been buried,[6] but as there was snow on the ground any unburied dead would not have been visible. Ellen would have been given an account of the fighting as they rode over the battlefield and, as she described the scene,

> *tho' the snow was on the ground and the cold most intense. We rode over the whole battle field, saw the hill where the Russians planted their artillery, the ground where our troops were advancing and retreating like waves of the ocean, and the celebrated Two Gun battery where the Guards fought so desperately and where the awful slaughter took place. We advanced long past the present line of our position, dismounted, and went into a redoubt on 'Shell Hill' just facing the Russian batteries and which they were firing occasionally.*

Shell Hill, of strategic importance, had been the scene of some particularly fierce fighting and had been taken by the Russians. In the chaotic conditions which had prevailed owing to the dense fog that enveloped the plain of Inkerman, the troops could scarcely tell who was friend and who was foe. When Raglan brought up two heavy 18-pounder cannon, blasting through the Russian batteries on Shell Hill, the Russians, who greatly outnumbered the British, were ordered to retreat and fled in panic, turning the battle into a massacre. Shell Hill was still under fire when Ellen visited.

> *We were warned first of all not to go in, and secondly not to stand near together, or else we should be shot at immediately. Indeed we had scarcely quitted the battery when the large 34 pounder came whizzing in behind us. We rode back through the Guards camp, past the windmill, and it froze so dreadfully hard that the horses could scarcely keep their feet, and when the sun went down it was really dreadful. However between slipping, sliding, stumbling and walking we managed to get home about ½ past 5 (nearly dark) after the very coldest ride I ever recollect. We saw numbers of horses lying about both dead and dying, it is really heartbreaking to look at the poor brutes suffering such agonies.*

Possibly because she did not actually see the men suffering in the same way, Ellen remarked without comment, '*men died in the trenches of cold last night*', followed by '*Capt. Peel and his cousin came in the evening and we played cards*'.

William Peel was a strikingly handsome young man, with dark hair, large, lustrous eyes, an aquiline nose and a generous mouth. He had already made a name for himself for bravery. He and a party of his men had been tasked with the movement of ammunition for the Allied gun batteries laying siege to Sevastopol. A Russian 42-pounder shell landed in among the powder kegs. With the fuse still burning Peel quickly picked up the shell and threw it over the parapet, where it exploded harmlessly. He was later awarded the VC for his bravery. There is no doubt that Ellen was attracted by this charismatic young officer, and he for his part was obviously intrigued by this unusual girl, beautiful, courageous and so full of energy. His less flamboyant young cousin, Archy Peel, had come out to the Crimea to be with his much-admired older cousin. It is no wonder that the Peels were frequent visitors to the *Caradoc*, ending the evening playing cards, often till one o'clock in the morning.

The following Sunday the Palmers went in a party to the cavalry camp and lunched in Roger's tent. '*Afterwards we roved about outside the harbour and saw the very spot where the transports were sunk on November 11th.*[7] *It is still freezing hard and the ground is almost too slippery to walk upon. They are beginning to build huts for the soldiers at last.*'

The dangers were not confined to the occasional shells landing at Inkerman; a far more serious cause for concern was the risk posed by the powder ships anchored in Balaclava in case of fire. Ellen's account of one such fire was brief and laconic – not that she did not understand the danger. On 9 January she wrote, '*A powder ship with 700 tons on board caught fire this morning and was very near exploding close to us, in which case every soul in the harbour would have been blown to pieces. Visitors all day. Lord F Paulet, Major Taylor, Captain Peel and his cousin dined here.*' Mrs Duberly was even nearer the action, on board the *Star of the South,* which had just taken on 1,000 tons of powder when a fire broke out in the hold. As may be imagined, her description of the action was very much more dramatic. When a sergeant asked her if the letter she was writing was finished, she replied, 'Not yet, you must wait a moment.' The sergeant's reply was, 'I cannot wait – for – the ship's on fire!'[8] Mrs Duberly was unwillingly taken off the ship and she watched the rest of the action from the shore. She wrote that she had had no thought of fear but that she was possessed of a strange exultation contemplating so magnificent a death, 'to die with hundreds in so stupendous an explosion, which not only would have destroyed every vessel in the harbour and the very town itself, but would have altered the whole shape of the bay and the echoes of which would have rung through the world!'

On 15 January a walking party was organised to visit the hut of their Irish neighbour, Major Taylor. For the first time Ellen seems aware of the plight of the troops, or at least mentions their suffering. There was no false sentimentality as she recorded,

> *the snow was deep on the ground and it had frozen over besides, so that it was like walking on glass, and we slid the whole way down the mountain. The troops are suffering terribly in this weather; the number of sick is enormous the men frequently brought in with the limbs frost bitten and sometimes they are frozen to death.*

But life went on and, as usual, the day ends with, '*and there was company in the evening*'. Two days later, after breakfast with Col. Somerset, the Peels and others, they all went out walking.

> *We walked a party to the summit of the highest mountain hereabouts to see the Rifle camp by special invitation. Major Bradford, the commandant and Captain Colville received us and showed us their residence, a very snug hut with a roof of gutta-percha*[9] *to keep out the damp. We were about 1,600 ft above the sea, so we had a splendid view over the magnificent mountain scenery, the fearfully precipitous coast, and the whole British positions, from Balaclava to the plains of the field of Inkerman. We also saw some Cossacks in the valley and Russian pickets on the hills. The snow was tremendously deep in some places and it was rather hard work to climb the steep sides of the mountain.*

For the first time, only one Peel came to dinner: it was Mr A. Peel without his cousin William, who perhaps had other duties to attend to.

Ellen had been pushing to be allowed to visit the 'Diamond Battery' only a few hundred yards from the Sevastopol, well within firing range and so dangerous that no one went there except those who had to man the trenches. Captain Peel was very unwilling to allow this; however, in an unguarded moment he had promised Ellen that she might go and despite all the risks she was determined '*coute que coute*' to go. She gloried in the idea that her dare-devil attitude to danger would further enhance her reputation to amaze and shock. Perhaps she and William Peel had argued about the proposed visit on their walk and he had shown his disapproval by not coming to dinner that night. But William Peel kept his promise and, together with Roger and Mr Roberts, they set off up the Vorontsov Ravine, the only way to the trenches until the railway was built. The road lay between high, rocky escarpments on either side, nicknamed 'The Valley of the Shadow of Death'[10] because so many people had been killed passing through. Ellen may have annoyed William Peel still more by finding it '*most comical*' to see the amazement on the faces of the people who watched them venture into the range of fire. He knew what real danger meant, and to see Ellen treating the expedition as some kind of public dare, together with her tendency for reckless exhibitionism and her determination to get her own way, might have made him think twice about his relationship with her. There is no doubt he had been attracted by Ellen because he had told his cousin Archy, whom he had taken into his confidence. They would have made a dashing couple, both so good-looking and spirited, she with her energy and intelligence, he already with a reputation for bravery, but it was not to be.

Roger and Mr Roberts accompanied Ellen and William Peel on the expedition:

> *The roads were dreadful and we had a long distance to go, as the 'Diamond Battery' is only a few hundred yards from the town of Sebastopol. We rode under fire for about a mile, partly sheltered by hills, and partly in view of the enemy, who were however polite enough not to fire on us. The amazement of all the people who saw us quietly venture in range was most comical. The last part of the road lay through a gorge called the 'Valley of the Shadow of Death' from the immense number of people who have been killed there. The round shot and shell lay on the ground as thick as hailstones and one could hardly move without stepping on them. We dismounted and went into the battery on foot and where the parapet was low we were obliged almost to crawl on all fours to avoid being picked off by Russian riflemen who were posted about in all directions. One poor fellow was killed by them just before we came in. We walked through the whole battery regardless of the shot and our cannon balls flying about and shells bursting in all directions. I had been told of 'Whistling Dick' and now I heard the peculiar noise they make quite close to me. The firing grew heavier while we remained, so our homeward route was more hazardous than our approach to the battery had been. Several shots came over the 'Valley of the Shadow of Death'*

whilst we were riding through and one shell in particular passed close to where we had been standing a few minutes before and burst on the other side. One rifle bullet fell a few yards behind Mr Roberts while we were in the battery. We got home safe enough after all our risks, perfectly delighted to think that we had seen the trenches and been the first visitors to the celebrated 'Diamond Battery'. It is actual fact that nobody ever ventured there unless called to it by duty.

So ended Ellen's triumphant account of her great adventure, but so may also have ended the attraction that William Peel had undoubtedly felt for Ellen, as he would have been relieved rather than triumphant at their safe return.

Undaunted by the exploits of the day before, they took a 13-mile walk to the Monastery of St George, where the Palmer party found a regiment of Germans quartered in the buildings. They accepted an invitation to sit down by their fires and share their bread. The monks had been allowed to remain and there were also some families who had taken refuge in the monastery. The *Caradoc* was sometimes used as a meeting place, and on Wednesday the 24th Lord Raglan, Rear Admiral Sir Edmund Lyons[11] and others came on board for a council of war. Rumours must have been flying round because Ellen mentions that there was great talk of peace, but concludes, '*I am afraid it is all moonshine*'. Another visitor was William Simpson,[12] the war artist who had arrived in the Crimea a month before the Palmers, commissioned by Colnaghi's to make sketches for the company. He came on board the following day and showed them his drawings, which might have included the Monastery of St George they had just visited. '*Mr Simpson, the artist, came and showed us his drawings which are really splendid. The Peels came in and joined us in our walk on the opposite side of the harbour. We scrambled down the face of the precipice, right down to the sea, rather a difficult proceeding. Company in the evening. Weather glorious.*'

The Palmers were due to leave Balaclava on the *Golden Fleece*, and the captain gave a lunch party for them when they came on board to inspect their new quarters. Sunday the 28th was their last day and the visitors who came to wish them goodbye included the Peels, Lord Burghersh,

Captain Colville, Colonel Seymour, Mr Dacre and others. '*Walked for the last time to the Genoese Castle, another favourite haunt of ours. A very sad evening; we were all anticipating our departure with sorrow. Poor Roger will have to return to his tent. The navvies have arrived at last and road from Balaclava to the camp will be commenced. Better late than never.*' They finally left on Monday after more farewell visits. Ellen was very sad indeed:

> *We embarked on the Golden Fleece at 4 and were about an hour getting clear of the harbour. When we were out in the open sea Capt. Derriman's boat came alongside and took away dear Roger and our other sorrowing friends. It was a very mournful parting from the former, but I trust the separation may not be for long. The sea was rather rough that evening, but we were not sick. Dined at ½ past 5, a party of about 40, there being a number of sick officers on board. We have also about 100 sick soldiers going down to the hospital at Scutari.*

Two days later they anchored near the hospital.

> *8 poor souls have died during the voyage. We landed this morning and called at Misseri's and Mrs Cumberbatch's. Found numerous letters and papers awaiting us. Dined and slept on board the Golden Fleece. Left the ship this morning and went down by the afternoon steamer to Buyulderch. Great joy at our arrival. This is the first day we have dined and slept on 'terra firma' and it seems quite odd and strange to be in a home after living on board ship for so long.*

The great adventure was over and Ellen was going to find life very dull in consequence.

This was almost her last full entry in the little blue notebook. From then on the entries were no more than a series of one- or two-line notes, apart from a full entry on 28 February giving details of an earthquake. By the month of March, diary entries were even less informative. In a final and typical entry on 22 March she says: '*Wrote letters, walked to the Burying Ground in the afternoon.*' After that, diary silence. What follows in the next chapter is taken from a very different source. Found inside the blue notebook were two small, thin sheets of paper measuring 5 by 4 inches, written in a microscopically small hand, even tinier than that used by the Brontë sisters, but perfectly legible. Had it not been for these secret writings nothing would have been known of the events which were to change Ellen's life for ever.

CHAPTER 15

Love at Last

Back at Buyerderch, Ellen had nothing to do but write long letters to her friends, walk on the quay and look forward to the arrival of the *Caradoc* and seeing Captain Derriman again. But suddenly, to her great surprise, on 9 February they were joined on their walk by '*Mr A Peel*', who had landed that morning from the Crimea. He was invited to join the Palmers for a musical evening, which he accepted gladly. The following day, Bevan the footman returned from Constantinople where he had gone to buy stores to be shipped to the Crimea, including a deer as a present for Lord Raglan. He also brought a note from William Peel, hoping that Ellen had not thought him rude, but also mentioning his cousin. Archy Peel again joined the Palmers the following day and told Ellen that '*Derry low after our departure; as soon go to h-ll as to the ship deserted as it was*', which must have pleased Ellen, as she certainly had enjoyed Derriman's company.

Having been attracted to the elder of the Peel cousins, Ellen was somewhat mystified by the sudden arrival of Archy. Three days after his unexpected arrival, trying to understand his reason for coming, Ellen wrote, '*Observed Peel look admiringly and earnestly several times, a thought darted through me. Could it be possible he is in love with me himself? He comes without any ostensible object.*' Already tired of Buyuderch, where there was no social life and nothing to do, the following day the Palmers left, with Archy accompanying them, sitting on deck with Ellen as they sailed back to Constantinople. At Misseri's, where they again took up residence, Ellen found letters awaiting her, including one from her brother but perhaps more importantly one from Derry. He had promised to write, and now gave the reason for not writing sooner, '*as he couldn't write coldly, didn't dare write affectionately so that was the reason that he had not kept his word and written before*'. Ellen had put him in an awkward situation. Attracted to him as she undoubtedly was, she had also been flirting with the Peel cousins, most particularly with William. Ellen, who always liked to have two strings to her bow, could not, or would not see that Captain Derriman was obviously at a loss as to know where he now stood.

Archy called again the next day to discover their plans and walked with them to the Galata Bridge. Whittaker, Ellen's maid, perhaps rather mischievously told Ellen that Peel had been very tipsy at a masked ball he had attended. When Ellen teased him about it he snatched her hand and kissed it. Learning that Ellen had been invited to an embassy ball that evening, he immediately said he would get an invitation as well. At the ball Ellen was in her element; a list of her partners preceded her account of the occasion: '*great success, crowds of introductions, great talk about the Crimea, Ld Napier*[1] *civil, knew all about it. Engaged 8 deep, threw over numbers [...] Peel waiting patiently to get a dance, it was claimed by three others, everybody striving, admiring looks from strangers, Stratfords very kind and Graziani and Moore insist upon me going to the French Embassy.*' Among all the other necessities Ellen had brought with her for the journey, ball dresses had been included and on this occasion she wore her pink one with diamonds in her hair.

The following day Archy joined them for a walk in the Champs des Morts, described by Murray in his *Guide to Turkey* as vast forests extending for miles around the city and its suburbs. The tombstones of white marble were not infrequently shaped from ancient columns and monuments. With its cypresses and the tombs, and the breathtaking view over the Golden Horn with the domes and minarets of Constantinople silhouetted against the sky, the Champs des Morts, despite its name, was a favourite walk. Archy tried to get her to join him at the opera, asked for a lock of her hair and if she would let him call her Nelly in private. Ellen did not go to the opera, and in all probability did not give him a lock of her hair, but does not seem to have objected to his asking. Whether she allowed him to call her Nelly is not known, but she did not rebuff him and wrote that he was '*very sweet, talked Buyukdere. I preferred staying here, "then he should stay also", I was enough to addle anyone's brains.*' But when he asked her to keep a waltz that night at the French Embassy Ball, she said he had to take a chance. Dressed this time in a gold dress with ornaments in her hair, Ellen was '*entourée and accablée*' (surrounded and overwhelmed) at the ball and enjoying her success when Archy arrived at half past twelve, '*Drunk. I wouldn't let him dance with me and told him to go to bed*'. It was all right for Archy to be tipsy at a carnival ball, but to come to an embassy ball drunk was not only bad form but, as a friend of Miss Palmer's, not to be tolerated.

Archy had the sense to stay away the following day, and Ellen, possibly to console herself for his lapse, notes with more than usual enthusiasm the effect she had out walking, even underlining twice the word 'tremendously': '*tremendously stared at, charmante, jolie constantly repeated, "there goes the prettiest girl in Turkey"*'. But however much she was stared at and complimented, that did not make up for Archy's absence and she '*read and moped*' in the evening. When Archy did come the following day, Ellen scarcely spoke to him and he left with Lane Fox, an old friend and one-time admirer, who had called in. Ellen took what comfort she could in her new purple bonnet, which attracted a further wave of compliments when she went out walking. But by Tuesday Ellen was glad to see him and he stayed a long time, called her dearest, and begged, in the small time they had alone, that she would forgive him. Ellen was also upset by the fact that she had not received an invitation to the Embassy and found it strange.

Archy, out walking with Ellen, then took a step too far.

> *He said he was going to write to his mother and he should tell her that he had met a young lady on the shores of the Bosphorus and loved her and might he add that she loved him a little? I was obliged to say that he must not say anything about me whereupon he rejoined, 'then I have been mistaken' in the tone of one deeply hurt. Told me that the feeling had crept on him unawares, that for long after our first acquaintance he had regarded me with indifference and wished his cousin to marry me. He liked you very much he said very earnestly. It was not till within two*

> *days of our departure that he confessed his feelings to himself. He told me all this in a tone of deep manly sincerity and says he loved me better than perhaps I thought and when I told him perhaps rather abruptly that I liked him but could not reciprocate his feelings, he seemed really too much overcome to speak; not violent like Derry but outwardly calm as such natures are. He advised me strenuously not to marry anyone whom I did not love.*

Ellen had been so deeply wounded by the behaviour of the Count de Bark, that she was still unable to commit to any deep relationship, although her final entry in the diary for that day showed that she perhaps regretted having rebuffed Archy so abruptly: '*Quite sorrowful thinking of Archy*'.

Archy, however, was not about to give up and he followed up with a kind and thoughtful letter, writing that he had been told she was beautiful and rich, '*but what was that to him, he wished his cousin to marry me [...] but then thrown into my society, watched me was interested, pitied my lonely position, and the thought flashed into his mind that he was alone too*'. Archy's understanding of her loneliness, and his belief that she should only marry for love must have touched a chord, for Ellen then continued, '*It is the first time since count de Bark that the possibility of my marrying for love has crossed my mind.*' But despite half admitting to herself that she felt more than just liking for Archy, when he called again, such was her lack of confidence and fear of being let down a second time, when he asked if she could love him, she replied, '*Would it be better not to try? I did like him very much but not in the way he liked me. He wanted an opportunity to speak openly. Did I like him better than I thought? I said I liked him very much and had felt unwilling for him to go, but still I thought it was better he should go.*' The following day, with her emotions in turmoil, Ellen chose to rake up his drunkenness at the embassy party as a reason to disbelieve in his love for her. Archy, desperately hurt, came to dinner that evening with Lane Fox. '*Stupid evening, Archy in wretched spirits, had scarcely a word to say – no invite from the embassy, strange!*' Things went from bad to worse on Sunday, when Archy did not call. '*Read service, everything desperately dull.*'

By Monday, Archy could hold out no longer and wrote, '*I fly like a moth into the flame that burns me. Ellen I cannot live without you. What am I to do?*' Ellen, now knowing that he was in love, decided to play it cool, and wrote that he was still to come as usual and that she liked him very much, but as a friend. She was rather more vexed by the fact that Archy was going to the ball at the Embassy. '*Lady Stratford, manoeuvering woman not invited us. Unkind, world very ill natured.*' But when the invitation did eventually arrive, Ellen had a bad cough and cold, then discovered that she had measles, so could not accept after all. For five days she could not eat or sleep, her throat became dangerously inflamed and she lost her voice. Archy was in constant attendance, and sat with her father and Aunt Mary for hours while she was ill. Even Ellen began to admit to herself that Archy must care: '*I think he must care something about me or he couldn't sit for hours together and come three times a day as he does.*'

But it was not long before Ellen was again doubting Archy's love for her. He had asked her to help him write a letter in Italian and had been amazed at her facility and stayed writing it all afternoon. When he did not return in the evening she wrote, '*He never came in the evening tho' he has a general invitation. He is getting tired of it and does not evidently love me well enough to prefer my society to anything else. I never thought he did so am not mistaken.*' This over-reaction could perhaps be put down to her weakened state after her illness. Her emotional turmoil was not helped by the arrival of Derry, who called, but took pains to appear indifferent. However, Archy was soon back, spending his evenings with the Palmers and staying late.

It was difficult for the young people ever to be alone. Time and again Ellen records snatched conversations whenever Aunt Mary left the room for a short time. Archy was just able to tell her that Derry had chaffed him about her,

> *also that everyone had got hold of it, Lord Raglan, the ADC's in the Crimea etc., Told me also that he had written to his mother. Really this is most deplorable, he seems to think I have accepted him, though I have definitely told him to the contrary. We must have an explanation as soon as I can get an opportunity. I dread it for I am afraid he will be offended and I should be very sorry if he were to go.*

But at the same time Ellen continued to see Derry. Her need to be loved and wanted was so great that it blinded her to the fact that, although it was obvious Derry had been in love with her, he could see the way the wind blew and knew there was no hope for him. When he would not call the following day she wrote,

> *A few weeks since he seemed to live but in my presence and I really did think his love was a little more deeply seated than it has proved. Everybody is deceitful. I think I am destined never to excite a real passion. He carefully abstained from asking me to revisit the Caradoc, a scheme he was so full of when we parted.*

Two days later Derry left and she could not believe that he had not even said goodbye. Perhaps Ellen, who had preferred the handsome William Peel to his less flamboyant cousin, sometimes wondered how it was that Archy was now courting her. Archy told her that William had sometimes been disgusted with her, possibly over her insistence on going to the Diamond Battery and putting herself and her companions in unnecessary danger, and during one of these occasions Archy had confided in his cousin his feelings for Ellen. As a result, the cousins had agreed that William would leave the field to Archy.

When Ellen was invited to dine at the Embassy she again had a great success, but not everyone was so forthcoming: '*Lady George civil, de Stratfords ditto but not cordial, I am not to be an amie de la maison, that is clear.*'[2] Perhaps part of the reason was that the de Stratfords had a daughter of their own to marry off, but most probably it was for the same reasons that had made it so difficult for the Palmers to move in the top social circles in London. What also must have hurt was the fact that Archy was part of the Embassy circle, acceptable and invited to go out riding with them. Ellen urged him to accept and commented, '*they never ask me, how unkind*'.

March became April, and the diary entries continued to record the lovers' tiffs: Ellen seized on the most trivial evidence to accuse Archy of not caring for her; Archy in despair begged to be forgiven. When Ellen received a letter from her brother she was devastated by the contents.

He wrote unkindly that he was not coming down, although many other officers came for visits to Constantinople, and made no mention of selling his commission. Ellen was utterly wretched and miserable and Archy wrote her a consoling letter sympathising with her. But life had to go on. The Palmers went sightseeing and Ellen was now taking music lessons. Her teacher, Pisani, was astonished at her facility. '*Read two things from "Il Trovatore". He said I understand them directly and really seemed quite amazed at my performance, interrupting me in his own songs frequently with "brava", and "molte bene".*'

Ellen was also pleased to learn that the Wrexham papers had printed an account of her expedition to the Crimea, calling her 'the beautiful heroine'.

Matters progressed, but not before one disagreement so serious that Archy wrote to say that he intended to go away and never see her again. Ellen was really distressed and sent Mr Roberts, or Bobby as they called him in the family, to call on Archy. He found him very ill and low, too much out of sorts to do anything. However, when invited to call, Archy came and as was usual took all the blame for the quarrel. The lovers were reconciled.

By 11 April, Ellen could write, '*I think I could be very happy for he is capable of loving deeply and I sometimes think I have at last found what has been the dream of my life but what I have always despaired of obtaining, a heart wholly and solely devoted to me – now and forever.*'

On the following Sunday, Archy proposed formally and asked her to be his wife; Ellen, although she did not say she had accepted him, recorded that they had a long talk about the future, which would have included the problem of her father, who all along had disapproved of Archy's courtship, as he would have done for any suitor, since he never wanted Ellen to leave his side and marry.

Then came the bombshell. A letter from Lady Alice Peel,[3] Archy's mother, was enclosed with one from Archy.

> *Instead of jumping at the proposal as I had thought, she wrote very coldly and disapprovingly tho' she said she did not know me so nothing personal intended. Archy was very indignant and wrote saying he*

> *would be frank at all hazards [...] my love, my wife you must be or I shall die he wrote. My pride however revolted at the bare idea of any objection being made to me who am so accustomed to be courted.*

They met to talk over the problem, Archy solemnly vowing never to see his mother again if Ellen persisted in saying they must part. Ellen said that she must have his mother's cordial acquiescence if she was to say anything positive to him, but they agreed that he was to stay and let matters go on quietly. Ellen had been wounded where she was most vulnerable: her need for acceptance from those she thought of as her social equals. Yet none of the people whose approval Ellen was so keen to have were particularly nice. Although de Stratford may have been a distinguished diplomat and a cousin of Canning's, he and his wife were not popular, being seen as more interested in social activities than in supporting the war effort in the Crimea. Alice Peel, who clearly did not think Ellen good enough for her son, was dismissed as a dinner companion by Lord Clarenden, who wrote that, 'as I sat between Ladies Salisbury and Alice Peel, I was not fatiguingly merry'.[4]

Archy was of course devastated at the thought of losing Ellen on account of his mother. But although Ellen had reacted strongly to what she considered an insult, she too had a lot to lose. If she really broke off her engagement to Archy the alternatives remained bleak, a return to England without her brother, with her father to care for, the estates to run, and the ritual of the annual visits to Kenure, Cefn and London. The very thought of another London season must have filled her with dismay. But above all she was now very much in love with Archy, having got over her unspoken disappointment that William Peel had withdrawn and allowed his cousin to pay court to her. So it was in both their interests to find a way of getting round Lady Alice's disapproval.

Two days later, both of them were dining at the de Stratfords' and Ellen was asked to sing. Although still hoarse and

> *dying with fright but I nerved myself to the task and got through triumphantly. Duet from Nabucco with Pisani and 'Come e Bello'. Succés éclatant and tumult of applause and everybody rushed forward*

> *to congratulate me. About 40 people there and the audience is usually very cold but I warmed to a tremendous pitch of enthusiasm and they applauded violently, the Embassy people were especially delighted [...] I was glad of my triumph before Archy and he looked so delighted with me.*

Archy came round to show Ellen the letter he had written to his father telling him that she had broken off the engagement and describing the conversation they had had the night before. Perhaps the de Stratfords had heard about the broken engagement because Ellen writes that Lady de Stratford was quite motherly, and two days later Ellen was invited to tea. Perhaps unable to really believe that Archy's family would accept her, she continued to see and flirt with Derry, who was in Constantinople at the time, preparatory to sailing with the Embassy party to the Crimea. The de Stratfords, perhaps inspired by Ellen's account of her adventure in Balaclava, were planning to attempt a visit now that the weather was warmer. Ellen had certainly been the first lady tourist, but after the de Stratfords' visit, and as the siege of Sevastopol continued to drag on, it became a fashionable pastime to sail to the Crimea and visit the battlefields. Archy, naturally, became jealous and cross, seeing Ellen walking and talking with Derry. Ellen, still uncertain of her own feelings, continued to find reasons to be cold and distant, writing casually, '*Archy had offended me somehow so I was cool to him and he abruptly took his leave in a great state of mind.*' Ellen was not the only one to have a romance while in Constantinople. Her maid Whittaker announced that she had become engaged to a Mr Simmonds, but there are no details as to who he was or how she met him.

Archy could never remain apart from Ellen for long nor could she bear his absences and soon after their latest tiff, while walking in the Valley of the Nightingales, one of the many walks round Constantinople, Ellen described Archy as anticipating the future with delight. It is clear that Ellen had not wanted to break the engagement, as she then stipulated that they must wait a year to test their feelings, and probably also to allow time for Lady Alice to accept her son's choice of bride, which Archy agreed to. By this time Roger had at last arrived, but Ellen hardly mentioned his arrival and there were few diary entries concerning him; rather the diary is full of the small disagreements between the lovers. They had obviously been discussing their future relationship when the question of where authority should rest arose:

> *We had rather a discussion of a husband's authority over a wife. Archy said he ought to have control and in certain cases to exercise it. He has expounded these sort of views before so I thought it was best to come to an understanding on the subject. I told him of this and also said plainly that if I ever married him I could never submit to be dictated to on any subject. I had been accustomed to act independently and I could not give up the habit. Advice I could bear, not control and I told him fairly that unless he would promise never to attempt to exercise authority he must make up his mind to give me up. I made many sacrifices for him and he must make this one for me.*

This was the most serious argument they had had and at first Archy said he was still of the same opinion as before, adding,

> *that he sometimes felt afraid of me (he meant marrying me) for if I continued to tease and bully him he might in time not like me. I was nettled at this for I saw it was a determined struggle on his part for mastery and if he wishes that now what will it be like afterwards so I said that if it had come to that and he could coolly contemplate the prospect of no longer loving me he had better have nothing more to do with me.*

Ellen also noticed that Archy had learnt how to deal with her mood swings, and, '*instead of showing grief when I am cool to him he quietly lets matters take their course in a sort of "wait till you get pleased" spirit*', which slightly annoyed her as she liked to decide when and how to end their disagreements.

It was lucky for Ellen that her brother was with her. It is probable that Ellen had written telling him of Archy's proposal and wanted him to talk it over with her. As she had done so many times before during her stormy relationship with Count de Bark, she also made use of Roger as a go-between. After this latest disagreement she immediately told him the whole story and she wrote that he listened most kindly.

> *He finally advised me to wait a fair time, say a year, to try the strength of my own feelings and then if we both continued the same he promised me his help to bring matters to a happy termination. It was very late when we had done talking but he went afterward to find out Archy and I spent a very uncomfortable night.*

Roger found Archy sitting under Ellen's window, wretchedly unhappy. After talking with Roger and finding that Ellen had forgiven him, '*he solemnly promised that I should always do as I liked in everything and he would give himself to me. It was a solemn abjuration of all his ideas of authority and all his expectations of exerting any control over me should I ever be his wife.*' The following afternoon on Friday, 5 May the Palmers went in caiques to the Sweet Waters of Europe with Archy and, '*we were very happy, perfectly reconciled too*'. That was Ellen's final written conclusion. She never transferred the minuscule notes she had made into her diary, and perhaps, now that she had found happiness and someone to confide in, she no longer needed the comfort of the diaries so she stopped writing.

Ellen had got what she wanted, marriage to a man whom she believed could truly love her for herself, at the same time ensuring her own independence within the marriage. Ellen was being true to herself, to her long held belief that she, as a woman, had as much right to have her judgement respected as any man. Perhaps more surprisingly, Archy, after some initial resistance realised that Ellen, having managed her father's affairs for three years, was never going to play the role of a submissive wife and accepted her terms. In the context of the times, Ellen's success in drawing up what was in effect a marriage contract giving her specific rights and limiting Archy's authority over her was a significant achievement and could perhaps be seen as a precursor of the women's movement. Ellen's diaries reveal her to have been a character larger than life, disciplined and dutiful, passionate yet vulnerable, self-confident and courageous, with an almost reckless disregard for danger. Although feeling trapped by the conventions of her day and the expectations of her family, she nevertheless remained true to her core beliefs and her desire to excel in whatever she attempted. What she might have become had she lived longer will never be known. This is the story of a remarkable woman, a woman ahead of her time as revealed in her diaries, and it deserves to be told.

EPILOGUE

The course of true love rarely runs smooth, and there were surely many arguments and disagreements between the happy couple before the wedding date could be settled, so much so that Roger advised that they should both wait a year before taking matters any further. In fact it was more than two years before they eventually got married. Little is known about Ellen's life after her last joyous diary entry. She completely gave up 'diarizing' as she called it. Perhaps now that she had found someone who really cared for her the emotional comfort she had found in confiding her thoughts to paper was no longer necessary, so tracing her life after she stopped writing presents something of a challenge. It is only thanks to the interest taken by the Taylors in her affairs, some brief entries in her brother's diaries, the newspaper accounts of her wedding, the records of the births of her children and that of her death that we are able to piece together a picture of her married life during those few brief years. There is nothing to say how she coped with the arrival of four children in five years, or whether her husband lived up to his promise to her or how she dealt with the problem of caring for her father. But marriage to Archy seems to have given her the entry into high society that eluded her earlier on and, financially secure, she was able to indulge her taste for theatricals as well as entertaining on a grand scale.

The Palmers stayed on in Constantinople until 4 June when they left for home, almost certainly by sea. Richard Taylor wrote to his mother from Constantinople, 'the Palmers left this place on their way home. I am sorry I missed them as should have liked to have had an account of the fair Ellen's proceedings since we last met'.[1]

Ellen's engagement to Archy Peel had not yet been made public, but Ellen must have felt confident enough of the future to entertain lavishly. Emboldened by the thought of her new status as the future wife of the nephew of the late prime minister she had given a series of dinner parties at Kenure, culminating with an invitation to the Lord Lieutenant of Ireland, Lord Carlisle.[2] In a further letter to his mother, who had been a guest at Kenure, Richard Taylor writes, 'I am charmed to find that you keep up your dissipation and are none the worse for it. A Kenure dinner party even I always considered an infliction so I think you deserve praise for thus performing the duties of neighbourly hospitality'.[3] To his sister Richard Taylor writes rather unkindly, 'I am anxious to hear of the Kenure Vice Regal festivities, and can well imagine the fuss they occasion in that establishment. I have often had the same idea as you of the Thackeray like style of that family, and if I had either his pen or pencil I am afraid I might be very ill natured.'[4]

Ellen cared little about what the Taylors thought, entertaining the Vice Regal Court at Kenure was most certainly a social triumph for her. The occasion was reported in the press and must have shown Kenure at its glorious best. Sadly, 120 years later it was a crumbling ruin and was demolished.[5] But on 3 March 1856, Kenure was *en fête*. Special trains had been laid on from Dublin to bring the 400 guests to the house. Lord Carlisle, the Lord Lieutenant, was met at the station by the Palmers' carriage drawn by four grey horses and driven through an arch of evergreens at the entrance to Kenure Park. The band of the 16th Lancers was stationed in the entrance hall and played during dinner and the whole suite of apartments was thrown open for the ball.[6] Ellen's triumph was complete.

Ellen had also won over her future in-laws, because there is a charming letter from Archy's father, Sir Jonathan Peel, to Ellen written on 20 August 1856. 'My Dear Miss Palmer,' he wrote, 'I cannot express to you the pleasure that Archibald's letter has afforded me or the happiness I have in assuring the affection I already entertain for you. I think Archy has been truly fortunate and I trust may prove himself worthy of it. There is one thing which cannot be doubted, which is his love for you and I am quite delighted at his being relieved of all suspense and anxiety he has suffered. Pray tell Sir Roger Palmer how anxiously I look forward to the pleasure of making his acquaintance and give my regards to your brother whom I have always liked exceedingly. Believe me, dear Miss Palmer, Yours very affectionately, J Peel.'[7]

Written over a year after Ellen and Archy had decided to give themselves time to consider their future together, Sir Jonathan's letter reads as a response to their formal engagement, so Lady Alice's initial misgivings as to the suitability of Ellen as a wife for her son must have been overcome. There was still much to be discussed because it took a further eight months before they were married. Ellen, besides being in charge of the management of the Palmer estates, also had to deal with the problem of her father's frailties and her duty of care to him. It would seem that she made living with her father a condition of the marriage, thus solving the conflict between love and duty. Emma, Jane Austen's fictional heroine, faced the same challenge, with a frail father who objected to her marrying. She solved the problem likewise by Mr Knightley agreeing to live with his father-in-law.

Although this was not the great marriage her family had worked so hard to achieve, to which Ellen had reluctantly agreed and seen as a duty to her family, nonetheless it was a step up the social hierarchy. Archy was the third of Sir Jonathan Peel's nine children and as Sir Jonathan kept a racing stable there cannot have been much money left over for the children. However, he was the brother of a prime minister, and Lady Alice Peel provided the aristocratic credentials. Back in London Ellen and her father would have driven to Marble Hill, an elegant Palladian villa set in 66 acres of parkland by the side of the Thames, to call on her future in-laws. They in turn would have dined at Portland Place and family legend has it that Lady Alice complained that the Irish servants wiped the plates with their sleeves.

Archy and Ellen's wedding was widely reported in the press. The *Morning Post* on 26 May 1857 under the heading 'Marriage in High Life' reported that 'The marriage of Miss Palmer, only daughter of Sir Roger Palmer with Mr Archibald Peel, younger son of General and Lady Alice Peel, took place yesterday at St Georges Church, Hanover Square in the presence of a very large circle of friends of both families.'

There followed a long list of guests, headed by the Duchess Dowager de Gramont and including Lady Tankerville and the Earl and Countess of Harrington. The *Liverpool Mercury* reported that the youthful bride, 'who was most magnificently attired in white silk bordered with emerald green, was attended to the altar by a bevy of ten bridesmaids'. The service was conducted by the Dean of Worcester, and after the ceremony the company adjourned to Portland Place, where no expense had been spared to celebrate the event. A pavilion had been constructed in the garden at the rear of the house by Mr Benjamin Edgington,[8] the superb breakfast for 150 guests was provided by Conrad Tauer[9] of South Audley Street and we are even told that the bridesmaids' dresses were made by Madame Levilly of St George's Hanover Street. It was a very much grander affair in comparison with the more modest wedding of Emma Mackinnon to the Duc de Guiche that Ellen had attended as a bridesmaid. The health of the couple was proposed by Sir Robert Peel, elder son of the late Prime Minister, after which Archy and Ellen left for the Isle of Wight to begin their married life. They were back in London in July for there is a note in the *Morning Post*[10] to say that Ellen had attended a fête given by Lady Holland at Holland House. That invitation, given to her in her own right, must have pleased Ellen.

It would seem, from the sparse entries in Roger Palmer's diaries, that Ellen continued to enjoy her social life to the full as a married woman. The following year, despite being pregnant with the baby imminently expected, Roger notes that he called on Lady Manners to explain about Ellen. The following day's entry records, 'Baby arrived and we went to the opera.'[11] From this brief entry it would seem that Ellen was not prepared to let her pregnancy interfere with her social life and was ready to accept invitations right up to the end. The baby was christened Archibald Roger.

From Roger we learn that Ellen had had a theatre built in the grounds at Cefn so that she could indulge her love of acting and singing. In January 1860, Roger was staying at Cefn, part of a large house party. The first week of January was spent rehearsing for and acting in a play. By 5 January they were able to perform for the local farmers and the evening went well. The next day there was a grand performance followed by a ball at Cefn. It is owing to Roger's note in his diary of a chance encounter with a woman on the train on the way to Kenure that we know that Ellen, not content with a theatre at Cefn, had one built at Kenure as well. The unknown woman told Roger that she 'thought Archy was a lunatic. Reason? For allowing Ellen to build a theatre'.[12]

Although Roger's diary is mostly concerned with accounts of how he fared out hunting, family news is also chronicled. On 26 January comes an ominous little note simply saying 'baby ill'. To judge by her earlier remarks about small children in her own diaries, Ellen did not much care for babies. The family story is that she sent poor little Archy, then aged 19 months, to stay with a farmer's wife in a cottage without drains, where he contracted typhoid whilst his mother entertained her friends at Cefn. Although the baby rallied, Roger's diary entry records that on 31 January 'poor baby very bad in the evening' and finally on 1 February Roger notes that 'baby died at 5.30 this morning'. He was buried eight days later in the family vault at St Giles's Church, Wrexham. It was probably the first time Ellen had ever been to a funeral as she had not been to her mother's or aunt's. Roger makes no mention of his brother-in-law, Archy, either attending the funeral or walking with Ellen and her father in the grounds the following days. Again it is only family hearsay, but Archy was said to be so angry with Ellen over the death of poor little Archy that he flew out of the house and did not come back for a year.[13] It cannot have been that long because Ellen was soon pregnant again and William Frederick was born on 21 March the following year. However upset he might have been with his wife, Archy was very much in love with her and he had clearly forgiven her, for one of the few pieces of documentary evidence which survives is a shockingly bad poem indicating this. And to help console her, he had also commissioned his friend, Thomas Woolner,[14] to make a memorial sculpture for Ellen commemorating the death of baby Archy. It shows Ellen with clasped hands kissing the baby as the angel prepares to take him to heaven and is in St Giles's Church, one of the 'seven wonders of Wales'. Woolner later wrote, 'have been modelling the child in your group and a pretty tough job it was to keep the horrid little squealer of a child quiet that I had to study from'.[15] Sentimental it may seem but the Pre-Raphaelite sculpture was very much in keeping with Victorian taste; its message was to console the bereaved family.

Not content with theatres in the grounds of Kenure and Cefn, Ellen must have been the moving spirit behind the restoration of the Wrexham Theatre Royal. This would have enabled her to put on public performances and there is an account of the play *The Two Buzzards or Whitebait at Greenwich,* a one-act farce,[16] being performed to great acclaim. Ellen appeared on the stage probably playing the part of Miss Lucretia Buzzard, allowing her to fulfil her long-held wish to perform in public. Costumes had been brought in from Nathan's and musicians from Liverpool had been engaged. Afterwards there was a supper at Cefn and dancing went on until four o'clock in the morning.[17] Performances continued at both theatres; another play had been produced the following year at Kenure, with a grand performance to amuse their guests and neighbours, followed by a ball. *Aladin* was played at the Cefn theatre, again followed by a ball.

Ellen and Archy stayed at Portland House each year for part of the London season, giving big dinner parties and, according to brief entries in Roger's dairies, going to Ascot and taking part in all the usual social activities. Once the season was over, the Peels were in the habit of taking a house for the rest of the summer in Brighton at 30 Adelaide Crescent, where they entertained, bathed in the sea, and went to the races at Goodwood. In Brighton, in 1862, Ellen awaited the birth of her third child, Mary, born on 30 August. The following year, *The Morning Post* recorded that on 23 July 'a second ball given by Mrs Archibald Peel on Tuesday night at Portland House was a brilliant reunion considering the lateness of the season'. Ellen possibly had chosen to have a second ball as she was heavily pregnant and would have wanted to enjoy dancing and to extend the season for as long as possible before the next baby arrived. A month later, exactly a year after she had given birth to Mary and again while staying in Adelaide Crescent, Ellen gave birth to her fourth child, a second daughter. All seemed well, but it is said that Archy was walking in the garden 10 days later when Ellen called out to him; as he rushed upstairs it was already too late – Ellen was dead. Her beloved brother's laconic entry in his diary simply reads, 'Ellen died'. The little motherless baby was christened Ellen. She was my grandmother.[18]

After due expressions of sorrow and regret at Ellen's death, the obituary in *The Wrexham Advertiser*[19] continued with, 'The deceased lady was well and favourably known in the district, not only for her full possession of all those gentle and amiable qualities that distinguish and adorn womanhood,' and then rather surprisingly it went on: 'but for the most unusual vigour and strength of her intellect, which we believe, caused her to be playfully called by some of her friends, the masculine minded.' It was almost as if the obituarist wanted to say that Ellen was not only a remarkable woman but an unusual personality and didn't quite dare to put it into words, using the word 'playfully' to soften the meaning of the words 'masculine minded'. Edward Lear, a friend of her husband's, is reported to have called her 'an oddish person'. Ellen had more than words to keep her memory alive. The graceful little church standing in the grounds of Kenure was built as a memorial to her by her brother and is still in use 150 years later. The beautiful round stained-glass window at the east end of the church has her entwined initials MEP (Mary Ellen Peel) at its centre and her name is spelled out under the window over the altar.

Archy Peel was devastated by Ellen's death and, leaving his children, he travelled incessantly, visiting North America, Nova Scotia, South America and Cuba, where he stayed for almost a year, frequently in the company of Edward Lear.[20] But Archy needed a mother for his children and on his return from his travels proposed to Lady Georgina Russell, daughter of Lord John Russell,[21] at a ball at Strawberry Hill, Twickenham, near to both Marble Hill and Pembroke Lodge, Richmond, where the Russells lived. Ten years after his marriage to Ellen, Archy married Georgina in 1867 at Petersham Church and he became father to a second family. Ellen's three motherless children had a difficult childhood and lacked love and affection, although no doubt Lady Georgina tried her best.[22] William, the only son, unfortunately inherited some of his grandfather's frailties and was always in debt; he was prone to assaulting women and ended up in an asylum. In her book, *A Victorian Young Lady,* Betty Askwith recounts how her mother (the baby Ellen), when she was only 21 took her brother to Australia to try to keep him out of trouble. On the return journey she met Henry Graham and rather unwillingly married him to escape from a useless existence as an unwanted, unmarried step-child. Henry and Ellen had two sons, Archie and Miles. When Henry had to be admitted to a home for alcoholics, although he paid for the boys' schooling, Ellen Graham turned to writing to earn some money to supplement her meagre allowance. She continued to visit Henry and was genuinely sad when he died in 1907. She married George Askwith,[23] a rising young lawyer, the following year. They had one daughter, Betty Askwith, who became a distinguished writer and biographer.

Cefn Park now belongs to Archie Graham Palmer, the great-great-grandson of Ellen Palmer Peel, which makes it one of the few important houses in North Wales mentioned in Ellen's diaries still in private hands. On the other hand, Kenure Park fell into disrepair and, after the sale of the contents, was pulled down in 1972. The then Dublin County Council felt they had no option but to demolish the house. Nothing now remains except the columns and the massive portico, forlorn and lonely amid a new housing estate. The house in Portland Place, where Ellen once danced with Louis Napoleon, was also demolished, to make way for the headquarters of the Royal Institute of British Architects.

Roger Palmer married Millicent Roper but he died childless; Mary, Ellen's older sister, had only one son, Roddy Fenwick Palmer, who never married, but Ellen's descendants continue to flourish and multiply. Now her numerous family of great-grandchildren and great-great-grandchildren, thanks to the discovery of her diaries, can appreciate what a very remarkable woman Ellen Palmer was, ahead of her time in so many ways.

NOTES

Introduction

1 Diary, 15 October 1854.

Chapter 1: A Strange Family

1 Napoleon III, 1808–73, nephew and heir to Napoleon 1. Elected president in 1848.
2 Cefn MSS 463.
3 Diary, 15 December 1852.
4 Cefn MSS 463.
5 Gretna Green Records, 14 March 1847.
6 Cefn MSS 578.
7 Irish Record Pedigrees Vol. XXVI, pp. 239–44.
8 Eleanor Ambrose (1694–1773), daughter of Michael Ambrose, a wealthy Dublin brewer. A celebrated beauty and Catholic heiress, described as witty, intellectual and a fervent patriot, she became the darling of the viceregal court in Lord Chesterfield's time.
9 Lord Chesterfield (1694–1773), statesman, man of letters, Lord Lieutenant of Ireland, 1746-8.
10 Tiffany Potter (ed.), *Women, Popular Culture in the 18th Century* (Toronto: University of Toronto Press, 2012), p. 99. The white rose was the symbol of the Jacobites.
11 Introduction to Cefn MSS.
12 Cefn MSS 873 Will of John Matthews.
13 Cefn MSS 578.
14 Cefn MSS 463.
15 Diary, 13 May 1854.
16 Diary, 25 October 1849.
17 Diary, 12 August 1850.
18 Diary, 3 May 1850.
19 Diary, 1 January 1847.
20 Diary, 1 January 1848.

Chapter 2: The Grand Tour

1 *A Handbook for Travellers on the Continent: Being a Guide through Holland, Belgium, Prussia, Northern Germany and along the Rhine from Holland to Switzerland* (London: John Murray, 1836).
2 Luke Hopkinson, coachmaker, introduced the briska-landau around 1838 which led to improvements in the landau.
3 Ellen's Travel Journal, 2 September 1844.
4 T.A. Heathcote, *British Field Marshals 1736–1997: A Biographical Dictionary* (Barnsley: Leo Cooper, 1999), p. 236.
5 'Here lies the leg of the illustrious and valiant Earl Uxbridge, Lieutenant General of His Britannic Majesty, Commander in Chief of the English, Dutch and Belgian cavalry, wounded on 18th June 1815 at the memorable battle of Waterloo, who by his heroism, assisted in the triumph of mankind, gloriously decided by the resounding victory of the said day.'
6 *Notes and Queries*, 1862.
7 See Fiona Macarthy, *Byron, Life and Legend* (London: Faber and Faber, 2003), pp. 286–7.
8 *Table d'hôte* refers to shared dining where every guest at the hotel can join the meal sitting round a large table.
9 Frankfurt is now famous for its Book Fair, the largest in the world, and its Christmas Market.
10 Mount Rigi, 1,797 metres high.
11 The waterfall is located just above Lauterbrunnen and drops 300 metres. It is one of the highest in Europe.
12 See MacCarthy, *Byron*, pp. 311–12.
13 Ibid., p. 300.
14 The Simplon Pass had been made passable for vehicular traffic by Napoleon between 1802 and 1805.
15 Mary Shelley (1797–1851), writer, best known for her gothic novel *Frankenstein*. Married to Percy Bysshe Shelley, the poet. Wrote *History of a Six Weeks Tour* in 1817.
16 Giuditta Pasta (1797–1865), soprano, among the greatest of opera singers.
17 The fresco suffered further damage during and after World War II. The latest restoration took 21 years and was not without its critics. The painting went on public display in 1999.
18 MacCarthy, *Byron*, p. 322.
19 Travel Journal, 4 November 1844.

Chapter 3: Preparing for the London Season

1 Diary, 11 January 1847.
2 Diary, 14 January 1847.
3 Diary, 17 January 1847.
4 Diary, 24 January 1847.
5 Diary, 30 January 1847.
6 *The Times*, 16 February 1847.
7 Hôtel Lambert was designed by Louis le Vau and built between 1640 and 1644 at the tip of the Isle St Louis in the centre of Paris. Bought in 1843 by Prince Adam Czartoryski, who played an important part in keeping alive 'the Polish Question' in European politics by promoting the Polish cause. Badly damaged by fire in July 2013.
8 Diary, 5 February 1847.
9 Princess Anna Zophia Sapieha married Prince Adam Czartoryski in 1817, a powerful Polish nobleman.
10 After the Congress of Vienna, Poland was divided between Prussia, Russia and Austria. The kingdom of Poland was created from the Russian part with the tsar as monarch. Polish dissatisfaction led to a rebellion which was crushed by the invading Russian army in 1831.
11 Diary, 12 March 1847.

Chapter 4: The London Season

1 Diary, 27 March 1847.
2 Lady Jersey (1785–1867), eldest daughter of 10th Earl of Westmorland, married 5th Earl of Jersey in 1804. She was the queen of London society, patroness of Almack's and introduced the quadrille. She inherited Osterley Park, was a senior partner in Child's Bank and influential in political circles.
3 Diary, 21 April 1847.
4 Captain Gronow (1794–1865), Welsh Grenadier officer, celebrated author of *Reminiscences of Captain Gronow 1862.*
5 Lady Agnes Duff (1829–69), daughter of 18th Earl of Erroll, married Earl of Fife 1846. Only son, Alexander, married daughter of Edward VII and Alexandra.
6 J. Hall, 'The Refashioning of Fashionable Society: Opera-Going and Sociability in Britain, 1821–1861,' PhD thesis, Yale University, 1996.
7 Pamela Horn, *Ladies of the Manor, Wives and Daughters of Country House Society, 1830–1916* (Stroud: Sutton, 1997), p. 120.
8 *I due Foscari* was first produced in London on 10 April 1847 at Her Majesty's Theatre.

9 Giulia Grisi (1811–69), Italian opera singer, considered to be the leading dramatic soprano of the nineteenth century. She played an important part in helping to establish Italian opera in London.

10 Jenny Lind (1820–47), Swedish opera singer, also known as the Swedish Nightingale.

11 *Irish Record Pedigrees*, Vol. XIV, pp. 239–44. See Anthony Wagner, *Records and Collections of the College of Arms* (*Burke's Peerage*, 1952).

12 The Comte de Montemolin (1818–61) was the Carlist pretender to the Spanish throne. Isabella II had succeeded as queen aged 3 in 1833 in disregard of Salic Law. Carlos IV, from a branch of the Bourbon family, did not recognise female succession and the Carlist wars (1847–9) were fought to put Carlos IV on the Spanish throne. When he abdicated in 1845, his son, Carlos V, took the title Comte de Montemolin and was known as the Conde. He had come to London to organise a fresh Carlist uprising, and was later taken prisoner by the French on his way to Spain, to be later released.

13 Diary, 5 May 1847.

14 Rotten Row, a riding track running along the south side of Hyde Park. A fashionable place to be seen on horseback in the nineteenth century.

15 Lord Ranelagh (1812–85), became 7th Viscount in 1820 on the death of his father. Known for involvement in the volunteer movement and links to glamorous women.

16 Diary, 21 May 1847.

17 Bethlem Royal Hospital, founded in 1247, rebuilt after the great fire of 1666: public visiting had been allowed as early as 1598.

18 Diary, 28 June 1847.

19 Prince Louis Napoleon (1808–73), was the nephew of Napoleon I and became his heir at the death of his father in 1846. He lived in London after an attempted coup in 1840. In 1848 he returned to France and was elected to the presidency by an overwhelming majority.

20 Diary, 9 July 1847.

21 Count de Bark (1820–87) was the son of Count Nils Bark (1793–1822. His first name was also Nils, but Ellen never mentions it. The family finances were undermined by a failed agricultural experiment and Count Nils de Bark (also spelt Barck) came to live in London and Paris. His good looks and his title enabled him to mix in society both high and low, and he was known as the 'Swedish adventurer'.

22 23 July 1847.

23 *Morning Post*, 24 July 1847.

24 Ibid., 9 August 1847.

25 Diary, 4 August 1847.

Chapter 5: Country Life in Ireland

1 Diary, 10 September 1847.
2 Domenico Crivelli (1793–1857) was Principal Professor at the Royal Academy of Music.
3 Joseph Robbins, *Champagne and Silver Buckles: The Vice Regal Court at Dublin Castle, 1700–1922* (Dublin: Lilliput Press, 2001), p. 121.
4 Diary, 31 August 1847.
5 Diary, 19 September 1847.
6 The Vernons could trace their ancestry back to its French origins, having come over with William the Conqueror and received estates in England. Captain John Blackwell had been granted the Clontarf estate by Thomas Cromwell who sold it in 1649 to John Vernon, Quartermaster General in Cromwell's army.
7 Diary, 17 December 1847.
8 Ardgillan Castle was built by Reverend Robert Taylor on land he had purchased in 1738. The estate with its Gothicised house is situated in a 200-acre park above Barnegeera Beach, 18 miles north of Dublin with views stretching to the Mountains of Mourne. It remained in the Taylor family until 1982. It was purchased by Fingal Council in 1992 and is now open to the public.
9 Diary, 10 March 1848.
10 Louis Philippe, 1773–1850, proclaimed King of France in 1830 in succession to Charles X, who abdicated. After his abdication in 1848 he lived in exile in England until his death.
11 Diary, 25 January 1848.
12 Ardgillan Letters, 8 January 1848.
13 Howth Castle, home of the St Laurence family since 1180. Sir Edwin Lutyens restyled the fourteenth-century castle overlooking Dublin Bay in 1837.
14 Diary, 10 February 1848.
15 Elizabeth Balcombe, *From the Archives, More Ardgillan Letters*. Letter from M.N. Taylor to Richard Taylor, 18 January 1848. *Skerries News*, 1992.
16 Diary, 29 February 1848.
17 Diary, 15 March 1848.
18 Diary, 29 March 1848.
19 Diary, 9 April 1848.

Chapter 6: A Fatal Attraction

1 Diary, 24 May 1848.
2 Diary, 17 July 1848.

3 Dr Travers Twiss (1809–97). Called to the bar in 1840, lawyer, friend and adviser to the Palmers, knighted on 4 November 1858.
4 Diary, 12 August 1848.
5 Ibid.
6 Diary, 15 May 1848.
7 Agénor de Guiche (1819–80), Duc de Guiche, eldest son of the Duc de Gramont. Succeeded his father in 1855.
8 Raymond Ritter, *La Maison de Gramont de 1529 à nos jours* (privately published, 1968), p. 585.
9 Julie Kavanagh, *The Girl Who Loved Camellias* (New York: Knopf, 2013), pp. 69–79.
10 Virginia Rounding, *Les Grandes Horizontales* (London: Bloomsbury, 2003).
11 Count Alfred d'Orsay (1801–52), French aristocrat, man of fashion, of striking good looks, had returned to London with the widowed Lady Blessington in 1829.
12 Lady Blessington (1789–1849) was of Irish descent; after a difficult early life married Lord Blessington in 1818. They lived lives of extravagant socialising. After Lord Blessington's death in 1829, widowed Lady Blessington returned to London with Count d'Orsay and made Gore House the centre of fashionable, literary and artistic society in London. No ladies would visit owing to the scandalous relationship between the two.
13 Quoted in Kavanagh, *The Girl*, p. 182.
14 James Morton, *Lola Montez: Her Life and Conquests* (London: Portrait, 2007), p. 54.
15 Kavanagh, *The Girl*, p. 102.
16 Rachel (1821–58), famous French actress, born Elisa Félix but always known as Rachel. She never married but had numerous lovers.
17 Kavanagh, *The Girl*, p. 218.
18 *La Maison de Gramont*, p. 579.
19 In his *Recollections of a Long Life* (New York: Charles Scribner's Sons, 1910), Vol. V, p. 8, Lord Broughton wrote that Lord Ossulston was 'a very intelligent agreeable young man, a sort of Liberal Conservative. An accomplished sportsman, sings very prettily'.
20 Diary, 6 May 1849.
21 Lola Montez (1821–61), see James Morton, *Lola Montez*.
22 Diary, 15 May 1849.
23 Diary, 23 May 1849.
24 Miss de Horsey later became the Countess of Cardigan.
25 Diary, 29 May 1849.
26 Adeline, Countess of Cardigan and Lancastre, *My Recollections* (London: Eveleigh Nash, 1909), p. 74. The marriage was opposed by Miss de Horsey's father when he realised that the Conde did not have the means to support his daughter.
27 Diary, 13 June 1849.

28 Diary, 16 July 1849.
29 Diary, 26 July 1849.
30 Francis Grant (1803–78) was known as a fine painter of sporting subjects, but became a fashionable portrait painter; his subjects included Queen Victoria and the Earl of Cardigan. He became President of the Royal Academy in 1866 and was knighted the following year.
31 Diary, 7 August 1849.
32 Diary, 10 August 1849.

Chapter 7: A Bleak and Cheerless Future

1 Carden Hall, magnificent black and white timber-framed house dating back to the sixteenth century. The earliest known link between Carden and the Leche family dates back to 1570, but the family had held property in Carden as early as 1346.
2 Diary, 16 January 1849.
3 Diary, 23 January 1849.
4 Diary, 2 February 1849.
5 Diary, 1 May 1849.
6 Diary, 25 July 1849.
7 Sackville George Lane Fox, 1827–74, succeeded as Duke of Leeds his uncle Francis Godolphin D'arcy who died of diphtheria in 1859. He also succeeded to the baronies of Conyers and Darcy, *Complete Peerage*, Vol. VII, p. 408.
8 Diary, 13 August 1849.
9 Diary, 15 August 1849.
10 Joseph Robins, *The Miasma, Epidemic and Panic in 19th Century Ireland* (Dublin: Institute of Public Administration, 1995), p. 139.
11 Diary, 28 August 1849.
12 Diary, 2 September 1849.
13 Robert James Graves (1796–1853), eminent Irish physician.
14 Diary, 9 September 1849.
15 Robins, *The Miasma*, p. 148.
16 Diary, 3 November 1849.
17 Germany is credited with starting the tradition of Christmas trees. Prince Albert introduced the idea to Queen Victoria. The *London Illustrated News* in 1848 published a print of the young royal family round a decorated tree, which helped to popularise the custom. A decorated yew branch had been customary before that.
18 Diary, 12 February 1850.
19 Sir Benjamin Brodie (1783–1862). Appointed Surgeon to the King in 1828, elected President of the Royal College of Surgeons in 1844; *Annals of the Royal College of*

Surgeons 65 (1983), pp. 418, 419.
20 Diary, 30 April 1850.
21 Diary, 25 May 1850.
22 Diary, 3 May 1850.
23 Emily Glegg was sent back to her family home where she gave birth to a son and where she would appear to have remained and never married. *Burkes Landed Gentry 1850–53, A Genealogical Dictionary of the Landed Gentry of Great Britain and Ireland* (London, 1850).
24 Diary, 14 May 1850.
25 Diary, 17 May 1850.
26 Diary, 27 June 1850.
27 Ibid.
28 Diary, 17 July 1850.
29 Richard Butler, 2nd Earl of Glengall (1794–1858).
30 Diary, 25 July 1850.
31 Diary 27 July 1850.
32 Diary, 2 August 1850.
33 Diary, 14 August 1850.
34 Diary, 15 August 1850.
35 Diary, 12 August 1850.
36 Diary, 28 August 1850.
37 Diary, 29 December 1850.

Chapter 8: Heartbreak

1 William, Duke of Manchester (1823–90), styled Viscount Mandeville 1843–55. *Complete Peerage*, p. 377.
2 Helen Kelen, *The Mistresses, Domestic Scandals of the Nineteenth Century Monarchs* (New York: Avon Books, 1966), pp. 73–86.
3 Diary, 6 February 1851.
4 Diary, 17 February 1851.
5 Diary, 28 February 1851.
6 Diary, 11 March 1851.
7 Diary, 9 April, 1851.
8 Diary, April 8 1851.
9 Diary, April 10 1851.
10 Ibid.
11 Diary, 3 March 1851.
12 Diary, 2 May 1851.

13 Diary, 22 April 1851.
14 Henry Cole (1808–82) secured the backing of Queen Victoria for the Royal Commission for the exhibition in 1850. Managed the exhibition under the presidency of Prince Albert.
15 Joseph Paxman (1803–65), English gardener and architect. Designed the Crystal Palace.
16 Diary, 13 June 1851.
17 Diary, 20 June, 1851.
18 Diary, 25 July 1851.
19 Diary, 13 August 1851.
20 Diary, 15 August 1851.

Chapter 9: Music Her Only Solace

1 Oteley Park, neo-Elizabethan stone mansion of 1826–30, built for Charles Kynaston Mainwaring. Lies splendidly above the mere.
2 Charles Kynaston Mainwaring, 1803–61.
3 Diary, 24 September 1851.
4 Spencer Lucy (1830–89), second son of George and Mary Lucy, succeeded his brother in 1848 aged 18.
5 Sir Henry Vane, a relative of the Duke of Cleveland.
6 Lord St Lawrence (1827–1909), styled Viscount St Lawrence until 1874; principal residence Castle Howth near Dublin; died unmarried.
7 Lady Delamere (1786–1852), wife of Thomas Cholmondeley (1811–87), who was created Baron Delamere of Vale Royal in 1821.
8 Mr Peel took his mother's surname of Peel on inheriting Bryn y Pys.
9 Diary, 13 October 1851.
10 *The Mistress of Charlecote, The Memoirs of Mary Elizabeh Lucy* (London: Gollancz, 1984).
11 Vale Royal was originally a Cistercian Abbey, but with the dissolution of the monasteries came into the hands of the Cholmondeley family in 1615. Extensively rebuilt and altered after the Civil War, it was eventually sold in 1947.
12 Diary, 14 January 1852.
13 Diary, 29 March 1852.
14 Diary, 25 April 1852.
15 This was confirmed to me by the late Lord Blake, historian and author of *The Conservative Party from Peel to Churchill* (London: Faber and Faber, 1970).
16 Diary, 17 October 1852.
17 Diary, 19 May 1852.

18 Diary, 25 June 1852.
19 Diary, 19 July 1852.
20 Lord Frederick Fitzclarence (1799–1855), third son of the Duke of Clarence, subsequently William 1V, and Mrs Jordan. He was raised to the rank of the son of a marquess in 1831.
21 Diary, 7 July 1852.
22 John Alexander Hope (1831–73) succeeded his father as 6th Earl of Hopetoun in 1843.
23 Diary, 5 August 1852.
24 Luigi Lablache (1794–1858), Italian opera singer, excelled in comic and tragic part, taught Queen Victoria singing in 1836/7.
25 See the *Gentleman's Magazine*, 14 November 1811, for an account of his death.
26 Diary, 17 August 1852.
27 Duc de Valentinois, ancient French title of nobility, now claimed as one of his hereditary titles by the Prince of Monaco.
28 Prince Frederick Wilhelm Ludwig of Prussia (1794–1863), Prussian prince, served in the Royal Cavalry. Moved to the Jagerhof Castle in 1820 and made it a centre of social and cultural life.
29 Diary, 6 September 1852.
30 Diary, 16 September 1852.

Chapter 10: Joy and Despair

1 Diary, 30 September 1852.
2 Diary, 8 October 1852.
3 Lady Hester Stanhope (1736–1839). Known as a passionate and intrepid traveller in an age when women were discouraged from being adventurous, she was independent and outspoken.
4 Diary, 6 October 1852.
5 Diary, 16 October 1852.
6 Sir Benjamin Brodie (1783–1862). Physiologist and surgeon. He was Sergeant Surgeon to William 1V and Queen Victoria.
7 The severe muscle spasms of tetanus (or lockjaw) are caused by the toxins released by the tetanus bacterium (*clostridium tetani*), which must have settled on tissues exposed during the mastectomy operation in unsterile conditions. It would take several days for the bacteria to multiply and produce sufficient toxin to enter the blood.
8 Louis Pasteur (1822–95). World-renowned biologist and chemist, responsible for the breakthrough in the prevention and treatment of infectious disease.

9 Sir Joseph Lister (1827–1912). British surgeon and pioneer of antiseptic surgery.
10 Diary, 15 November 1852.
11 Diary, 19 November 1852.
12 Lady Palmer and Alice Palmer were subsequently brought back to North Wales and buried in the family vault in Wrexham Church.
13 Diary, 23 November 1852.
14 Ibid.
15 Diary, 29 November 1852.
16 Diary, 15 December 1852.
17 Diary, 28 December 1852.

Chapter 11: A Parting of the Ways

1 Diary, 6 March 1853.
2 A motte and bailey castle built *c.*1100, Chartley Castle itself, now a ruin, was abandoned in 1485 and Chartley Manor, a moated and battlemented timber mansion, was built nearby.
3 Diary, 23 April 1853.
4 Lady Tankerville, née Corisande Armandine Sophie Léonie de Grammont (1783–1865), married 5th Earl of Tankerville in 1806.
5 Earl of Tankerville (1776–1859).
6 Charles James Fox (1749–1806), prominent British Whig statesman, spent all his political career in opposition.
7 *The Complete Peerage, A History of the House of Lords and All Its Members from Earliest Times*, ed. Geoffrey White (London: George Bell & Sons, 1953), Vol. XII, p. 634.
8 Ist Marquis of Breadalbane (1796–1862), Scottish nobleman and Liberal politician.
9 Diary, 4 June 1853.
10 Diary, 7 June 1853.
11 Diary, 22 June 1853.
12 Diary, 29 June 1853.
13 Lady Harrington (1798–1867) was an actress until 1831. She was the mistress of Colonel Berkeley, and in 1824 sued Mr Hayne Cairns for breach of promise. She married the Earl of Harrington in 1831. He died in 1851. *Complete Peerage*, ed. H.A. Doubleday, Duncan Warrand and Lord Howard de Walden, Vol. VI, p. 327.
14 Ernesto Dentice, Prince of Frasso, of San Vito and of Crucoli (1825–86), became an Italian politician.
15 Prince Felix Constantin Alexander Johann Nepomuk of Salm-Salm (1828–70), Prussian military officer of princely birth, soldier of fortune, served in United States Army and Mexican army.

16 Breakfast would probably have been eaten late in the morning in the nineteenth century.
17 Diary, 13 July 1853.
18 Diary, 20 July 1853.
19 Diary, 24 July 1853.
20 Diary, 6 April 1854.
21 Sir Philip Crampton (1777–1858), eminent Irish surgeon and anatomist.
22 Diary, 11 April 1854.
23 Diary, 13 May 1854.

Chapter 12: To Constantinople

1 Alexander Kinglake (1809–91), travel writer and historian. Published *Eothan; Or Traces of Travel Brought Home from the East* (London: John Olliver, 1844). His *magnum opus* was *The Invasion of the Crimea,* in 8 volumes (London and Edinburgh: William Blackwood, 1863–87).
2 Diary, 12 July 1854.
3 Diary, 3 June 1854.
4 Diary, 14 July 1854.
5 Fanny Duberly, *Mrs Duberly's War, Journal and Letters from the Crimea*, ed. Christine Kelly (Oxford: Oxford University Press, 2007), pp. 19–22.
6 Ibid., p. 44.
7 Omar Pasha (1806–71), Commander-in-Chief of the Ottoman Army. He was born Michael Lotis, son of a Croatian army officer, converted to Islam and took a Turkish name. Married a wealthy heiress and had a successful army career.
8 Duberly, *Mrs Duberly's War*, p. 41.
9 Araba, a wagon or cart drawn by horses or oxen used in Turkey and neighbouring countries.
10 Duberly, *Mrs Duberly's War*, p. 44.
11 Lord Raglan, Lord Fitzroy James Henry Somerset, 1st Baron Raglan (1788–1855), Commander-in-Chief of the British Expeditionary Force. Had fought with the Duke of Wellington in the Peninsular War. Thanks to automatic promotion through seniority he had become a general in 1854, but had never held a command or led troops in battle.
12 Marshal de St Armand, Jacques Leroy de St Armand (1798–1854). Minister of War under Napoleon III, he accepted command of the French forces in the Crimean War although gravely ill. He died at sea *en route* for France.
13 Diary, 4 September 1854.
14 Diary, 6 September 1854.

15 Ibid.
16 Richard Chamber Hayes Taylor (1819–1904), son of Rev. Henry Taylor and Marianne Taylor of Ardgillan Castle, Co. Dublin. Captain, 1844, promoted to Lieutenant-Colonel in 1854, Colonel, 1858, Lieutenant-General, 1863, General, 1883.
17 *Letters of General Sir Richard Taylor of Ardgillan, 1855–1856*, ed. Elisabeth Balcombe (Crimean War Research Society, 6 September 2002).
18 Diary, 18 September 1854.
19 Diary, 19 September 1854.
20 Diary, 24 September 1854.
21 Diary, 29 September 1854.
22 Diary, 30 September 1854.
23 Diary, 1 October 1854.
24 Diary, 3 October 1854.
25 Ibid.
26 Diary, 5 October 1854.
27 Ibid.
28 Orlando Figes, *Crimea, the Last Crusade* (London: Allen Lane, 2010), p. 184.
29 Diary, 6 October 1854.
30 Diary, 7 October 1854.
31 Diary, 8 October 1854.
32 Diary, 10 October 1854.
33 Diary, 11 October 1854.
34 Diary, 12 October 1854.
35 Misseri had accompanied Kinglake during his eastern journey recorded in *Eothen* and acted as his interpreter 20 years earlier. His hotel was rated as the best in Constantinople.

Chapter 13: The Crimea, So Near and Yet So Far

1 Bashi Bazouks, irregular soldiers belonging to the Ottoman army.
2 Diary, 15 October 1854.
3 Ibid.
4 Rear-Admiral Edward Boxer (1784–1855) was appointed as Admiral Superintendent 'from the entrance to the Dardanelles to East entrance of the Bosphorus at the Black Sea', which gave him control over all the shipping in the area. Died of cholera in 1855.
5 Fanny Duberly, *Mrs Duberly's War, Journal and Letters from the Crimea*, ed. Christine Kelly (Oxford: Oxford University Press, 2007), p. 94.

6 Lord George Paget, *The Light Cavalry Brigade in the Crimea* (London: Murray, 1881), p. 248.
7 Paget, *The Light*, p. 228.
8 *London Gazette*, 24 February 1857.
9 Alexander Roberts Dunn VC (1833–68). Awarded the VC for his actions in the Charge of the Light Brigade.
10 I am grateful to Dr Douglas Austin for this information.
11 Diary, 26 October 1855.
12 Sweet Waters of Asia: name given by foreigners to the confluence of two small rivers at the mouth of the Golden Horn.
13 Private Gregory Jowett enlisted in 1847, promoted sergeant in 1855, attended first Balaclava Commemoration in 1857. Portrait in the *London Illustrated News*, 30 October 1875.
14 John Thadeus Delane (1817–79), editor of *The Times*, 1841–77.
15 William Russell (1820–1907), reporter for *The Times*, spent 22 months covering the Crimean War. First and greatest war correspondent.
16 *Wrexham and Denbigh Weekly Advertiser*, 27 October 1855.
17 Diary, 10 November 1854.
18 Paget, *The Light*, p. 228.
19 Orlando Figes, *Crimea: The Last Crusade* (London: Allen Lane, 2010), p. 273.
20 Hutting: troops were supplied with wood to make huts to replace their tents.
21 Diary, 4 December 1854.
22 Diary, 2 December 1854.
23 Mark Bostridge, *Florence Nightingale: The Woman and Her Legend* (London: Farrar, Straus and Giroux, 2008), p. 219.
24 Diary, 9 December 1854.
25 Diary, 15 December 1854.
26 Saul David, *The Homicidal Earl: The Life of Lord Cardigan* (New York: Little, Brown, 1997), p. 427.

Chapter 14: Balaclava

1 Fanny Duberly, *Mrs Duberly's War, Journal and Letters from the Crimea*, ed. Christine Kelly (Oxford: Oxford University Press, 2007), p. 118.
2 *Letters from the Crimea of Colonel Richard Chambre Hayes Taylor, Ardgillan Castle, 1819–1904* (National Library of Ireland).
3 Colonel Poulett Somerset was the grandson of the 5th Earl of Beaufort.
4 Lord Burgersh, eldest surviving son of the Earl of Westmorland.
5 William Peel (1824–55) was appointed captain of the frigate HMS *Diamond* in

1854 and transferred to the Black Sea. Awarded the VC in October 1854. *Illustrated London News*, 20 June 1857.
6 Orlando Figes, *Crimea: The Last Crusade* (London: Allen Lane, 2010), p. 270.
7 A gale sank many of the transports carrying supplies for the winter months.
8 Duberly, *Mrs Duberly's War*, p. 130.
9 Gutta-percha is a tough plastic substance made from the latex of several Malaysian trees.
10 The valley of the shadow of death has been popularly associated with the poem by Tennyson, 'Into the valley of Death/Rode the six hundred', but at the time the Voronzov Road was known by that name.
11 Rear Admiral Sir Edmund Lyons was in command of HMS *Miranda*. Both he and Lord Raglan died the following year, one through illness, the other through enemy action.
12 William Simpson (1823–99), war artist. He arrived in the Crimea in November 1845 and produced many sketches and watercolours.

Chapter 15: Love at Last

1 Napier of Ettrick, Francis Lord (1829–98), diplomat, attached to the British Embassy during the Crimean War.
2 Stratford Canning, Viscount Stratford de Redcliffe (1786–1880), diplomat and politician. He was a cousin of George Canning, Foreign Secretary and briefly Prime Minister in 1827. Created Viscount in 1852, Ambassador to the Ottoman Empire from 1853 to 1858.
3 Lady Alice Peel, née Kennedy, daughter of the Earl of Ailsa, one of the oldest Scottish families. Married in 1824 to General Sir Jonathan Peel, brother of Sir Robert Peel.
4 Betty Askwith, *Crimean Courtship* (London: Hurlingham Books, 1985), p. 130.

Epilogue

1 Ardgillan Letters, 4 June 1855.
2 George Howard, 7th Earl of Carlisle (1892–1969). Appointed by Lord Palmerston as Lord Lieutenant of Ireland from 1855 to 1858.
3 Ardgillan Letters, 29 February 1856.
4 Ardgillan Letters, 10 March 1856.
5 *The Irish Times*, 7 September 1976.
6 Accounts taken from *Morning Post*, 8 March 1856 and *Freeman's Journal and Daily*

Commercial Advertiser, 7 March 1856.

7 Quoted in Betty Askwith, *Crimean Courtship* (London: Hurlingham Books, 1985), p. 135.

8 Benjamin Edgington made and rented marquees, by appointment to the Queen. His shop was at 32 Charing Cross Road.

9 Conrad Tauer, a Bavarian confectioner who received British naturalisation papers in 1851.

10 *Morning Post,* Thursday, 30 July 1857.

11 Roger Palmer's diaries, 30 May 1858.

12 Roger Palmer's diaries, 15 April 1862.

13 Askwith, *Crimean Courtship*, p. 138.

14 Thomas Woolner RA (1825–92), one of the founding members of the Pre-Raphaelite Brotherhood and the only sculptor among its founding members.

15 Askwith, *Crimean Courtship*, p. 140.

16 *The Two Buzzards or Whitebait at Greenwich*, a one-act farce of 1850 by John Maddison Morton.

17 *North Wales Chronicle*, 14 January 1860.

18 *The Wrexham Advertiser*, 12 September 1863.

19 Ibid.

20 Georgiana Adelaide Russell Peel, *Recollections of Lady Georgiana Peel* (London: John Lane, 1920), p. 251.

21 Lord John Russell (1792–1878) served twice as Prime Minister, taking over for the first time from Robert Peel after Peel's resignation in 1846.

22 See Betty Askwith, *A Victorian Young Lady* (Norwich: Michael Russell, 1978).

23 Alison Heath, *The Life of George Rankin Askwith* (London: Pickering and Chatto, 2013).

BIBLIOGRAPHY

Primary Sources

Cefn MSS: 403, 463, 578, 873
Denbighshire Record Office
Ellen Palmer's Diaries: 1847–55
Ellen Palmer's Travel Diary 1855, including 8 pages of notes found inside
Ellen Palmer's Travel Journal 1844
Gretna Green Records
Guildhall Library, Manuscripts Library, London
Irish Record Pedigrees, Vols XIV and XXVI
Principal Registry, Family Division
Roger Palmer's Diaries 1857–63
Shropshire Archives

Newspapers and Periodicals

Daily Commercial Advertiser
Freeman's Journal
The Gentleman's Magazine
The Illustrated London News
Liverpool Mercury
The Morning Post
North Wales Chronicle
Notes and Queries
Skerries News
The Times
The War Correspondent: The Journal of the Crimean War Research Society
Wrexham and Denbighshire Advertiser

Background Reading

Askwith, Betty, *A Victorian Young Lady* (London: Michael Russell, 1978).
———, *Crimean Courtship* (London: Michael Russell, 1985).
Austen, Jane, *Emma* (London: Macmillan, 1929).
Balcombe, Elizabeth, *From the Archives, Ardgillan Letters* (*Skerries News*, 1992).
Blackwood, Lady Alicia, *A Narrative of a Residence on the Bosphorus during the Crimean War* (London: Hatchard, 1856).
Bonython, Elizabeth and Anthony Burton, *The Great Exhibitor: The Life and Work of Henry Cole* (London: Victoria and Albert Museum Catalogues, 1903).
Bostridge, Mark, *Florence Nightingale* (London: Penguin Books, 2009).
Burke, Sir Bernard, *Burkes Landed Gentry: A Genealogical Dictionary of the Landed Gentry of Great Britain and Ireland* (2nd ed., London, 1850–3).
Burney, Fanny, *Evelina: Or the History of a Young Lady's Entrance into the World* (4th ed., London: T. Lowndes, 1779).
Cardigan, Adeleine, Countess of, *My Recollections* (London: Eveleigh Nash, 1909).
Coates, Tim, *Delane's War: How Front-line Reports from the Crimean War Brought Down the British Government* (London: Biteback Publishing, 2009).
Cokayne, G.E. (ed.), *The Complete Peerage* (London: George Bell & Sons, 1913).
Compton, P., *Colonel's Lady and Camp-Follower: The Story of Women in the Crimean War* (London: Hale, 1970).
Cowen, Ruth, *Relish: The Extraordinary Life of Alexis Soyer, Victorian Celebrity Chef* (London: Weidenfeld and Nicolson, 2006).
David, Saul, *The Homicidal Earl: The Life of Lord Cardigan* (London: Abacus, 1998).
Fairfax-Lucy, Alice, *The Mistress of Charlecote* (London: Victor Gollancz, 1984).
Figes, Orlando, *Crimea: The Last Crusade* (London: Allen Lane, 2010).
Freely, John, *Istanbul, the Imperial City* (London: Penguin Books, 1998).
Griffin, Susan, *The Book of the Courtesans* (New York: Broadway Books, 2001).
Gronow, Rees Howell, *Captain Gronow: His Reminiscences of Victorian and Regency Life 1810–1860*, ed. Christopher Hibbert (London: Kyle Cathie, 1991).
Hall, J., 'Refashioning of Fashionable Opera', PhD dissertation, Yale University, 1996.
Heath, Alison, *The Life of George Rankin Askwith, 1861–1942* (London: Pickering and Chatto, 2013).
Hibbert, Christopher, *The Destruction of Lord Raglan* (rev. ed., London: Wordsworth Editions, 1999).
Horn, Pamela, *Ladies of the Manor: Wives and Daughters of Country House Society, 1830-1916* (Stroud: Sutton Publishing, 1999).
Hurd, Douglas, *Robert Peel: A Biography* (London: Weidenfeld and Nicolson, 2007).
Kavanagh, Julie, *The Girl Who Loved Camellias: The Life and Legend of Marie Duplessis* (New York: Alfred K. Knoff, 2013).

Kelen, Betty, *The Mistresses: Domestic Scandals of the Nineteenth Century Monarchs* (New York: Avon Books, 1968).

Kelly, Christine (ed.), *Mrs Duberley's War: Journal and Letters from the Crimea 1854–6* (Oxford: Oxford University Press, 2007).

Kineally, Christine, *This Great Calamity* (Dublin: Gill & Macmillan, 1994).

———, *A Death-Dealing Famine: the Great Hunger in Ireland* (London and Chicago: Pluto Press, 1997).

Kinglake, Alexander William, *The Invasion of the Crimea: Its Origin and an Account of Its Progress down to the Death of Lord Raglan*, Vols 2 and 3 (Cambridge: Cambridge University Press, 2010).

Lady Morgan's Memoirs: Autobiography, Diaries and Correspondence, Vol. II (London: Wm. H. Allen, 1863).

Lane-Poole, Stanley, *The Life of the Right Honourable Stratford Canning*, Vol. 1 (London: Longmans, Green and Co., 1888).

Lummis, W.M. and K.G. Wynn, *Honour the Light Brigade* (London: J.B. Hayward and Son, 1973).

MacCarthy, Fiona, *Byron: Life and Legend* (London: Faber and Faber, 2003).

Maddison Morton, John, *The Two Buzzards; or, Whitebait at Greenwich: A Farce, in One Act* (n.p., 1888).

Massie, Alastair, *A Most Desperate Undertaking: The British Army in the Crimea, 1854–56* (London: National Army Museum, 2001).

———, *The National Army Museum Book of the Crimean War* (London: Pan Books, 2005).

Morton, James, *Lola Montez: Her Life and Conquests* (London: Portrait Books, 2007).

Murray, John, *A Handbook for Travellers on the Continent: Being a Guide through Holland, Belgium, Prussia, Northern Germany and along the Rhine from Holland to Switzerland* (London: John Murrary, 1836).

Paget, Lord George, *The Light Cavalry Brigade in the Crimea* (London: John Murray, 1881).

Peel, Jonathan, *The Peels: A Family Sketch* (London: Richard Bentley and Son, 1877).

Peel, Lady Georgiana, *Recollections of Lady Georgina Peel. Compiled by Her Daughter Ethel Peel* (London, 1920).

Potter, Tiffany, *Women, Popular Culture, and the Eighteenth Century* (Toronto: University of Toronto Press, 2012).

Robins, Joseph, *The Miasma: Epidemic and Panic in Nineteenth-Century Ireland* (Dublin: Institute of Public Administration, 1995).

———, *Champagne and Silver Buckles: The Viceregal Court at Dublin Castle, 1700–1922* (Dublin: Lilliput Press, 2001).

Robinson, Rod, 'The Travelling Heiress: Ellen Palmer's Excursion', *War Correspondent* 20.3 (October 2002), pp. 14–16, and 20.4 (January 2003), p. 11.

Ruiter, Raymond, *La Maison de Gramont, de 1529 à nos jours* (privately printed).
Russell, William Howard, *Despatches from the Crimea* (Barnsley: Frontline Books, 2008).
Small, Hugh, *The Crimean War: Queen Victoria's War with the Russian Tsars* (Stroud: Tempus Publishing, 2007).
Smith, William, *Napoleon III: les derniers feux de l'Empire* (Paris: Hachette, 1882).
Snowman, Daniel, *The Gilded Stage: A Social History of Opera* (London: Atlantic Books, 2010).
Soyer, Alexis, *A Culinary Campaign* (Lewes: Southover Press, 1995).
Thackeray, William, *Vanity Fair* (London: BCA, 1998).
Troubettzkoy, Alexis, *The Crimean War: The Causes and Consequences of a Medieval Conflict Fought in a Modern Age* (London: Constable and Robinson, 2006).
Vickery, Amanda, *A Gentleman's Daughter* (Princeton, NJ: Yale University Press, 2006).
Walpole, Spencer, *The Life of Lord John Russell*, Vol. II (London: Longmans, Green and Co., 1889).
Woodham Smith, Cecil, *Florence Nightingale* (London: Constable and Co., 1950).
———, *The Reason Why* (London, Constable and Co., 1953).

INDEX